BASIC CARPENTRY

By the Editors of Sunset Books

Sunset Books
President and Publisher: Susan J. Maruyama
Director, Finance & Business Affairs: Gary Loebner
Director, Manufacturing & Sales Service: Lorinda Reichert
Director of Sales & Marketing: Richard A. Smeby
Editorial Director: Kenneth Winchester

Sunset Publishing Corporation
Chairman: Jim Nelson
President/CEO: Robin Wolaner
Chief Financial Officer: James E. Mitchell
Publisher, Sunset Magazine: Stephen J. Seabolt
Circulation Director: Robert L. Gursha
Editor, Sunset Magazine: William R. Marken

Basic Carpentry was produced by
St. Remy Press
President: Pierre Léveillé
Managing Editor: Carolyn Jackson
Senior Editor: Heather Mills
Senior Art Director: Francine Lemieux
Art Director: Solange Laberge
Assistant Editors: Neale McDevitt, Rebecca Smollett
Designers: François Daxhelet, Hélène Dion,
    Jean-Guy Doiron, Michel Giguère, François Longpré
Picture Editor: Christopher Jackson
Contributing Illustrators: Michel Blais, Jacques Perrault
Production Manager: Michelle Turbide
System Coordinator: Eric Beaulieu, Jean-Luc Roy
Photographers: Robert Chartier, Christian Levesque
Proofreader: Judy Yelon
Indexer: Christine M. Jacobs
Administrator: Natalie Watanabe
Other Staff: Lorraine Doré, Dominique Gagné,
    Alfred LeMaitre

Book Consultants
Karl Marcuse
Don Vandervort

Acknowledgments
Thanks to the following:
Alcan Building Products (division of Alcan Aluminum
    Products), Woodbridge, NJ
American Hardboard Association, Palapine, IL
American Plywood Association, Tacoma, WA
Jon Arno, Troy, MI
Arrow Fasteners, Saddle Brook, NJ
Asphalt Roofing Manufacturers Association, Rockville, MD
Association of the Wall and Ceiling Industries-International,
    Falls Church, VA
Daniel Ball, Ellicott City, MD
Black & Decker, Towson MD
Cedar Shake and Shingle Bureau, Bellevue, WA
The Celotex Corporation, Tampa, FL
Delta International Machinery/Porter-Cable, Guelph, Ont.
Dewalt Industrial Tool Co., Hampstead, MD
The Dow Chemical Company, Granville, OH
Freud Inc., Mississauga, Ont.
Lee Valley Tools Ltd., Ottawa, Ont.
Makita Canada Inc., Whitby, Ont.
Maze Nails, Peru, IL
Giles Miller-Mead, Brome, Que.
Milwaukee Electric Tool Corp., Brookfield, WI
National Particleboard Association, Gaithersburg, MD
National Roofing Contractors Association, Rosemont, IL
Norandex Inc., Cleveland, OH
North American Insulation Manufacturers Association,
    Alexandria, VA
Northwestern Steel and Wire, Sterling, IL
Marty Obando, Elizabeth City, NC
Occupational Safety and Health Association,
    Washington, DC
Skil Canada, Markham, Ont.
United Solvents of America, Sumter, SC
United States Public Health Department, Washington, DC
Western Wood Products Association, Portland, OR

Picture Credits
Photos courtesy of the following:
p. 14 *(upper)* Skil Canada
p. 16 Dewalt Industrial Tool Co.
p. 20 *(left)* Dewalt Industrial Tool Co.
p. 21 *(left)* Makita Canada Inc.
        (right) Black & Decker Inc.
p. 26 *(both)* Black & Decker Inc.
p. 28 Delta International Machinery/Porter-Cable
p. 29 Makita Canada Inc.
p. 31 Milwaukee Electric Tool Corp.

CONTENTS

TOOLS AND TECHNIQUES

The first step to becoming a skillful carpenter is choosing the correct tool for the job and knowing how to use it properly. This chapter will help you acquire a firm foundation. You can put the information to work in two ways. If you read consecutively, you'll gain an overview of the classic carpentry tools and learn about some new tools that fill the gaps in today's do-it-yourself world. But when you're simply looking for the best way to execute a procedure, such as measuring, cutting, or drilling, you can turn directly to the appropriate section. We'll help you select the most useful tool by discussing the function and design of each one, as well as adjustment and operating techniques.

Knowledge alone won't produce an ace carpenter, of course. The best way to achieve good results is to get acquainted with your tools by practicing on scrap materials. Consider looking for home improvement classes in your community, or for other opportunities to acquire some "hands-on" experience—without making expensive mistakes on your own materials.

In deciding what tools you need to get started, you may find yourself wavering between two strategies: buy nothing until you need it, but then buy every tool required for a particular project; or buy a core of basic tools that will cover most of the tasks you'll encounter, and then add more sophisticated tools as you need them. If you're likely to need an expensive power tool only once, consider renting it; if you find yourself needing it again, that may be the time to buy your own.

Working with tools—especially power tools—always requires a knowledge of safety procedures. We begin the chapter with a few guidelines and show some equipment that will make your job safer.

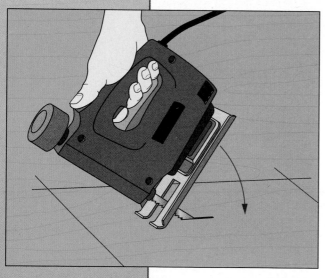

Plunge cutting with a saber saw is one of the handy techniques you will learn in the pages that follow.

SAFETY WITH TOOLS

Every carpenter should attempt to decrease or to completely remove the dangers that are inherent in using tools and carpentry materials. Start your personal safety campaign by looking at your workplace: It should be clean and well organized, and not dangerously crowded, with adequate lighting and proper ventilation. Next, consider your work clothing and personal safety equipment. Power tools, because of their operating speed, demand special attention, too. Furthermore, when you're working with electricity, you introduce yet another potential hazard. The following pages present some basic guidelines for safe carpentry.

A SAFE WORKPLACE

Working in a cluttered or poorly lit area is asking for an accident to happen, and you should keep in mind that certain types of materials can give off potentially toxic fumes, particles, or dust. The following pointers can help promote safety, whether you're on a jobsite or in your home shop.

A clean, well-lit workplace is the key to safe and efficient carpentry. Keep tools and materials organized to allow maximum working space. Plan your setup carefully before you begin work. Whenever possible, avoid working with a partner in cramped quarters; you can

DRESS FOR SAFETY

Eye protection
Wear goggles, glasses, or face mask to operate power tools and high-impact hand tools. Should be made of scratch-resistant, shatterproof plastic that won't fog; must fit comfortably. Glasses with side-guards best for heavy-duty work; goggles good for dust, but may scratch more easily.

Hand protection
Wear all-leather or leather-reinforced cotton work gloves to handle wood. Wear disposable rubber or plastic gloves for work with solvents, wood preservatives, or adhesives; use heavy-duty type for heavy work with caustic materials.

Respiratory protection
Wear a respirator to prevent breathing harmful vapors, dust, or insulation fibers; interchangeable cartridges and filters are rated for special requirements. Disposable painter's dust mask can protect from heavy sawdust, joint compound dust, or insulation fibers.

Protective headgear
Wear a hard hat when working with others in tight quarters, or if there is a possibility of anything falling on your head. Wear any hat to help keep dust and other particles out of hair.

Hearing protection
Wear earmuff protectors (most effective) or earplugs when operating a power tool for any length of time, or even when pounding nails in close quarters; high noise levels can be painful and can cause permanent damage.

Protective footwear
Sturdy work boots or shoes—especially models with steel toes—protect your feet from blades and dropped tools; puncture-proof insole protects from stepped-on nails—especially important when framing.

too easily be injured by the swing of another's hammer, or by a wrecking bar dropped from above. Carpentry can be messy work. Clean up as you go, preventing an accumulation of bent nails or wood scraps, or spills that might cause uncertain footing.

Good lighting (natural or artificial) leads to neater and safer work. Clip-on electric lights, powered by extension cords, make handy supplements; in tight quarters, try a work light—the type housed in a metal cage with a built-in hook.

Some of the materials you encounter in carpentry can be dangerous to your health: wood preservatives; oil-based enamel, varnish, and lacquer—and their solvents; adhesives (especially resorcinol, epoxy, and contact cement); insulation (asbestos fibers and urea formaldehyde); and even sawdust or the dust particles from wallboard joint compound.

These simple safety rules can help decrease the risks:
• Ventilate the workplace adequately to get rid of particles and fumes.
• Clean the work area frequently with a vacuum, or by wet-mopping. A vacuum will remove most sawdust, but will exacerbate problems of airborne asbestos.
• Read all the precautions on product labels and follow them exactly.
• Wash skin and workclothes regularly (and separately from your other laundry) to remove toxic particles.
• Wear sturdy clothing and the appropriate safety gear *(page 5)* to avoid contact with dangerous materials.

SAFETY WITH POWER TOOLS

The advent of portable power tools introduced a new potential for injury, but these tools can be quite safe if they are handled with respect, and if you adopt some basic safety habits:
• Read the owner's manual carefully before using the tool to understand its capabilities and limitations.
• Be absolutely certain to unplug any tool before servicing or adjusting it, and after you're finished using it.
• Before you plug in a tool, tighten any clamping mechanisms on the tool, ensure that the blade or bit is securely installed, and double-check that you've removed any keys or wrenches.

• Check that any safety devices, such as guards on the tool, are in good working order.
• Never stand on a wet floor or ground when using a power tool.
• Have any necessary supports *(page 13)* or clamps for securing the work set up before turning on the tool.
• Make sure there are no fasteners in the stock to be sawn or drilled.
• Never cut wet wood, and if you can't avoid cutting warped boards or through a knot, be on your guard for kickback.
• Always stand to one side of a circular saw in case of kickback.
• When you operate a power tool, arrange to do so without interruptions or distractions; block off the work area to keep all visitors away—especially youngsters and pets—while the tool is running.
• Never wear loose-fitting clothing that could catch in the tool's mechanism; do wear safety goggles or glasses. Tie back long hair.
• Never use a power tool if you're tired, or under the influence of alcohol or drugs.
• Ensure that your hands and body—and the power cord—are well away from the blade or bit.
• To keep your balance, don't reach too far with the tool; move closer to it and keep a stable footing.
• If a blade or bit jams in the stock, turn off and unplug the tool before trying to extricate it.
• When you've finished the operation, let the bit or blade stop on its own before setting down the tool.
• Follow the manufacturer's specifications to clean and lubricate power tools, and make sure all blades and bits are sharp and undamaged.

WORKING WITH ELECTRICITY

Unless it's double-insulated, a power tool has to be properly grounded. Power tools that are neither grounded nor double-insulated can give a serious—and even fatal—shock. Double-insulated tools are the best defense against a questionable electrical source. These tools contain a built-in second barrier of protective insulation; they are clearly marked and should not be grounded (they'll have two-prong plugs only). If you are working

Grounding a tool

TOOLKIT
• 3- to 2-prong adapter
• Screwdriver

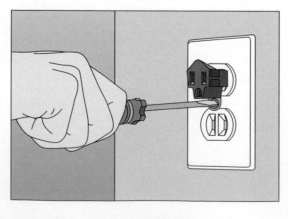

Installing an adapter
A tool is grounded if its three-prong plug is connected to a three-hole, grounded outlet. You can also plug a three-prong plug into a two-hole outlet with an adapter, as shown, but only if adapter's grounding lug is itself grounded—otherwise, you won't be protected. If the outlet is properly grounded, simply attach the lug to the outlet's cover plate screw *(left)*. If you aren't positive that the outlet is grounded, as is often the case in older homes, call in an electrician to check.

in a damp area or outdoors a ground-fault circuit inter-rupter (GFCI)—either built into the outlet or the portable type—is an essential piece of equipment.

Use the shortest extension you can for the job. A very long cord can overheat, creating a fire hazard. Further-more, the longer the cord, the less amperage it will deliver, which translates into less power for the tool's motor. The most important factor to consider is the maximum amp load your extension cord will need to carry. Look for the nameplate on the tool containing its amperage requirement. Add up the requirements of all the tools you plan to plug into the cord at the same time; the extension cord selected must have an amp capacity that equals or exceeds this sum. A cord with a larger load capacity will have bigger wires, but a lower gauge number. The chart shown below will help you to select an extension cord of the correct gauge, depend-ing on the length of cord you need for the job and what the amperage requirements are. For instance, a 50-foot cord to be used for 10 amps must be at least 14-gauge wire.

Follow these tips for safe extension cord use:
• Never use an extension cord outside unless it's indi-cated that it is acceptable for exterior use.
• To keep the plugs on the extension cord and the tool's power cord from being pulled apart, tie the ends of the cords together in a loose knot before plugging them together.
• If you must use long extension cords in heavily traf-ficked areas, tape them to the floor. Never tack or staple a cord in place; this could result in a short circuit.
• Avoid crimping the extension cord; do not run it over or under a door that will be continually opened and closed.
• Inspect extension cords frequently for defects; replace a cord with frayed or cracked insulation.

RECOMMENDED EXTENSION CORD SIZES FOR PORTABLE POWER TOOLS

Nameplate ampere rating	Length of cord in feet			
(115V tool)	25 ft.	50 ft.	100 ft.	150 ft.
0-2	18	18	18	16
2-3	18	18	16	14
3-4	18	18	16	14
4-5	18	18	14	12
5-6	18	16	14	12
6-8	18	16	12	10
8-10	18	14	12	10
10-12	16	14	10	8
12-14	16	12	10	8
14-16	14	12	10	8
16-18	14	12	8	8
18-20	14	12	8	6

Chart courtesy of Delta International Machinery/Porter-Cable

SAFETY WITH RENTAL TOOLS

Every tool has limitations, and trying to force a tool to perform a task it isn't designed for is a good way to hurt yourself or damage the tool or workpiece. Unless you're a professional, you may not own many of the tools or equipment needed for specialized or big jobs. This is where your local rental store comes in. The most reli-able outlets have liability insurance, well-maintained tools, and a straightforward policy on tool failures. The staff should be able to help you select the proper tool for your needs as well as demonstrate its safe use. If you need to buy or rent accessories for a tool, make sure they are appropriate for that model. You can rent virtu-ally anything from hand and power tools to forklifts and steamrollers. Here are some of the more commonly rented tools, with specific safety tips:

Air-powered nailer:
Popular with professionals, this tool can greatly reduce the time it takes to do long and arduous jobs, like installing underlayment. Specialized nailers are available for roof-ing nails and staples. The tool must be seated on the work-piece to drive a nail. Wear eye protection.

Drywall lift:
This platform safely raises heavy gypsum wallboard sheets to the ceiling and holds them in place for fastening. It can be set at an angle for sloping ceilings. Respect the load limit of the model you're using, and double-check that the sheet is securely held on the lift.

Posthole digger:
Unrivaled for digging quick, accurate holes, this back-saving tool is available in models that can be operated by one or two people. It usually runs on gas; be careful not to touch the hot muffler. Dig only about one foot at a time, keeping a keen lookout for rocks and roots.

Scaffolding:
For large interior or exterior projects such as painting, re-siding, or roofing, scaffolding is safer and more effi-cient than ladders. Make sure all the frame pieces and working platforms are in good repair. Outdoors, planks under the base plates will assure a solid footing for the scaffold. Install a guardrail on the working level.

Power miter saw:
This circular saw mounted on an adjustable table can cut wood at virtually any angle, essential for jobs where you need to cut numerous miter joints accurately. Follow the general safety rules for power tools as well as specific instructions for the particular saw.

Electric pavement breaker:
This electric version of the pneumatic jackhammer has enough power to break concrete slabs. Protective cloth-ing and work gloves, steel-toed boots, goggles or face shield, and respirator or mask are a must, as is a clear understanding of how to use the tool.

MEASURING AND MARKING

The same procedures—accurate measurement, layout, and marking—launch all successful carpentry projects. While there are a great number of tools you can buy for these vital preliminary steps, you only need a few for basic carpentry. A tape measure, a combination square, and a pencil will see you through many tasks; buy more specialized tools, such as a reel tape, carpenter's square, or chalkline as you need them.

An investment in the best measuring and layout tools you can afford will pay off in the long run, since the ultimate quality of every project depends on precise dimensions. Keep in mind the old rule "Measure twice, cut once," and develop careful work habits right from the start, and you'll be satisfied with the results.

Measuring tools: To measure distances of a foot or two, you can get by with either a combination square or a rigid bench rule. But for accurate gauging of greater distances, a tape measure is generally the answer; in fact, the flexible steel tape measure is considered the modern carpenter's workhorse. For laying out distances beyond 25 feet or so, choose a reel tape.

Layout tools: The main tools for laying out cutting lines for marking are squares. Most indicate 90° angles; some, in addition, indicate 45° miter angles. Adjustable bevel squares can be set to duplicate any angle. To lay out a curve, your best tool is a French or flexible curve; both are available at woodworking or drafting supply stores. (To mark full circles, see page 10.) Layout tools are illustrated on page 9.

Any layout tool must be true, or your most careful work will be wasted. To test a square, hold the body tight against the edge of a perfectly straight board and draw a line along the blade. Then flop the square over and draw another line; both lines should match exactly.

Marking tools: Not surprisingly, the trusty pencil serves as your basic marking tool. But don't use a lead so soft that it needs constant resharpening. Flat-sided carpenter's pencils are also handy, although some people may find they're awkward for scribing irregular lines or curves.

Mark off distances with a sharp pencil, then carefully recheck each one. Many carpenters find that a V mark or "caret" is more effective than a straight line to mark a point on the edge of a board. When you draw a cutting line, tilt the pencil so that the lead lies flush against the layout tool.

A few additional tools (*page 10*) will refine and guide your marking process.

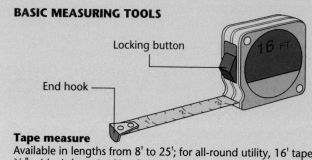

BASIC MEASURING TOOLS

Locking button

End hook

Tape measure
Available in lengths from 8' to 25'; for all-round utility, 16' tape, 3/4" wide, is best. Locking button prevents tape from retracting, an advantage when you're working alone. End hook should be loosely riveted to adjust for precise "inside" and "outside" readings. Although case may be an even 2" or 3" in length, test this carefully before adding the case length to inside measurements. Most tapes are marked in 1/16" increments; good tapes also have special marks every 16", the most common spacing for wall studs and floor joists.

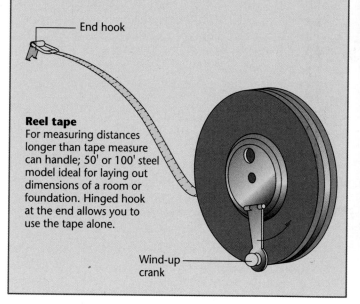

End hook

Reel tape
For measuring distances longer than tape measure can handle; 50' or 100' steel model ideal for laying out dimensions of a room or foundation. Hinged hook at the end allows you to use the tape alone.

Wind-up crank

ASK A PRO

HOW DO I MEASURE WALLS USING A TAPE MEASURE?
To measure a wall's height from the floor, butt the tape measure's end hook against the floor. Pull several feet of tape from the case, and "walk" the slack tape up the wall, bending it at the ceiling. Read the measurement right at the bend. A 1-inch-wide tape can come in handy for measuring openings and distances from corners; these wide tapes will remain rigid horizontally for 8 to 10 feet if pulled from the case gently.

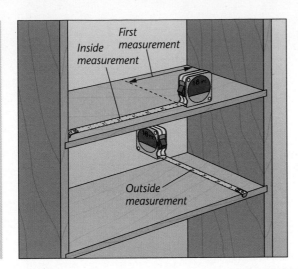

First measurement
Inside measurement
Outside measurement

Using a tape measure

Making accurate measurements

Your tape measure must be parallel to the edge of the material. To make an inside measurement, press the end hook against the vertical surface. To avoid possible inaccuracies from including the length of the case, measure partway (to an even inch mark), then make a second measurement and add it to the first *(left, above)*. For an outside measurement, pull the tape taut against the end hook before marking the distance *(left, below)*. When handling wide sheet materials, measure and mark at several different points. When letting the tape back in, don't allow it to slam into the case; this can damage the tape. Instead, guide the tape with light pressure from your finger, but watch the sharp edges.

LAYOUT TOOLS FOR CARPENTRY

French curve
Used to lay out irregular contours and arcs; available in different sizes and shapes. Place curve between two points or, with line lightly sketched, position French curve so one of its contours matches line, then draw along curve's edge.

Flexible curve
Handy for laying out contours and arcs; most effective for creating irregular paths between points you've marked or copying irregular contours. Bend to desired shape, then draw along edge. Comes in sizes from 12" to 48".

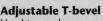

Blade

Try square
Used to check 90° angles or to lay out cutoff lines across boards and framing lumber; handle may have bevel for 45° miters. Typically available with either 6", 8", or 12" blade; larger models are best for general work.

Rafter scales — Body — Tongue

Heel

Carpenter's square
For laying out lines and checking square on large stock. Standard model has 16" x 1½" tongue and 24" x 2" body, meeting at exact 90° angle at heel. Most durable squares are made from steel; because accuracy depends entirely on square's exact shape, store it where it can't fall or be banged and bent by other tools. Useful information printed on face and back; "rafter" or "framing" squares are normally most complete.

Blade

Adjustable T-bevel
Used to mark any angle between 0° and 180°, or to copy existing angle; tighten wing nut to lock blade at desired angle. Determine correct setting either with aid of protractor or simply by matching angle to be duplicated.

Square gauges
Also known as stair gauges; allow repeated marking of same angle; useful for laying out rafters, or treads and risers of stairs. Attach to body and tongue of carpenter's square to set the angle when gauges rest against edge of stock.

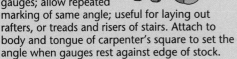

Combination square
Serves as both try and miter square; sliding head can be locked anywhere along blade, or can be removed. May include spirit level for spot-checking level and plumb; optional removable scribe used to mark fine lines. Versatility shown at far right. Test square carefully; make sure there's no play between head and blade. Check blade's increments against your tape measure.

Scribe

Spirit level

Locking nut

Blade

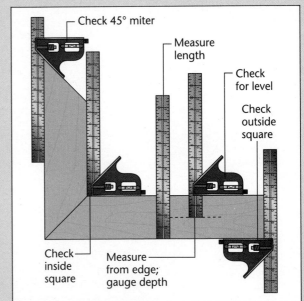

Check 45° miter

Measure length

Check for level

Check outside square

Check inside square

Measure from edge; gauge depth

Checking a board's squareness

TOOLKIT
• Try or combination square

Using a try square
Test the squareness of a board's end or edge by positioning the square as shown. If light shows between blade and board, the board is out of square. To check a board's face, simply lay the blade across the surface with the handle on the adjacent face.

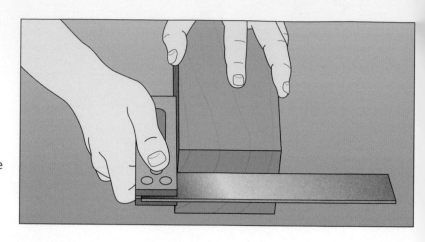

Using a carpenter's square

TOOLKIT
• Square gauges (optional)

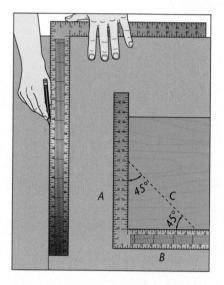

Marking straight lines and angles
To mark a straight line across a board or sheet, hold the square's tongue against the stock's edge and mark along the body *(far left)*. This is particularly useful for plotting long lines on plywood or other sheet material. Lay out accurate 45° angles by matching the inch graduations on both body and tongue *(near left)*; you can also align these figures on the same edge of the stock, attaching square gauges if you want to repeat the angle. The figures and tables embossed on the square's face and back enable you to quickly lay out roof rafters, stairs, or wall bracing. The tables work on the principle of right triangles: $A^2 + B^2 = C^2$. Once you've determined the lengths of the two straight sides (A and B), the square helps you calculate the length and slope of C as well. For details, follow the instructions included with your square, and see the sections on "Ceiling and Roof Framing" *(page 69)* and "Basic Stairways" *(page 98)*.

TOOLS FOR EXACT MARKING

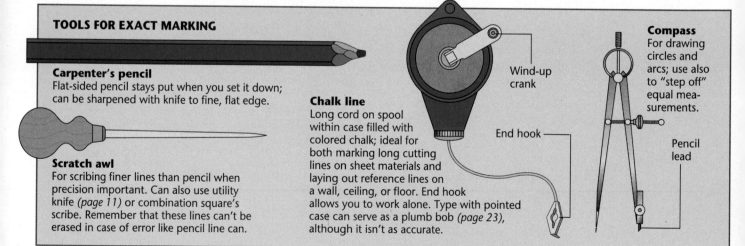

Carpenter's pencil
Flat-sided pencil stays put when you set it down; can be sharpened with knife to fine, flat edge.

Scratch awl
For scribing finer lines than pencil when precision important. Can also use utility knife *(page 11)* or combination square's scribe. Remember that these lines can't be erased in case of error like pencil line can.

Chalk line
Long cord on spool within case filled with colored chalk; ideal for both marking long cutting lines on sheet materials and laying out reference lines on a wall, ceiling, or floor. End hook allows you to work alone. Type with pointed case can serve as a plumb bob *(page 23)*, although it isn't as accurate.

Wind-up crank

End hook

Compass
For drawing circles and arcs; use also to "step off" equal measurements.

Pencil lead

Using a chalk line

Snapping the line
To mark a line, pull the chalk-covered cord from the case and stretch it taut between two points. Then, toward one end, lift the cord and release quickly, so that it snaps down sharply, leaving a long, straight line of chalk. For long lines over uneven surfaces, fasten the cord at both ends (it is useful to have a helper) and snap it from the center.

CUTTING WITH HANDSAWS

In any carpentry project, you'll need to start with accurate, consistent sawing, which is essential to strong, square joints and assembly. Along with precise measuring, careful cutting is the key to success.

Power saws aren't necessary; you could build an entire house with a crosscut saw, perhaps supplemented by a compass saw. And there are times when only the hand-saw will do—spots without electricity or where a power saw might be dangerous. As a rule, though, power saws perform much faster and more accurately, once you've had some practice.

The portable circular saw *(page 14)* and the saber saw *(page 15)* have become standard tools for carpenters. Learn to use the basic handsaws first, then move on to power tools as your needs—and wallet—dictate.

Saws differ in shape, blade size, and the position and number of teeth along the blade. Both tooth size and number of teeth per inch (tpi) are indicated by the term "point." An 8-point saw has only 7 teeth per inch, since the points at both ends of that inch are included. In general, you'll get a rougher but faster cut with fewer teeth; many teeth means a smooth but slower cut.

The degree to which the teeth are set, or bent outward, determines the thickness of the cut. Saw teeth are set to produce a cut wider than the blade; otherwise, the saw would bind in the kerf, or sawcut. The wider the set, the faster and rougher the cut will be; a smaller tooth set gives a fine kerf.

A basic collection of handsaws is illustrated at right; a utility knife, though not exactly a saw, is also handy.

The crosscut saw: When you choose a crosscut saw, be sure the handle feels comfortable in your hand. Sight down the back of the saw blade to make sure it's straight. Flex the tip; it should bounce back to the center position. Look for a "taper ground" saw; the blade's thickness tapers toward the back and the tip, preventing the saw from binding in the kerf and allowing a narrower set to the teeth. Premium saws are also "skew-backed," meaning the back is slightly cut away to improve balance and minimize weight, although this makes the saw impractical for heavy-duty work. High-quality steel, though more costly, will flex better and stay

---

HANDY HANDSAWS

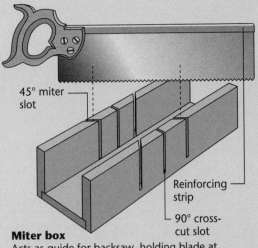

Backsaw
Designed for crosscutting fine finish work like moldings and trim; reinforcement along back prevents bowing and allows use of thinner blade, producing very fine, straight cuts. Typically has 12" to 14" blade with 12 to 16 tpi. A 12" saw with 12 tpi is a good first choice.

45° miter slot

Reinforcing strip

90° cross-cut slot

Miter box
Acts as guide for backsaw, holding blade at 90° or 45° angle. Integral backsaw/miter box units that cut to any angle are also available; saws in these units range up to 26" long.

Replaceable blade

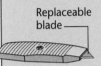

Utility knife
For scoring and light-duty cutting of gypsum wallboard and other thin materials.

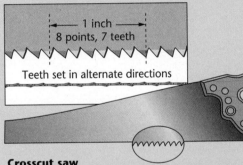

1 inch
8 points, 7 teeth

Teeth set in alternate directions

Crosscut saw
Designed to cut across wood grain; also all-purpose saw for plywood and other sheet products. Length varies from about 20" to 26"; a good first choice is 26" blade. For framing work, 8-point saw is most effective. To also cut plywood or paneling, choose slightly slower, but smoother, 10-point saw.

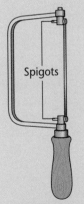

Spigots

Coping saw
For fine, accurate cuts and sawing tight curves. Limited by relatively shallow frame; typical throat depth 4³/4", although deeper models are available. Average blade length 6¹/2" with 10 to 20 tpi. Position blade with teeth up, down, or to either side; rotate spigots to adjust position.

Compass saw
For making cutouts and gentle curves; also called keyhole saw. Thin, 10" to 14" blade tapers to pointed tip; model shown has interchangeable blades. Typical blades 8 points per inch, producing fast but relatively rough cut. Smaller 6" to 8" version with straight handle designed for making cutouts in gypsum wallboard.

sharp much longer than lower grades. When sawteeth go dull, they must be leveled and filed and (after long, hard use) reset. You can do this yourself or take the saw to a professional sharpener.

The ripsaw is a variation of the crosscut saw, with bigger, chisel-like teeth that make fast cuts in line with the wood grain; they are generally available with 5, 5½, or 6 points per inch. However, most carpenters find that the power circular saw is the tool for ripping and that any occasional hand-ripping can be handled by a crosscut saw. If you do choose to use a ripsaw, use it in the same way as a crosscut saw, but hold the blade at a slightly steeper angle—about 60°.

The coping saw: This saw, with its thin, wiry blade strung taut within a small, rectangular frame, is very handy for cutting curves or making cutouts near an edge. Clamp the material to a sawhorse or vise for better control. For a cutout, first drill a pilot hole the size of the blade width, slip the blade through this hole and then reattach it to the frame.

You can install the blade with the teeth pointed away from the handle to cut on the push stroke, or toward the handle to cut on the pull stroke.

The backsaw: Unlike the blades of the crosscut saw and ripsaw, the backsaw's blade is held parallel to the stock. Commonly used with a miter box, backsaws are also found on integral backsaw-miter box units. Although these are more versatile and more precise than the traditional wooden miter box shown on page 11, they are quite expensive. Another option, the power miter saw, is an even handier tool; if you have a lot of finish work to do, consider renting one (*page 7*).

Cross-cutting technique

1 **Starting the cut**
Crosscut saws do about 75% of their cutting on the downstroke and 25% on the upstroke. Start a cut by holding the saw upright; slowly draw the blade up several times to cut a notch on the edge. At first, guide the blade with your thumb knuckle (*right*). A full kerf notched about ½" into the edge of the board will help guide the saw for the remainder of the cut. Make sure all of the saw's kerf is to the waste side of the marked cutting line—or your piece will be too short. (As some carpenters say, "Leave the line.")

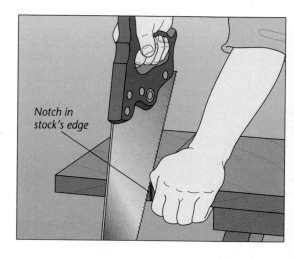

Notch in stock's edge

45°

2 **Cutting**
Once the cut is started, lower the saw's angle to about 45°—or 30° if you're cutting plywood—and make smooth, full strokes (*left*). Sight down the back of the saw from overhead to align it; your forearm and shoulder must remain lined up with the blade. Whenever the blade veers from your cutting line, you can get it back on track by twisting the handle slightly to the opposite side. If you have a persistent problem keeping the blade on the cutting line, clamp a straight board along the line to guide the saw. Don't let the saw tilt to one side or the other.

3 **Finishing the cut**
Toward the end of the cut, reach around the saw and support the waste piece with your free hand. Bring the saw to a vertical position once more (*right*) and make the last strokes slowly to avoid breaking off—and splintering—the board. For long plywood cuts, recruit a helper to hold the waste piece. If you are working alone, position the support so that the scrap piece will fall away.

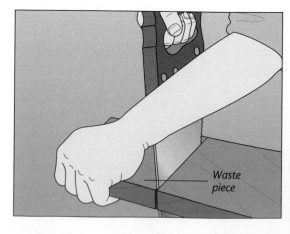

Waste piece

Making a cutout

TOOLKIT
• Drill and bit
• Compass saw
• Crosscut saw (optional)

Using a compass saw

To begin a cutout in wood, first drill a pilot hole large enough for the compass saw's blade (to cut out a square shape, drill holes in two opposite corners as shown). Insert the sawblade in the hole and saw *(right)*; after the cut is started, you can switch to a crosscut saw for a long, straight cut. If you're making a cutout in gypsum wallboard, you don't need to make a pilot hole: simply tap on the saw's handle end with your free hand or a hammer until the blade is started.

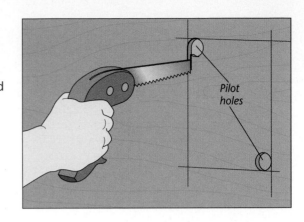

Pilot holes

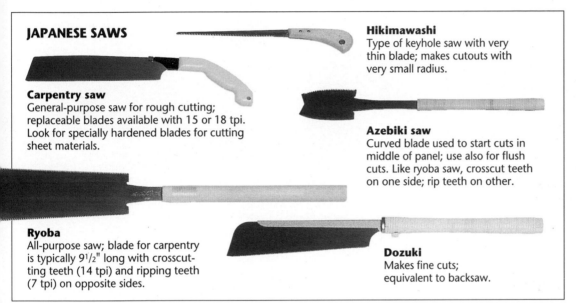

JAPANESE SAWS

Carpentry saw
General-purpose saw for rough cutting; replaceable blades available with 15 or 18 tpi. Look for specially hardened blades for cutting sheet materials.

Ryoba
All-purpose saw; blade for carpentry is typically 9$\frac{1}{2}$" long with crosscutting teeth (14 tpi) and ripping teeth (7 tpi) on opposite sides.

Hikimawashi
Type of keyhole saw with very thin blade; makes cutouts with very small radius.

Azebiki saw
Curved blade used to start cuts in middle of panel; use also for flush cuts. Like ryoba saw, crosscut teeth on one side; rip teeth on other.

Dozuki
Makes fine cuts; equivalent to backsaw.

Some carpenters are turning to Japanese saws, which are becoming more popular in North America. Look for them at woodworking specialty stores, or through mail-order catalogs. Unlike most other saws, they cut on the pull stroke. This design permits a thinner blade, since it doesn't need extra metal to prevent buckling. The resulting saw has less set, resulting in a finer cut.

SAWING SUPPORT

To support your lumber or sheet material securely at a jobsite, use a pair of sturdy sawhorses, or a folding, portable workbench. You have two options for sawhorses; build your own from scratch, or add 2x4 or 2x6 crossbraces to purchased folding metal legs.

When you're cutting lumber to length, you may need only a single support. For a short cut, simply hang the waste end off one edge. To crosscut a long board near the middle, or to cut across sheet materials, you'll need support on both sides of the cut so the waste neither tilts in, which could bind the blade, nor swings out, which could splinter the cut. Placing 2x4s across the sawhorses as shown will give you a solid platform.

If you're cutting with a portable circular saw, set the blade depth so that you cut through the material, but just nick the 2x4 support. With a handsaw, cut only up to the support, then slide the stock forward slightly for a little more unobstructed cutting. Reposition the stock and

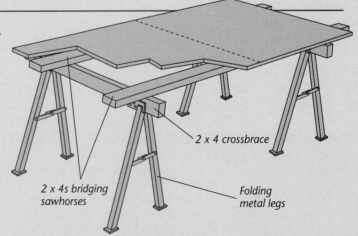

2 x 4 crossbrace

2 x 4s bridging sawhorses

Folding metal legs

continue cutting on the other side of the support. You should have a helper to hold the waste piece.

Ripping usually calls for two sawhorses and no 2x4s, but thin boards may need support to prevent sagging.

CUTTING WITH POWER SAWS

The circular and saber saw, or jigsaw, are the basic power saws. The circular saw makes straight cuts, while the saber saw's specialty is curves and cutouts. Wear eye protection when working with either tool. The reciprocating saw, also commonly used, is shown on page 31.

THE PORTABLE CIRCULAR SAW

This saw allows you to make cross-cuts much faster than with a hand-saw, and is unparalled for ripping. Common sizes are from 5½ to 8¼ inches; this refers to the largest diameter of blade that fits the saw's arbor (axle). The most common 7¼-inch model will go through surfaced 2-by framing lumber *(page 33)* at any angle between 45° and 90°. Look for a model rated at between 8 and 12 amps.

Two distinct styles are available: the standard, or "side-winder," shown at right, and the worm-drive, which is good for heavy use, but much more expensive, and is not recommended for the beginner.

Take the time to set up your unplugged saw properly. Choose the correct size and type of blade to suit your task; most are available with carbide tips on the teeth. Get blades resharpened as soon as they become dull.

To keep the blade from rotating when you're changing it, lightly dig the teeth into scrap lumber. Make sure the new blade's teeth are pointing forward and up. Check the blade angle: Unclamp the angle adjustment lever and push on the base plate until it stops in the horizontal position; lock the lever. If you're beveling, tilt the base plate to the desired angle. Always make a cut on scrap and measure it.

Finally, loosen the depth adjustment lever and set the correct blade depth. Use your tape measure or, with the base plate on the stock, set the depth by eye. For most materials, you'll want the blade to protrude only about ⅛ inch below the stock.

CIRCULAR SAW

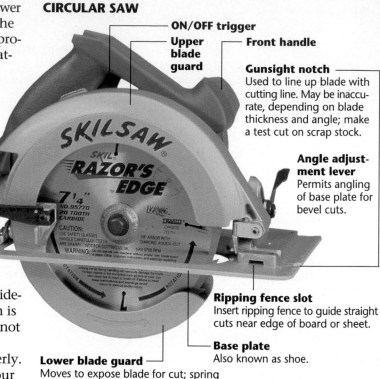

ON/OFF trigger

Upper blade guard

Front handle

Gunsight notch
Used to line up blade with cutting line. May be inaccurate, depending on blade thickness and angle; make a test cut on scrap stock.

Angle adjustment lever
Permits angling of base plate for bevel cuts.

Ripping fence slot
Insert ripping fence to guide straight cuts near edge of board or sheet.

Base plate
Also known as shoe.

Lower blade guard
Moves to expose blade for cut; spring returns it to closed position after cut.

A CARPENTER'S COLLECTION OF SAW BLADES

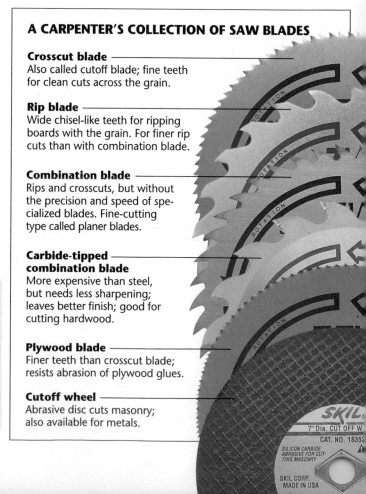

Crosscut blade
Also called cutoff blade; fine teeth for clean cuts across the grain.

Rip blade
Wide chisel-like teeth for ripping boards with the grain. For finer rip cuts than with combination blade.

Combination blade
Rips and crosscuts, but without the precision and speed of specialized blades. Fine-cutting type called planer blades.

Carbide-tipped combination blade
More expensive than steel, but needs less sharpening; leaves better finish; good for cutting hardwood.

Plywood blade
Finer teeth than crosscut blade; resists abrasion of plywood glues.

Cutoff wheel
Abrasive disc cuts masonry; also available for metals.

ASK A PRO

HOW CAN I CUT VERY THICK STOCK?
Mark the cutoff line on all four sides with a square. Set the saw blade to maximum depth, and cut one side. Then flip the piece over and cut through the back. Or, mark the cutting line on one side only, make the cut, then make the second cut on the adjacent side, using the kerf as a guide; repeat on the third side. For very big stock, make cuts on all four sides and finish off with a handsaw.

Basic operation of the circular saw

1 Starting the cut
Because the blade cuts in an upward direction, the material's top surface tends to splinter; place the best face down. Before plugging in the saw, carefully turn the blade by hand to ensure that it isn't jammed.

To start a cut, place the saw's base plate on the material and align the blade just to the waste side of your cutting line. Back the blade away to avoid jamming at startup. Check that the power cord or extension is away from the cutting path.

Kerf splitter

Ripping fence

2 Cutting
Once the motor has reached speed, slowly feed the blade into the stock. If you have trouble following the cutting line, use a straightedge guide, as shown below. If the saw binds, back it off an inch and try again. On long cuts—especially rips—place a commercially available kerf splitter *(inset)* in the kerf to prevent binding. To rip *(left)*, attach the ripping fence loosely; if the cut is too far in, use a guide *(step 3)*. Lining up the blade to the waste side of the width mark at the board's end, tighten the screw holding the fence.

Ripping can be slow, dusty work and is especially prone to kickback. Cut by pushing the saw slowly away from you. When you need to reposition yourself, let the blade stop, then back the saw off an inch in the kerf; move farther down the line, then start up the saw with the blade away from the material to be cut. For very long cuts, you may have to stop the saw, back it off, and reposition the kerf splitter.

1x4 hardwood straightedge guide

C-clamp

3 Using a guide
To make really straight cuts with a circular saw, clamp a straight length of hardwood lumber to the material to guide the saw's base plate. Measure from the blade to the edge of the base plate; clamp the guide at that distance from your cutting line (measure from two points for greater accuracy). Make sure the clamps won't interfere with the saw. As you make the cut, keep the saw's base plate riding against the guide for the length of the cut.

4 Finishing the cut
At the end of the cut, be prepared to support the saw's weight; you may need to grasp the front handle with your free hand. When you're crosscutting an unsupported piece, you can avoid splintering by accelerating right at the end of the cut. Always wait for the blade to come to a complete stop before you swing the saw up or set it down.

THE PORTABLE SABER SAW

This saw's high-speed motor drives one of many types of blades in an up-and-down (reciprocating) motion; the blade on an orbital model goes forward and up, then back on the downstroke, for faster cuts. The tool excels at cutting curves, circles, and cutouts, but you can also use it for straight cutting or beveling. Consider a variable-speed model for greater control on tight curves or different materials. Choose the right blade for the job *(page 16)*. Blades with 4 to 7 teeth per inch (tpi) are designed for rough, rapid cuts in wood. Fine finish work, tight curves, and scrollwork require blades in the 10 to 20 tpi range. For thick metals, use 14 to 18 tpi blades; thin metals demand even finer teeth (24 to 32 tpi). Specialty blades also are available to cut other materials.

SABER SAW

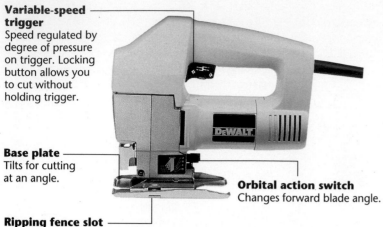

Variable-speed trigger
Speed regulated by degree of pressure on trigger. Locking button allows you to cut without holding trigger.

Base plate
Tilts for cutting at an angle.

Ripping fence slot
Insert adjustable fence to help guide straight cuts parallel to edge of board or sheet. Fence can usually be turned upside down to serve as circle guide.

Orbital action switch
Changes forward blade angle.

STANDARD SABER SAW BLADES

Fine wood-cutting blade
For smooth cuts in wood and sheet materials.

Coarse wood-cutting blade
For fast, but rough cuts in wood and sheet materials.

Scrolling blade
For smooth, intricate cuts.

Metal-cutting blade
Cuts metal, tubing, plastic. May require cutting oil to keep metal cool.

Carbide grit-edge blade
For materials like ceramic tile, slate, fiberglass, and metal.

Basic operation of the saber saw

Making a straight or curved cut

Because the saber saw's upward-cutting blade may cause the material's top surface to splinter, place the best side down. Guide the saw through straight cuts to the waste side of the cutting line. Cut slowly; fast cutting leads to snapped blades and an overheated motor. For straight cuts, clamp on a straightedge guide for the base plate to follow.

For tight curves, use the thinnest blade you can, and slow down even more the tighter the curve gets. In thick materials the blade may wander, giving inaccurate results; go more slowly or use a blade with more teeth (although this will give you a rougher cut). Don't brush sawdust off the base plate; blow it off instead.

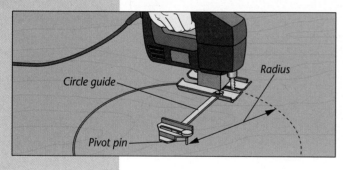

Circle guide

Radius

Pivot pin

Using a circle guide

Circles with a radius as large as 6 or 7 inches can be cut with a circle guide—often the ripping fence turned upside down. Before you install the circle guide, get the saw blade to the cutting line—you will need to drill a pilot hole or plunge the blade into the waste first if you are making a cutout. Align the pivot pin with the front of the blade and drive it into the midpoint of the desired circle; the length from the pin to the blade determines the circle's radius. Make the cut as you would any curved cut.

Making a cutout inside a panel

With a pilot hole or a plunge cut

Either drill a hole for the blade in the waste area, or, in thin, soft materials start by "plunge cutting" with a rough-cutting blade. Rock the saw forward onto the front edge of the base plate until the blade is free of the material—since it moves up and down, be sure it will clear the surface at its fullest extension. Turn the saw on and with the nose of its base plate planted solidly, lower it slowly to let the blade cut into the material *(right)*. Once the blade is through the stock and the base plate rests on the surface, make the cut as you would a normal cut. For a rectangular cutout, round the corners on the first pass, then go back and make two cuts to square each corner; for a perfect circle, use a circle guide.

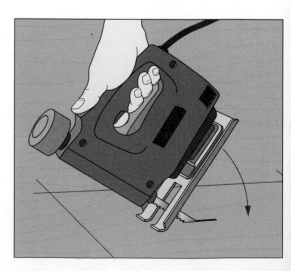

SHAPING

Once sawn, the stock for many projects still needs to be cut, shaped, or smoothed before being fastened; this is where the shaping tools come into play.

Planes: Turn to planes—either bench or block type—to smooth surfaces, square boards, and make fine joint adjustments. Bench planes smooth and square in line with the grain. Three main types are the jointer plane (about 22 inches long), the versatile and popular jack plane (14 inches long), and the smoothing plane (9¾ inches long). The shorter block plane—typically 6 inches long—smooths end grain and cuts bevels. To get the most from planes, you need to know their components, and keep them sharp and in fine adjustment.

Chisels: If kept sharp, chisels perform a variety of tasks—rough shaping of framing members, paring notches and grooves, and cutting mortises for door hinges and hardware. Concentrate on the basic types shown on page 18; for finish work or joinery, buy more specialized chisels.

Rasps and files: These should only be used when planes or sanding tools aren't suitable, such as on contours or cutouts. Files can handle metal as well, and perforated rasps will shape several materials. Tooth pattern, tooth coarseness, length (a longer tool has larger teeth), and shape determine performance. Common shapes include flat, half-round, and round. For general-purpose work, choose the half-round style.

The portable electric router: The router makes short work of many painstaking joinery and shaping tasks formerly done with chisels and specialty planes. Fitted with the proper bit, the router cuts dadoes and grooves, V-grooves, rounded grooves, and even dovetails. It can also round, bevel, or otherwise shape the board edges; trim plastic laminate at a single pass; and whisk out hinge mortises with the aid of a template.

Basically a motor within a flat-based housing, the router turns a bit at speeds up to 25,000 rpm, resulting in fast, clean cuts. When choosing router bits for normal use, the high-speed steel type is sufficient. Carbide-tipped bits cost more but stay sharp longer—they're recommended for hard woods, particleboard, plastic laminate, or synthetic marble. When it comes to edge-cutting bits, ball-bearing pilots are best for smooth edge-forming without burning the stock.

Adjusting a bench plane

TOOLKIT
- Screwdriver or edge of lever cap

Preparing to use a jack plane

The lever cap holds the cutting iron and cap iron under tension against the "frog"—the sloped body. Lift up the locking lever to remove the lever cap, freeing the irons to set their clearance. Loosen the cap iron screw (you can use the edge of the lever cap for this) and adjust the irons to expose about 1/16" of the cutting iron beyond the cap iron.

Tighten the screw; then reassemble the plane. Check the angle and exposure of the blade by turning the plane over and sighting down its sole. If the blade is out of square, push the lateral adjustment lever toward the side that's further out. Turn the depth adjustment knob until the blade is just protruding from the mouth.

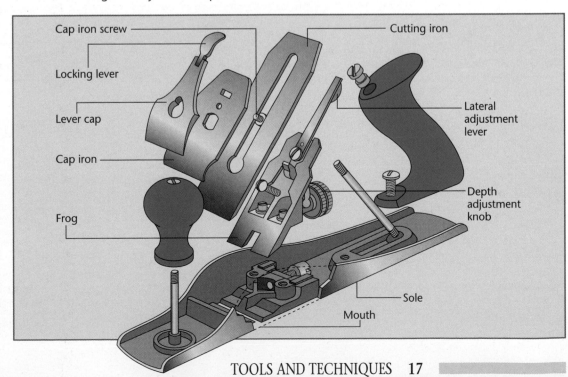

Cap iron screw — Cutting iron

Locking lever

Lever cap

Cap iron

Frog

Lateral adjustment lever

Depth adjustment knob

Sole

Mouth

HOW DO YOU USE A BENCH PLANE ON THE EDGE OF STOCK?

Grip the rear handle with one hand, and the front knob with the other. Or, you can press down on the front of the plane with your thumb as shown, bracing your fingers against the edge of the stock to guide the plane. Angle the plane slightly in relation to the direction of travel to make a shearing cut. Always cut in the direction of the grain. For clean, shallow cuts, determine how the grain slopes and cut "uphill" with the grain.

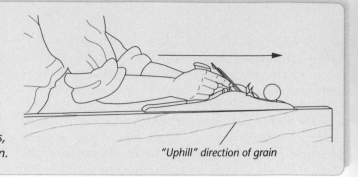

"Uphill" direction of grain

Adjusting and using a block plane

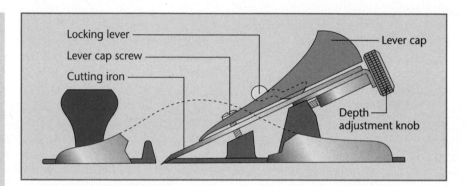

Locking lever
Lever cap screw
Cutting iron
Lever cap
Depth adjustment knob

Setting the block plane and planing

Depending on your model of block plane, the adjustments will be different. On "fully adjustable" models you'll find both a lateral adjustment lever and a depth adjustment knob, while "adjustable" block planes may have a depth adjustment nut and/or a locking lever for the cutting iron assembly. On these models *(above)*, you'll need to loosen the locking lever and adjust blade angle (and possibly the blade depth) by hand. To operate a block plane, hold it in one hand, applying pressure to the front knob with your forefinger. Use short, shearing strokes to cut end grain; to prevent splitting the edge of a board plane inward from both edges, slightly bevel the edge first, or clamp a piece of scrap wood to the far edge.

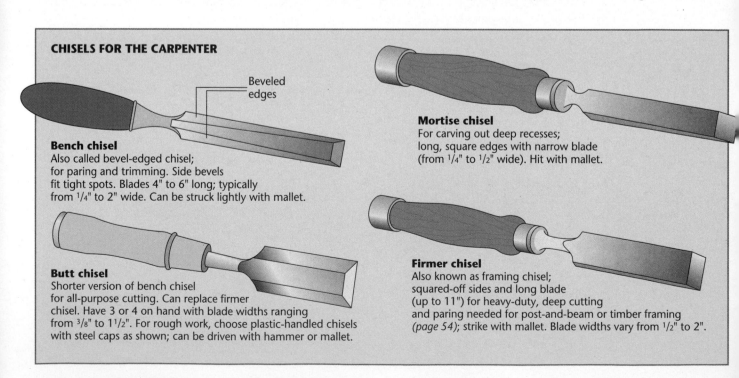

CHISELS FOR THE CARPENTER

Beveled edges

Bench chisel
Also called bevel-edged chisel; for paring and trimming. Side bevels fit tight spots. Blades 4" to 6" long; typically from 1/4" to 2" wide. Can be struck lightly with mallet.

Butt chisel
Shorter version of bench chisel for all-purpose cutting. Can replace firmer chisel. Have 3 or 4 on hand with blade widths ranging from 3/8" to 1 1/2". For rough work, choose plastic-handled chisels with steel caps as shown; can be driven with hammer or mallet.

Mortise chisel
For carving out deep recesses; long, square edges with narrow blade (from 1/4" to 1/2" wide). Hit with mallet.

Firmer chisel
Also known as framing chisel; squared-off sides and long blade (up to 11") for heavy-duty, deep cutting and paring needed for post-and-beam or timber framing *(page 54)*; strike with mallet. Blade widths vary from 1/2" to 2".

Shaping a notch

TOOLKIT
- Saw
- Bench chisel
- Mallet

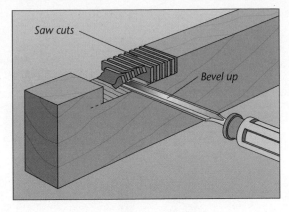

Saw cuts

Bevel up

Chiseling out the waste

To easily chisel a notch or groove, first cut the outlines to the proper depth with a handsaw or a circular saw. Then make several additional cuts through the waste area, as shown. Remove the waste wood with a chisel held horizontally, bevel up *(left)*. (You can also turn the chisel's bevel down and hold the tool at an angle with the bevel flat on the bottom of the recess.) Drive the chisel lightly with taps of a mallet; then finish smoothing the bottom with hand pressure alone, bevel up.

Shaping a hinge mortise

TOOLKIT
- Bench or mortise chisel
- Mallet

1 ▶ **Making preliminary chisel cuts**
To chisel a recess for a hinge or other hardware, first trace its outline. Score the lines with a sharp knife, then hold a bench or mortise chisel vertically—bevel toward the waste—and give it some light taps with a mallet. Next, make a series of parallel cross-grain cuts to the proper depth *(right)*.

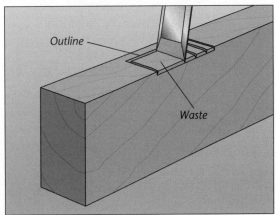

Outline

Waste

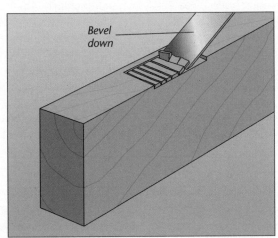

Bevel down

◀ **2** **Chiseling out the waste**
With the bevel facing down, lower the angle of the chisel so the bevel is lying flat on the surface; using hand pressure, chip out the waste wood *(left)*. Then work from the side, if possible, to clean across the grain; hold the chisel almost flat, bevel up. (For a hinge mortise starting at the edge of the stock like the one shown, you can also chip out the waste with the chisel horizontal and the bevel up.)

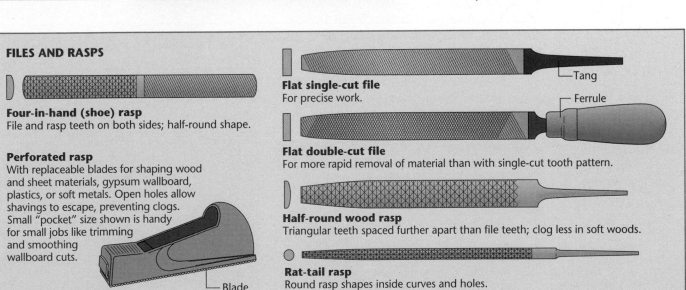

FILES AND RASPS

Four-in-hand (shoe) rasp
File and rasp teeth on both sides; half-round shape.

Perforated rasp
With replaceable blades for shaping wood and sheet materials, gypsum wallboard, plastics, or soft metals. Open holes allow shavings to escape, preventing clogs. Small "pocket" size shown is handy for small jobs like trimming and smoothing wallboard cuts.

— Blade

Flat single-cut file
For precise work.

— Tang

— Ferrule

Flat double-cut file
For more rapid removal of material than with single-cut tooth pattern.

Half-round wood rasp
Triangular teeth spaced further apart than file teeth; clog less in soft woods.

Rat-tail rasp
Round rasp shapes inside curves and holes.

ROUTER

ON/OFF switch

Base plate

Motor
Raised or lowered within housing to adjust cutting depth.

Housing
With comfortable hand grips at opposite sides.

Collet
Tighten to hold bit; ensure bit is properly installed.

BASIC ROUTER BITS

Straight bit

Rabbeting bit

Laminate-trimming bit

Arbor

Beading bit

Mortising bit

Ball-bearing pilot

Basic operation of the router

TOOLKIT
• Wrenches to fit collet

1 Setting up the router
Install the bit securely, following the instructions in the owner's manual. Unless your router has a shaft-locking button, you'll need two wrenches to tighten the collet. Next set the bit depth. Measure the clearance between the bit and base plate, or with the router overhanging the edge of the stock, lower the bit to a marked depth line. Wearing eye and hearing protection, test the depth on a piece of scrap wood. For a deep cut, make several passes to get to the final depth, lowering the bit slightly each time.

2 Routing
Line up router just outside stock. When motor gains full speed, feed the bit into the work carefully. The bit spins clockwise, so the router drifts or kicks the other way. To compensate, work router so the bit's leading edge bites into fresh stock, normally from left to right along an edge. To get a feel for the right speed, listen to motor's sound during a smooth cut; keep feeding at this speed. If the stock is rough you've cut too fast; if it's burned you're feeding too slowly. Turn the router off, but don't put it down until the bit stops.

Common router cuts

TOOLKIT
For routing grooves or dadoes:
• Stock for straight-edge guide
• Clamps
• Straight or decorative grooving bit
For rabbets or other edge treatment:
• Self-piloting bit
For a mortise:
• Template
• Top-piloted bit or a straight or mortising bit and guide bushing

Routing recesses, edges, and mortises
To rout a groove (in line with the grain) or a dado (across the grain), set up a guide for the router to follow. Determine the distance between the edge of the bit and the outside of the base plate to install the guide the correct distance from the cutting line. With a straight or decorative grooving bit, rout the dado *(right)* or groove. To shape a rabbet, trim edges, or cut any other type of edge-treatment, a self-piloting bit will guide the cut *(bottom right)*. Make sure the edge is smooth, since the pilot will follow any unevenness. A third type of cut is made by following a template, either store-bought or cut out of thin plywood. Use a top-piloted bit or install a guide bushing on the base plate, compensating for its width if you make the template. Keep the bushing in constant contact as you follow the template. For an interior cut, make a plunge cut: With the motor running, tilt the router back on part of the base plate, then slowly bring the router down to the surface while plunging the bit into the stock.

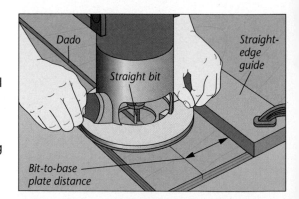

Dado

Straight bit

Straight-edge guide

Bit-to-base plate distance

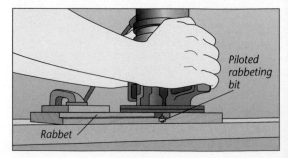

Piloted rabbeting bit

Rabbet

DRILLING

Carpenters drill holes for screws, bolts, dowels, door-knobs, locksets and hinges, masonry fasteners, picture hangers—even for nails in hardwoods. And if you double as a plumber or electrician, you'll need to drill holes for pipes or electrical cable.

The portable electric drill has virtually replaced its manual counterparts. A cordless model, with its rechargeable battery, is handy if you're working far from electrical power. However, you'll still find traditional hand drills in many carpenters' tool boxes.

The portable electric drill: An electric drill is classified by the biggest bit shank that can be accommodated in its chuck (jaws), most commonly 1/4-inch, 3/8-inch, and 1/2-inch. The bigger the chuck size, the higher the power output, or torque. Electric drills are rated light, medium, and heavy-duty. A heavy-duty model is only needed if you'll be using it daily or for long, uninterrupted sessions. As well as single-speed drills, there are variable-speed models which allow you to use the appropriate speed for the job—very handy when starting holes, drilling metals, or driving screws. Reversible gears are good for removing screws and stuck bits. For most carpentry, the 3/8-inch variable-speed drill is your best bet; it can handle a wide range of bits and accessories. If you're drilling large holes in masonry, you'll need a 1/2-inch drill or a hammer drill; both can be rented.

Tool catalogues and hardware stores are brimming with special drill bits, guides, and accessories for electric (or cordless) drills; a selection of the most reliable and commonly used bits is shown on page 22.

When operating an electric drill, clamp down the materials whenever possible beforehand, particularly when using a 3/8- or 1/2-inch drill. Wear safety goggles, especially when drilling metal. If your drill allows, match the speed to the job, using the highest speeds for small bits or soft woods, and slower speeds for large bits or metals. Don't apply much pressure when you're drilling, and don't turn off the motor until you've removed the bit from the material. If you're boring large holes in hard woods or metal—especially with oversize twist bits—first make a smaller pilot hole. Back the bit out occasionally to cool it and clear out the waste. When drilling tough metal, lubricate it with cutting oil as you go. If you want to stop at a certain depth, buy a stop collar designed for the purpose, use a pilot bit, or wrap tape around the bit at the correct depth.

Hand drills: The size of a hand brace is determined by its sweep, which varies from 6 to 14 inches; a 10-inch brace is a good choice. Using this tool is much like turning a crank with an attached bit: Position the center screw on the bit on your mark, then hold the butt knob and turn the offset handle clockwise. To drill horizontally, use your body to keep the knob in line. It takes some practice to keep the brace from wobbling.

The design of the compact push drill allows you to bore small holes quickly with one hand while holding the stock with the other. As you push down on the handle, a strong spring-and-spiral mechanism rotates the bit clockwise. The hand ("eggbeater") drill is used for holes up to 1/4 inch in diameter.

ELECTRIC DRILL

Jaws
Hold bit.

Reverse switch

Chuck
Opens or closes jaws when turned.

Locking button
Keeps motor running without pressing trigger.

Variable-speed trigger
Higher pressure increases speed.

CORDLESS DRILL

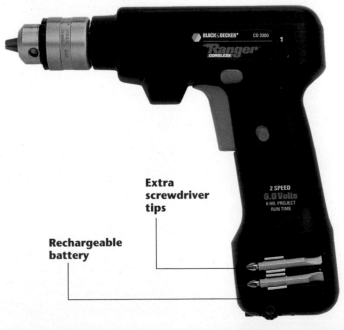

Extra screwdriver tips

Rechargeable battery

BITS FOR YOUR ELECTRIC DRILL

Masonry bit
Carbide-tipped; cuts slowly through concrete, stone, mortar joints, and brick. Hammer drill best for bits over 3/8".

Mandrel

Hole saw
For holes up to 4"; if bigger than 2 1/2", use 1/2" drill and heavy-duty mandrel (arbor). Standard depth 1", extra-deep models 2 1/2". Buy individual type with fixed blades; mandrel attachment with pilot bit fits drill chuck; hole saw snaps onto mandrel.

Oversize bit

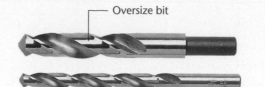

Twist bits
High-speed steel bits most durable. Sized from 1/16" to 1/2"; sets graduated by 32nds or 64ths. Increase reach with long-shank bit or extension shaft. Oversize bits bore holes up to 1".

Screwdriver and nutdriver bits
Transform drill into power screwdriver or wrench. Variable-speed drill required; screws or nuts must be started slowly or they'll strip.

Brad point bit
Bores cleaner holes than twist or spade bits, although more costly. Pointed tip prevents "skating" common with twist bits. Sizes range from 1/8" to 1".

Spade bit
Bores larger holes, from 3/8" to 1 1/2". Spur on tip keeps bit from "skating."

Pilot bit and adjusting hex wrench
Drills pilot hole for screw's threads, body hole for shank, countersink for head, and counterbore for wood plug—in one step. Match bit to screw size.

ASK A PRO

HOW CAN I AVOID COMMON DRILLING PROBLEMS?
Here are some time-tested techniques to help you center the spinning bit on its mark, drill a perpendicular—or correctly angled—hole, and keep the back of the stock from breaking away as the drill bit pierces. Tap an awl or center punch with a hammer to keep the bit from wandering when you're beginning a hole; a self-centering punch or bit is handy for door hinges. To keep a drill bit on the right path, a commercial doweling jig, as shown, or a portable drill stand helps increase accuracy. Or, simply line up the drill body with the help of a perpendicular try or combination square blade (use a T-bevel for an angled hole). With practice, you should be able to line up the drill by sight. To keep the back of the wood from tearing out, clamp a wood scrap against the back of your stock and bore through into the scrap; or, just as the tip of the bit pierces, flip the piece over and complete the hole from the opposite side.

Doweling jig

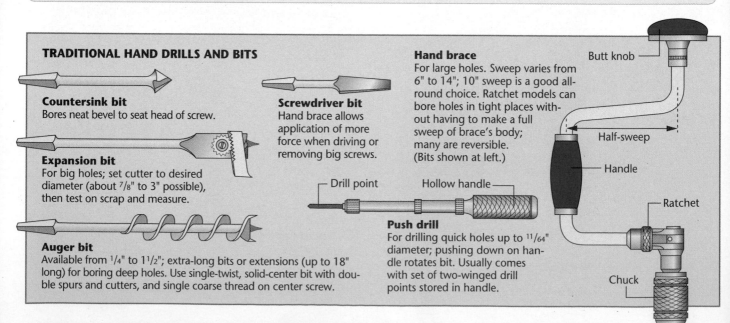

TRADITIONAL HAND DRILLS AND BITS

Countersink bit
Bores neat bevel to seat head of screw.

Expansion bit
For big holes; set cutter to desired diameter (about 7/8" to 3" possible), then test on scrap and measure.

Auger bit
Available from 1/4" to 1 1/2"; extra-long bits or extensions (up to 18" long) for boring deep holes. Use single-twist, solid-center bit with double spurs and cutters, and single coarse thread on center screw.

Screwdriver bit
Hand brace allows application of more force when driving or removing big screws.

Drill point

Hollow handle

Push drill
For drilling quick holes up to 11/64" diameter; pushing down on handle rotates bit. Usually comes with set of two-winged drill points stored in handle.

Hand brace
For large holes. Sweep varies from 6" to 14"; 10" sweep is a good all-round choice. Ratchet models can bore holes in tight places without having to make a full sweep of brace's body; many are reversible. (Bits shown at left.)

Butt knob

Half-sweep

Handle

Ratchet

Chuck

GAUGING LEVEL AND PLUMB

One of the carpenter's ongoing concerns is keeping all horizontal surfaces level and all vertical surfaces plumb. Problems with ill-fitting windows, doors, and finish work can often be traced back to inaccurate leveling and plumbing at an earlier stage. A collection of the tools you'll need are illustrated below.

Using a level: Test a level before using it: Place it on a surface that you've determined to be perfectly flat, then turn the instrument around and recheck it on the other edge. The readings should be identical in each case. To test a horizontal surface for level, place the tool on the surface; when the air bubble in liquid enclosed in glass tubing at the center lines up exactly between the two marks, you know the surface is level. When the level is held vertically, the tubes near each end indicate plumb.

Using a plumb bob: From above, maneuver the weight as close to the floor as possible without touching, using either your overhead or floor point as a reference. You'll find it helps to have a partner at the other end. Once the weight stops swinging, line up and mark the other point. If you're working outside, make sure that the wind isn't playing with the string.

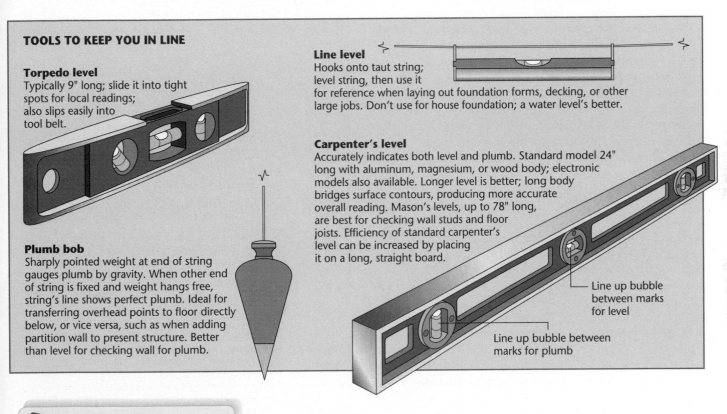

TOOLS TO KEEP YOU IN LINE

Torpedo level
Typically 9" long; slide it into tight spots for local readings; also slips easily into tool belt.

Line level
Hooks onto taut string; level string, then use it for reference when laying out foundation forms, decking, or other large jobs. Don't use for house foundation; a water level's better.

Carpenter's level
Accurately indicates both level and plumb. Standard model 24" long with aluminum, magnesium, or wood body; electronic models also available. Longer level is better; long body bridges surface contours, producing more accurate overall reading. Mason's levels, up to 78" long, are best for checking wall studs and floor joists. Efficiency of standard carpenter's level can be increased by placing it on a long, straight board.

Plumb bob
Sharply pointed weight at end of string gauges plumb by gravity. When other end of string is fixed and weight hangs free, string's line shows perfect plumb. Ideal for transferring overhead points to floor directly below, or vice versa, such as when adding partition wall to present structure. Better than level for checking wall for plumb.

Line up bubble between marks for level

Line up bubble between marks for plumb

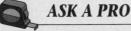 *ASK A PRO*

HOW DOES A WATER LEVEL WORK?
Trapped water always seeks its own level; when plastic tubing is filled with water, the water will be at the same height at both ends. You can use this to compare the heights of foundation forms or posts more precisely than with a line level, or you can easily transfer heights from one point to another around a room.

Water levels are sold commercially, but you can make your own from 1/4-inch-diameter clear plastic tubing or wider-diameter garden hose and water; food coloring may help make readings more visible. To operate a water level, make sure the tubing is free of air bubbles. Have a helper line up the water's height at one end with a reference point—post, foundation wall, or pencil mark. To transfer that point, hold up the other end at the appropriate location and mark the height of the water there. A pair of rubber stoppers or cork plugs allows you to store the device.

Clear garden hose filled with water

FASTENING

The art of fastening, like measuring and cutting, is one of carpentry's fundamentals, and you should become familiar with the tools that make it possible; hammers, staplers, and screwdrivers are the most basic. By taking time to master the techniques presented here, you'll reap immediate dividends in the form of a reduced number of bent nails and burred screws.

You'll also need wrenches for bolts and lag screws. The indispensable clamp keeps the pressure on while glue sets, or holds stock in place while you work on it.

For details on selecting the correct fasteners to complement these tools, turn to pages 45-48.

Hammers: Everyone knows what the claw hammer looks like, but not all are aware that differences in the tool's shape, weight, and head determine the one to pick for any specific project. Carpenters occasionally turn to other tools for driving nails or pounding stubborn joints together; the roofer's hatchet and an all-purpose mallet are two examples.

Hammer faces may be either flat or slightly convex. The convex, or bell-faced, type allows you to drive a nail flush without marring the wood's surface. Mesh-type faces are available for rough framing work—the mesh pattern keeps the face from glancing off large nailheads, and can help guide the nails. Don't use this face for finish work, since the pattern will imprint the surface. Head weights range from 7 to 28 ounces. Pick a weight that's comfortable but not too light: your arm may actually tire sooner swinging a light hammer for heavy work than it would wielding a heavier hammer. Though both steel and fiberglass handles are stronger, some carpenters may prefer the feel of wood.

Staplers and nailers: Hand and power-driven staplers make some carpentry jobs quicker and easier. Light-weight staplers are designed to be used one-handed, leaving your other hand free to hold the material. To operate the squeeze-type stapler, simply hold it flush against the material and squeeze down on the trigger. With the hammer-type, first position the material where you want it, then strike the stapler against its surface.

Most heavy-duty staplers and nailers are pneumatically or electrically driven, although flooring nailers are driven with a mallet. Some models hold two or three sizes of fasteners in large quantities, and thus are extremely useful for such "assembly-line" jobs as roof sheathing, framing, flooring, or fencing. These heavy-duty fasteners are expensive, so you'll probably want to rent one for a specific job.

Wrenches: You may be surprised how often you'll reach for a wrench on a carpentry job—to drive lag screws, tighten bolts and nuts, or remove existing structures such as cabinets and built-ins. The basic selection to add to your tool box is shown on page 26.

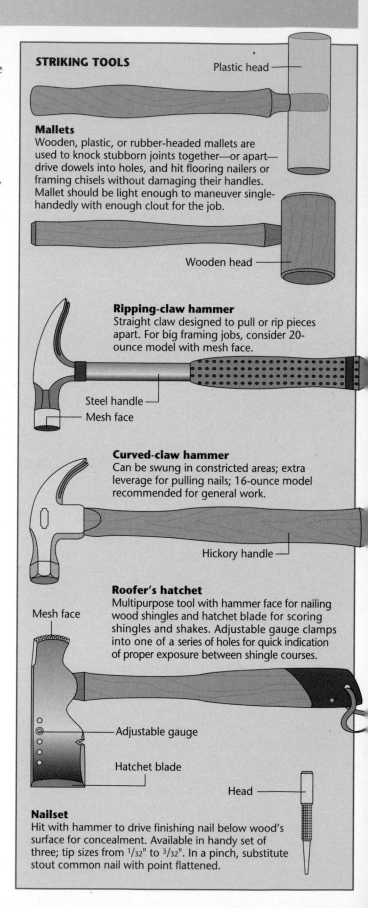

STRIKING TOOLS

Plastic head

Mallets
Wooden, plastic, or rubber-headed mallets are used to knock stubborn joints together—or apart—drive dowels into holes, and hit flooring nailers or framing chisels without damaging their handles. Mallet should be light enough to maneuver single-handedly with enough clout for the job.

Wooden head

Ripping-claw hammer
Straight claw designed to pull or rip pieces apart. For big framing jobs, consider 20-ounce model with mesh face.

Steel handle
Mesh face

Curved-claw hammer
Can be swung in constricted areas; extra leverage for pulling nails; 16-ounce model recommended for general work.

Hickory handle

Roofer's hatchet
Multipurpose tool with hammer face for nailing wood shingles and hatchet blade for scoring shingles and shakes. Adjustable gauge clamps into one of a series of holes for quick indication of proper exposure between shingle courses.

Mesh face

Adjustable gauge

Hatchet blade

Head

Nailset
Hit with hammer to drive finishing nail below wood's surface for concealment. Available in handy set of three; tip sizes from 1/32" to 3/32". In a pinch, substitute stout common nail with point flattened.

Screwdrivers: The screwdriver vies with the hammer as the most frequently employed tool in a do-it-yourselfer's collection. For best results, there are some fine points to consider when selecting and using screwdrivers.

When you're choosing a screwdriver, keep in mind that they fall into three main categories: standard, Phillips, and square drive. The screwdriver tip must fit the screw exactly; an ill-fitting tip may lead to a burred screw head or gouged work surface. A long screwdriver lets you apply more torque than a shorter one, but the long shank may not leave you room to maneuver. When buying a large, all-purpose screwdriver, choose one with a square shank; you can fit a wrench onto it to apply extra leverage to stubborn screws. Don't forget that you can also install a screwdriver bit in an electric drill or hand brace *(page 21)*. (If you choose an electric drill, you'll need a variable-speed model).

Clamps: These hold assembled parts tight while glue sets, and serve as an on-site helper to hold stock to be worked. They're also needed to keep saw or router guides in place. If you want to protect wood surfaces from being marred by the jaws of a metal clamp, fit a scrap block of wood, or fabric or newspaper, between the jaws and the wood surface. Tighten clamps until they're snug, but not too tight. Clamps come in many shapes and sizes, as illustrated on page 27.

Nailing

TOOLKIT
• Hammer
For finishing or casing nails:
• Nailset to drive finishing nails
• Wood dough or putty

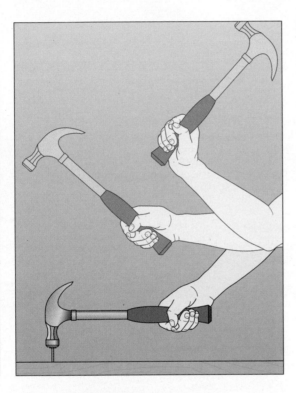

Special nailing situations

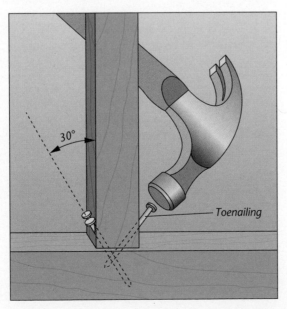

Toenailing

Basic techniques

To start a nail, hold it just below the head between your thumb and forefinger, and give it a few light taps with the hammer. This way, if you miss the nail, you won't smash your fingers and the work is protected. Once the nail is started, remove your fingers and swing more fully. The most effective hammer stroke combines wrist, arm, and shoulder action. At the top of the stroke, both wrist and elbow are cocked. The downstroke begins with the shoulder and elbow driving down; near the end of the stroke, the wrist snaps down. Experiment on scrap until you get the feel of a fluid stroke—most beginners use too much wrist. Think of the hammer as an extension of your arm, with your shoulder, elbow, forearm, and wrist working together.

Drive finishing or casing nails to within $1/8$" of the surface, beginning with full hammer strokes and ending with careful taps. Tap the nailhead below the surface with the point of a nailset. Use wood dough or putty to conceal the resulting hole.

Toenailing or clinching a nail

When you can't nail through the face of one board into the end of another (as when you're nailing wall studs into place), you must drive nails at an angle through one board into the other. This is called "toenailing." Drive the nails from both sides at about a 30° angle from the vertical; stagger the nails so they won't hit each other *(left)*. The nails should penetrate solidly into both pieces without splitting the wood. "Clinching" is a method used to face-nail or laminate two boards together: Hammer overlength nails through both boards until their heads are firmly seated. Turn the boards over, bend each nail end over perpendicular to its body, and then hammer it flat, driving the end into the wood. It's easier to bend the nails' ends—and bury the nails—in line with the grain, but this may dimple the wood; going across the grain is better.

Removing nails

TOOLKIT
- Steel-handled hammer and scrap wood block

OR

- Cat's paw or pry-bar and hammer

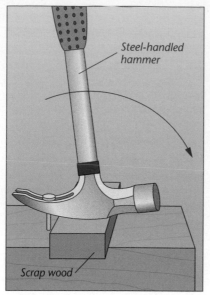

Steel-handled hammer

Scrap wood

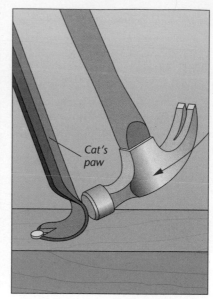

Cat's paw

Pulling a nail

There are two ways to pull out tough nails. You can use a hammer placed on top of a piece of scrap to lever out the nail *(far left)*—a wood-handled hammer may not be strong enough for this task; use a steel-handled model. Or, drive a cat's paw or prybar underneath the nailhead *(near left)* to pry the nail up.

LIGHTWEIGHT STAPLERS

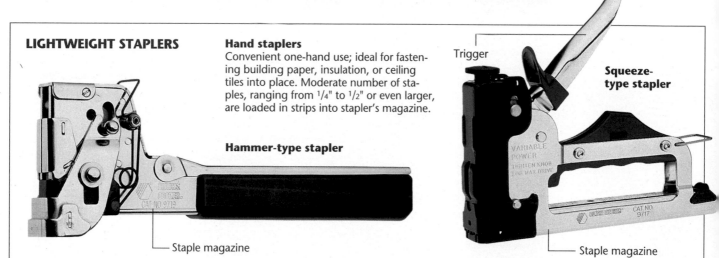

Hand staplers

Convenient one-hand use; ideal for fastening building paper, insulation, or ceiling tiles into place. Moderate number of staples, ranging from 1/4" to 1/2" or even larger, are loaded in strips into stapler's magazine.

Hammer-type stapler

Staple magazine

Trigger

Squeeze-type stapler

Staple magazine

WRENCHES FOR THE CARPENTER

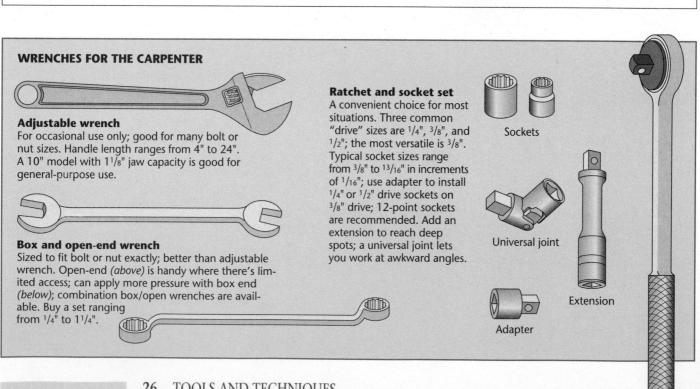

Adjustable wrench

For occasional use only; good for many bolt or nut sizes. Handle length ranges from 4" to 24". A 10" model with 1 1/8" jaw capacity is good for general-purpose use.

Box and open-end wrench

Sized to fit bolt or nut exactly; better than adjustable wrench. Open-end *(above)* is handy where there's limited access; can apply more pressure with box end *(below)*; combination box/open wrenches are available. Buy a set ranging from 1/4" to 1 1/4".

Ratchet and socket set

A convenient choice for most situations. Three common "drive" sizes are 1/4", 3/8", and 1/2"; the most versatile is 3/8". Typical socket sizes range from 3/8" to 13/16" in increments of 1/16"; use adapter to install 1/4" or 1/2" drive sockets on 3/8" drive; 12-point sockets are recommended. Add an extension to reach deep spots; a universal joint lets you work at awkward angles.

Sockets

Universal joint

Adapter

Extension

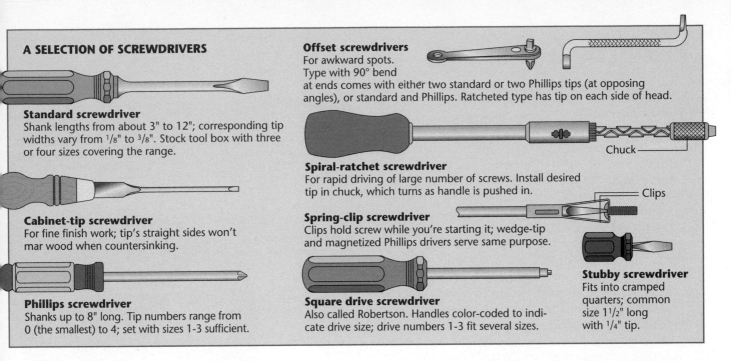

A SELECTION OF SCREWDRIVERS

Standard screwdriver
Shank lengths from about 3" to 12"; corresponding tip widths vary from 1/8" to 3/8". Stock tool box with three or four sizes covering the range.

Cabinet-tip screwdriver
For fine finish work; tip's straight sides won't mar wood when countersinking.

Phillips screwdriver
Shanks up to 8" long. Tip numbers range from 0 (the smallest) to 4; set with sizes 1-3 sufficient.

Offset screwdrivers
For awkward spots. Type with 90° bend at ends comes with either two standard or two Phillips tips (at opposing angles), or standard and Phillips. Ratcheted type has tip on each side of head.

Chuck

Spiral-ratchet screwdriver
For rapid driving of large number of screws. Install desired tip in chuck, which turns as handle is pushed in.

Spring-clip screwdriver
Clips hold screw while you're starting it; wedge-tip and magnetized Phillips drivers serve same purpose.

Clips

Square drive screwdriver
Also called Robertson. Handles color-coded to indicate drive size; drive numbers 1-3 fit several sizes.

Stubby screwdriver
Fits into cramped quarters; common size 1 1/2" long with 1/4" tip.

Driving screws

TOOLKIT
- Drill
- Screwdriver

Drilling a pilot hole

Screws require pilot holes in all but the softest materials. (Pilot holes are unnecessary if you're driving drywall screws into soft wood with a power drill.) Using a bit the diameter of the screw's shank, drill through the top piece of wood. In hard woods, also drill a smaller hole for the threads—about half as deep as the threaded portion is long. Use a bit the same size as the core between the threads. Flathead and oval head screws are countersunk flush with the surface, or can be counterbored and covered with wood putty or a plug. To deal with a stubborn screw, rub paraffin or wax on its threads. If it still sticks, enlarge the pilot hole and try again.

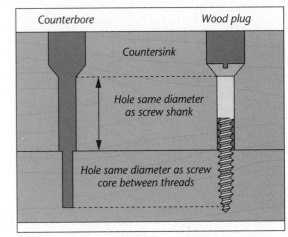

Counterbore   Wood plug

Countersink

Hole same diameter as screw shank

Hole same diameter as screw core between threads

A COLLECTION OF CLAMPS

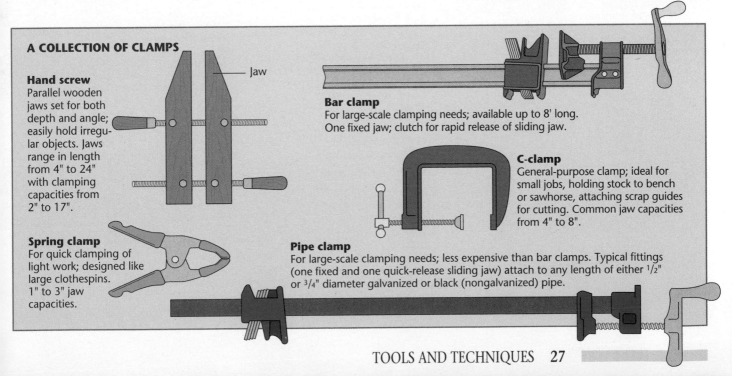

Jaw

Hand screw
Parallel wooden jaws set for both depth and angle; easily hold irregular objects. Jaws range in length from 4" to 24" with clamping capacities from 2" to 17".

Spring clamp
For quick clamping of light work; designed like large clothespins. 1" to 3" jaw capacities.

Bar clamp
For large-scale clamping needs; available up to 8' long. One fixed jaw; clutch for rapid release of sliding jaw.

C-clamp
General-purpose clamp; ideal for small jobs, holding stock to bench or sawhorse, attaching scrap guides for cutting. Common jaw capacities from 4" to 8".

Pipe clamp
For large-scale clamping needs; less expensive than bar clamps. Typical fittings (one fixed and one quick-release sliding jaw) attach to any length of either 1/2" or 3/4" diameter galvanized or black (nongalvanized) pipe.

FINISHING

Most projects require some careful touch-up—prepping, sealing, and sanding—before you're through. Once surfaces are smooth and clean, you're ready to apply paint, wallpaper, or any other finish.

Prepping, or rough patching before sanding, is your first step; when it comes time to sand, choose between traditional muscle power and electric power. For small areas, traditional hand-sanding produces a fine finish, and in tight spots or on contoured surfaces, it may be the only feasible method. On the other hand, portable power sanders save time and aching muscles. They fall into two main types: belt and finishing. Belt sanders remove a lot of stock quickly—they're best for rough, general sanding over large areas. High-speed finishing sanders offer a finer, more controlled finish, and they won't remove much stock, even with coarse paper attached. (For very fine finishes, do the final sanding by hand with a block, or consider getting a random orbit sander, which leaves less-visible swirls than the finishing type.) Most finishing sanders are available with either straight-line or orbital action; some allow you to switch from one to the other. Straight-line action usually produces a finer finish, since the stroke is always back and forth with the grain. An orbital sander moves in very tight circles, resulting in a polished look. Small "palm-grip" models are designed to be held in one hand, allowing comfortable sanding of vertical and overhead surfaces.

BELT SANDER

Sanding belt
Most common size is 3"x24"; its length and width identify sander's size. Make sure you buy the correct size replacement belts. Belt coarseness indicated by grit numbers like those on sandpaper sheets, but belt numbers tend to be consistently lower and more coarse; 36-50 is coarse, 50-80 is medium, 80-120 is fine.

Dust collector

Locking button
Keeps motor running without pressing switch.

Trigger switch

Tracking control knob
Turn to move sanding belt to middle of roller.

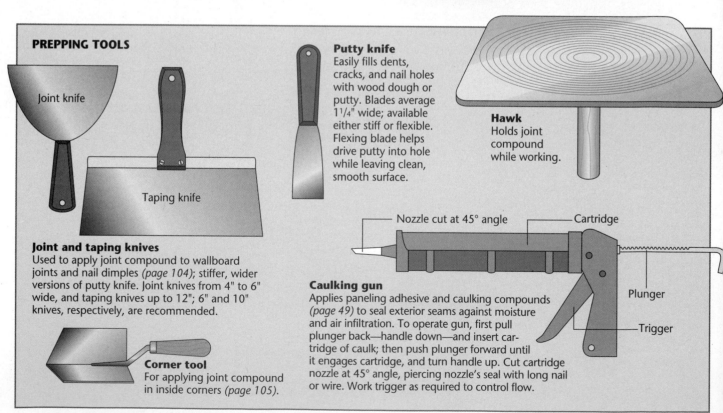

PREPPING TOOLS

Joint knife

Taping knife

Putty knife
Easily fills dents, cracks, and nail holes with wood dough or putty. Blades average 1¹/₄" wide; available either stiff or flexible. Flexing blade helps drive putty into hole while leaving clean, smooth surface.

Hawk
Holds joint compound while working.

Joint and taping knives
Used to apply joint compound to wallboard joints and nail dimples (page 104); stiffer, wider versions of putty knife. Joint knives from 4" to 6" wide, and taping knives up to 12"; 6" and 10" knives, respectively, are recommended.

Corner tool
For applying joint compound in inside corners (page 105).

Nozzle cut at 45° angle

Cartridge

Plunger

Trigger

Caulking gun
Applies paneling adhesive and caulking compounds (page 49) to seal exterior seams against moisture and air infiltration. To operate gun, first pull plunger back—handle down—and insert cartridge of caulk; then push plunger forward until it engages cartridge, and turn handle up. Cut cartridge nozzle at 45° angle, piercing nozzle's seal with long nail or wire. Work trigger as required to control flow.

FINISHING SANDER

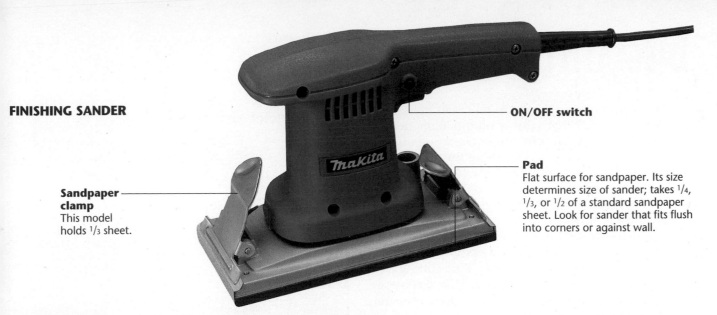

ON/OFF switch

Sandpaper clamp
This model holds 1/3 sheet.

Pad
Flat surface for sandpaper. Its size determines size of sander; takes 1/4, 1/3, or 1/2 of a standard sandpaper sheet. Look for sander that fits flush into corners or against wall.

Choosing sandpaper

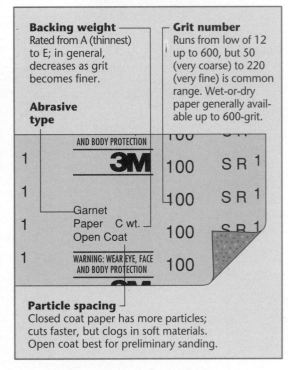

Backing weight
Rated from A (thinnest) to E; in general, decreases as grit becomes finer.

Abrasive type

Grit number
Runs from low of 12 up to 600, but 50 (very coarse) to 220 (very fine) is common range. Wet-or-dry paper generally available up to 600-grit.

AND BODY PROTECTION

3M   100   S R 1

1   100   S R 1

1   Garnet Paper C wt. Open Coat   100   S R 1

1   WARNING: WEAR EYE, FACE AND BODY PROTECTION   100

Particle spacing
Closed coat paper has more particles; cuts faster, but clogs in soft materials. Open coat best for preliminary sanding.

Deciphering the backing information

Choosing the correct type of sandpaper for the job involves knowing about all the different abrasive materials used in making it. Read the sheet's backing for sandpaper type and other information *(left)*. "Sandpaper" is a misnomer, since it's not made with sand. The most common materials are as follows: **Flint** paper (beige colored) is the most economical choice, but it won't last long. It's useful for very rough sanding or for removing an old finish. **Aluminum oxide**, light gray to light brown, is a very rugged synthetic paper, best for rough to medium sanding by hand and for power sanding. **Garnet** paper, reddish- to golden-brown, is the ideal selection for hand sanding, particularly in the last stages. **Silicon carbide**, blue-gray to charcoal in color, is known as "wet-or-dry" because its backing is waterproof; wetting the paper prevents the minute grains from clogging. Use it wet on metal, dry as a final polish on wood, or wet to sand joint compound when installing gypsum wallboard.

Sanding techniques

TOOLKIT
• Sanding block
OR
• Power sander

Sanding block

Hand or power sanding

Always divide the sanding procedure into at least three stages: rough-sand with 50- to 80-grit paper; sand again with 120-grit; finally sand with 180- to 220-grit paper. To provide a flat surface for the sandpaper when hand sanding, buy a sanding block, or make your own from a 2x4 scrap. Always sand in line with the wood grain *(left)*; cross-grain lines will show up as ugly scratches.

Power sanders require little muscle power; in fact, apply no pressure—the weight of the sander is sufficient. For the belt sander, remember always to keep the tool moving when it's in contact with the work. Move the sander forward and back in line with the grain. At the end of each pass, lift it and start again, overlapping the previous pass by half. For maximum removal, you can sand at a slight angle to the grain, but always finish directly with the grain. The finishing sander works best in line with the grain.

DISMANTLING TOOLS

From time to time you'll need to pull bent nails or replace a wall stud that's out of plumb. Remodeling may call for chiseling through tough plaster and lath, prying up a rotting subfloor, or cutting the opening for a new skylight. Dismantling often involves some outright bashing to separate old wall coverings from framing members or to knock apart the framing members themselves for removal.

General dismantling tools help supply the muscle for the bending, prying, and controlled bashing that are all facets of the demolition process. Heavy-duty cutting tools are designed to get through a variety of tough building materials. Pliers are invaluable for small-scale gripping, twisting, bending, and cutting.

Because dismantling is often rough and messy, wear protective boots, sturdy clothes and work gloves, hard hat, safety goggles, and respiratory protection (*see page 5*).

PLIERS FOR THE CARPENTER'S TOOLBOX

Pivot screw

Slip-joint pliers
Also known as combination pliers. Lightweight version of lineman's pliers with notch and pivot screw that adjust jaw capacity. Sizes typically range from 4" to 10"; buy larger size for maximum strength.

Moving pivot

Rib-joint pliers
Like slip-joint pliers, but for heavier work. Long handles offer more leverage; 7"- or 10"-long handles recommended. Ideal for grasping pipe. Set to desired width; jaws stay parallel for better grip.

Adjusting screw

Straight jaws

Release lever

Locking pliers
Keep pressure on material being gripped, letting you concentrate on turning or bending. Excellent for removing gnarled bolts or for holding nut tight while you turn bolt's head with wrench. Typical sizes 5", 7", and 10"; available with curved or straight jaws.

Cutters

Serrated jaws

Lineman's pliers
Perform heavy-duty gripping and bending; cutters behind serrated jaws cut wire and thin metals. Typical size is 9".

DEMOLITION TOOLS

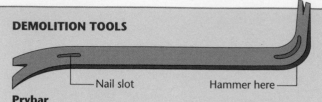

Nail slot — Hammer here

Prybar
Handy for removing wallboard or plaster and lath from wall studs, or for pulling exposed nails. Flat-shank type good for nail pulling and small jobs, but tends to flex too much for heavy prying. Typically 12" long; available longer. Be sure bar you choose provides good hammering surface; drive chisel end into crack or under tough nailhead with hammer blows on the opposite end; pry by hand or with hammer blows.

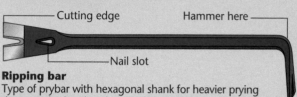

Cutting edge — Hammer here

Nail slot

Ripping bar
Type of prybar with hexagonal shank for heavier prying than standard prybar, but used same way; may have offset end or straight chisel (*shown*). Typically 18" long.

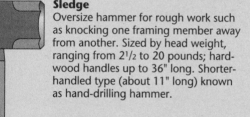

Sledge
Oversize hammer for rough work such as knocking one framing member away from another. Sized by head weight, ranging from $2\frac{1}{2}$ to 20 pounds; hardwood handles up to 36" long. Shorter-handled type (about 11" long) known as hand-drilling hammer.

Nail-pulling claw

Wrecking bar
For tough work; longer than prybar, giving much greater leverage, and hands kept farther from sharp materials like metal lath and nails. Run from 12" to 36" long; consider the trade-off between power and maneuverability in longer bars. Bar should have offset chisel at one end and hooked, nail-pulling claw at other end. For extra leverage, hammer on hooked end; place a block of scrap wood between hook and hard surface to further increase leverage, and to protect the surface if necessary.

Offset chisel

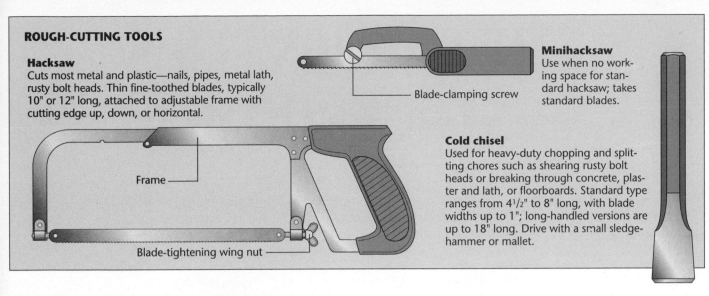

ROUGH-CUTTING TOOLS

Hacksaw
Cuts most metal and plastic—nails, pipes, metal lath, rusty bolt heads. Thin fine-toothed blades, typically 10" or 12" long, attached to adjustable frame with cutting edge up, down, or horizontal.

Blade-clamping screw

Frame

Blade-tightening wing nut

Minihacksaw
Use when no working space for standard hacksaw; takes standard blades.

Cold chisel
Used for heavy-duty chopping and splitting chores such as shearing rusty bolt heads or breaking through concrete, plaster and lath, or floorboards. Standard type ranges from 4 1/2" to 8" long, with blade widths up to 1"; long-handled versions are up to 18" long. Drive with a small sledge-hammer or mallet.

RECIPROCATING SAW

Trigger switch
Variable-speed for more precise control; use lower speeds for cutting metal and for finer work, and higher speeds for rough cuts in wood.

Blade
Varies in length, tooth size, and design. Blades with 3 1/2-10 teeth per inch (tpi) are best on wood; 14-32 tpi for metal. Also available: general-purpose blade (for wood, sheet products, and plaster) and plaster-cutting blade (also cuts through metal lath behind). Blades from 2 1/2" to 12" long.

Reciprocating saw
Designed for roughing-in window, skylight, or door openings; fit with proper blade to cut diverse materials such as wall studs, plaster and lath, old nails, steel pipe. Operates like freehand saber saw, but is expensive to buy; consider renting one.

Blade guard
Pivots; keep pressed against material being cut.

Using a reciprocating saw

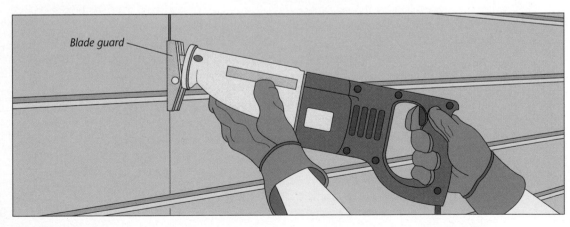

Blade guard

Making a cut
Always wear eye protection. Keep a firm grip on the rear handle with one hand, and cup the body with your other hand, as shown. Always keep the blade guard flush against the material being cut (*above*), for safety's sake and to prevent excess vibration. To make a wall cutout, start from a predrilled hole. The saw blades are flexible, which helps you make tricky cuts, but be careful—they can snap. Practice with the saw to keep the blade tip from bouncing against the work.

THE CARPENTER'S STOCKROOM

Carpentry's basic materials may lack glamour, but they certainly merit respect. Every carpenter embarking on a project should remember that the finished product will be only as handsome, functional, and durable as the components.

This chapter presents carpentry's everyday materials: lumber, sheet products, paneling and trim, roofing and siding, fasteners, and sealing products. You can use this information as a quick primer and reference to what's available, and as a dictionary for the mysterious jargon of lumberyards and hardware stores. For instance, you'll discover what is meant by a 10-penny galvanized finishing nail, or dimension lumber. The chapters on rough and finish carpentry will give you more detail on exactly what you'll need for a particular job—what size finishing nails, or plywood sheathing, or floor joists; you'll also find descriptions of many of the more specialized materials that are required.

A very important part of planning any project is estimating amounts and volumes of materials. Always leave a slight margin for waste and error, so that you can make all the purchases at once. Done well, estimating saves money; done carelessly, it will cost both time and money. This chapter will include guidelines to help you estimate the necessary materials once your plans are ready to go.

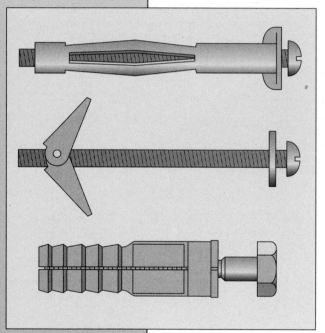

You may already be familiar with common screws and nails, but to hang shelves or pictures on gypsum wallboard or plaster wall, you'll need to use a special fastener. Shown above are the fasteners used for walls made of materials other than wood.

CHOOSING LUMBER

Lumber is the starting point for almost all carpentry projects. But the landslide of lumber sizes, species, and grades awaiting the uninitiated can be overwhelming at first. You may also be surprised at how unhelpful a busy lumberyard employee can be if you have no idea what you're looking for! On the other hand, armed with an understanding of some basic terms, you can usually secure friendly help and more detailed information.

If you're just building some simple garage shelves or patching a hole in the backyard fence, you can probably close your eyes and buy any boards. But for anything larger, you should do a little homework first.

Lumber is described as either hardwood or softwood. These terms refer to the origin of the wood: hardwoods come from deciduous trees, and softwoods come from conifers. As a rule, hardwoods are harder than softwoods. However, the terms can be misleading; some softwoods are actually harder than so-called hardwoods such as poplar or aspen.

You'll probably select one of the softwoods for your rough carpentry project because they are generally much less expensive, easier to work, and more readily available than hardwoods. Nearly all facets of house construction today are done with softwoods. The durable, handsomely grained hardwoods are generally reserved for fine interior paneling, flooring, and other finish work.

HOW LUMBER IS SOLD
Once you've chosen whether to work with softwood or hardwood, you'll need to know the size categories.

Lumber sizing: Generally, softwood lengths run from 6 to 20 feet in 2-foot increments. Lumberyards and lumber grading associations often divide softwood lumber into five size categories: **Strips** are small pieces, 1 inch thick or less and 6 inches or less in width, and are often used for furring strips. **Boards**, graded by appearance, are normally not more than 2 inches thick, and are 4 to 12 inches wide. They are typically used for shelves and paneling. **Dimension lumber**, graded mainly for strength, is intended for structural framing. Sizes range from 2 to 4 inches thick and at least 2 inches wide. **Beams and stringers** are structural lumber 5 inches thick or more used for beams and headers; the width must exceed the thickness by at least 2 inches. **Posts and timbers** are heavy construction lumber used for posts and heavy columns. Dimensions are 5 inches by 5 inches and larger. The cross section is nearly square—the width must not exceed the thickness by more than 2 inches.

Hardwoods typically come in standard thicknesses but random lengths. Check sizing standards with your lumberyard.

Nominal and actual sizes: Lumber dimensions such as 2x4 refer to the nominal size, or the size when sliced

STANDARD DIMENSIONS OF SOFTWOODS	
Nominal size	Surfaced (actual) size
1x2	$3/4$"x$1^1/2$"
1x3	$3/4$"x$2^1/2$"
1x4	$3/4$"x$3^1/2$"
1x6	$3/4$"x$5^1/2$"
1x8	$3/4$"x$7^1/4$"
1x10	$3/4$"x$9^1/4$"
1x12	$3/4$"x$11^1/4$"
2x3	$1^1/2$"x$2^1/2$"
2x4	$1^1/2$"x$3^1/2$"
2x6	$1^1/2$"x$5^1/2$"
2x8	$1^1/2$"x$7^1/4$"
2x10	$1^1/2$"x$9^1/4$"
2x12	$1^1/2$"x$11^1/4$"
4x4	$3^1/2$"x$3^1/2$"
4x10	$3^1/2$"x$9^1/4$"
6x8	$5^1/2$"x$7^1/2$"

from the log. This can be confusing for the beginner because nominal dimensions do not correspond to the actual dimensions when the piece is sold; the piece is first dried and surfaced (planed), reducing it to a smaller size. Almost all the softwood lumber that you'll find in the lumberyard is surfaced on four sides (designated "S4S"). Some lumber is sold "rough"—without being surfaced—so the actual dimensions are closer to the nominal dimensions.

Board foot versus lineal foot: The price of lumber is calculated either by the lineal foot or by the board foot.

ASK A PRO

HOW DO I ESTIMATE MY LUMBER NEEDS?
A good set of scale plans will come in handy in figuring out the amount of lumber you'll need for a particular job. The best way to estimate your lumber needs is simply to count up the pieces, noting the lengths of individual pieces. Remember, lumber is normally stocked in even sizes from 6 to 20 feet.

Decide whether you need to cover that $10^1/2$-foot span with a single 12-foot board, or if 7- and $3^1/2$-foot lengths cut from other pieces will do just as well. If you can use two 8-foot pieces rather than one 16-foot board, you'll not only save money, but find the stock easier and safer to transport home—unless you're having it delivered.

The lineal foot refers to only the length of a piece. For example, you might ask for "20 2x4s, 8 feet long" or "160 lineal feet of 2x4." The board foot refers to all three dimensions of the piece. A piece of wood 1 inch thick by 12 inches wide by 12 inches long equals one board foot. To compute board feet, use this formula: thickness in inches $\times$ (width in inches $\div$ 12 to convert to feet) $\times$ length in feet. For example, a 1x6 board 10 feet long would be computed: $1" \times \frac{1}{2}' \times 10' = 5$ board feet. And a 4x4, 16 feet long, becomes: $4" \times \frac{1}{3}' \times 16' = 21\frac{1}{3}$ board feet. Lumberyards often quote prices per 1000 board feet.

Moisture content: When wood is cut at the lumber mill, it's unseasoned, or "green." Before it's ready for use, most lumber is dried, either by air-drying or kiln-drying. Most hardwoods are kiln-dried, while softwoods may be air-dried or left green.

The highest grades of softwood lumber will normally be stamped "MC-15," indicating a moisture content not exceeding 15 percent. Dimension lumber may be stamped MC-15, "S-DRY" (indicating 19 percent moisture content or less), or "S-GRN" (meaning green, unseasoned lumber with a moisture content of 20 percent or higher). S-DRY is usually adequate. If you opt for green wood, you're asking for trouble later from splitting, warping, nail popping, and shrinkage.

Placing an order: When buying lumber, specify the amount required, the moisture content, the species, the nominal dimensions, the length, and the surfacing. For example, 700 board feet of S-DRY Douglas-fir, 2x4, 16 feet long, S4S. Also specify the grade, as discussed below.

HOW LUMBER IS GRADED

Lumber of the same species and size is graded on a sliding scale; the top grade may be almost flawless; the bottom grades are virtually unusable. At the mill, workers group lumber into grades; it is then stamped (*above right*) or inventoried according to species, moisture content, and grade name.

It is defects in the wood that define the different grades. Lumberyards sometimes refer to these grades by different names—look for a grading stamp or ask for assistance. To save money, decide what you can live with and what

local building codes require, and buy the lowest acceptable grade, unless it will be in view.

Softwood grades: There are two basic softwood categories: strength-graded dimension lumber and appearance-graded boards. Dimension lumber, rated primarily for strength in house framing, is used for wall studs, sole and top plates, floor and ceiling joists, support beams, and rafters (for a discussion of these terms, see the chapter beginning on page 51).

The American Lumber Standards (ALS) Committee has set up guidelines to establish consistent grading categories throughout the country. The grades available depend on the size of the lumber. Lumber 4 inches wide and less is generally available in Construction, Standard, and Utility grades. **Construction** and **Standard** are both strong and serviceable for framing. For blocking, plates, and bracing, **Utility** is a cheaper option, and is allowed for interior

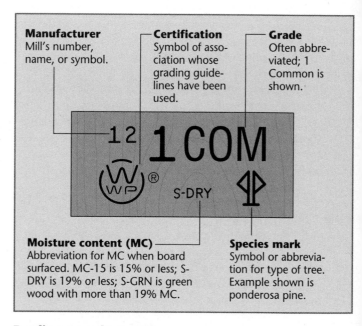

Manufacturer
Mill's number, name, or symbol.

Certification
Symbol of association whose grading guidelines have been used.

Grade
Often abbreviated; 1 Common is shown.

Moisture content (MC)
Abbreviation for MC when board surfaced. MC-15 is 15% or less; S-DRY is 19% or less; S-GRN is green wood with more than 19% MC.

Species mark
Symbol or abbreviation for type of tree. Example shown is ponderosa pine.

Reading a grade stamp
On higher grades of lumber, if a stamp appears, it will be on the edge or back. The Western Wood Products Association uses grade stamps like the one shown above.

 SAFETY TIP

PRESSURE-TREATED LUMBER SHOULD BE HANDLED WITH CARE.

Impressed by its resistance to decay, more and more carpenters are using pressure-treated lumber. It's important to note that this lumber has been treated with potentially toxic chemicals and should be handled with care.

Of the three most popular treating agents used, creosote, pentachlorophenol, and inorganic arsenic, the first two should not be used indoors at all. Don't use any type of pressure-treat-ed lumber for countertops, cutting-boards, or in applications where it will be in frequent or prolonged contact with skin (such as chairs or outdoor furniture). Avoid using this type of wood near vegetable gardens or drinking water supplies.

Always cut pressure-treated wood outside, and be sure to wear safety glasses, respiratory protection, long pants and long-sleeved shirt, and chemical-resistant vinyl-coated gloves.

studs in some parts of the country. For lumber 6 inches wide and up, the grades available are usually Select Structural, No. 1, No. 2, and No. 3. **Select Structural** is strong and rigid and looks good. **No. 1** grade is strong and rigid but less attractive in appearance. **No. 2** grade is appropriate for most standard construction uses, while **No. 3** grade is for applications where less strength is required. Finally, **Stud** grade is recommended for all kinds of studs, including load-bearing walls.

"Boards" are graded for appearance; they're not intended for structural framing, but would be used for non-weight-bearing finish carpentry applications instead. If you want a perfect natural finish, buy **Select** or **Finish** lumber. If you plan to paint, buy a lower grade—paint hides many defects. **Common 2** and **3** grades are often chosen specifically for their tight knot patterns. Let your eye be the judge. Certain species, notably redwood and Idaho white pine, have their own grades; check with your dealer or a lumber association.

Hardwood grades: Hardwoods are judged by appearance; the number of defects in a given length determines the grade. The National Hardwood Lumber Association lists the best grades as **Firsts, Seconds,** and a mix of the two called **FAS,** which applies to clear wood at least 8 feet long and 6 inches wide. Next comes **Select,** which permits defects on the back, and **Common 1** and **2. No. 3A Common** or **No. 3B Common** is generally unusable where appearance counts.

OTHER CHARACTERISTICS OF LUMBER

Even within the same stack of lumber, you'll often find differences between individual pieces. Ask if you can

MAJOR SOFTWOODS			
Species or species group	**Growing range**	**Characteristics**	**Uses**
Cedar, western red	Pacific Northwest from southern Alaska to northern California; Washington east to Montana	Similar to redwood in decay-resistance, but coarser. High resistance to warping, weathering. Strongly aromatic. Somewhat weak and brittle; moderate nail-holding ability; very easy to work.	Exposed beams, exterior siding, interior paneling and trim, shingles and shakes, decks, fences, saunas.
Douglas-fir/ western larch	Western states (Rocky Mountains and Pacific Coast ranges)	Very heavy, strong, and stiff; good nail-holding ability. Somewhat difficult to work with hand tools. Number one choice for structural framing. Resistant to decay and termites only if pressure-treated with preservatives.	Framing, sheathing, posts and beams, flooring and subflooring, decks.
Hem/fir (eastern and western hemlock; true firs)	Western hemlock and firs: Rocky Mountains and Pacific Coast ranges; Eastern hemlock: northeastern U.S. and Appalachians	Firs are generally lightweight, soft to moderately soft, with average strength. Hemlocks are fairly strong and stiff; below-average nailing ability. Firs are easy to work; hemlocks are somewhat more difficult. Shrinkage can be substantial. Resistant to decay and termites only if pressure-treated with preservatives.	Framing, sheathing, flooring and subflooring, interior finish work.
Pine, eastern white, northern, and western (Idaho white, lodgepole, ponderosa, and sugar)	Eastern white and northern pines: Maine to northern Georgia and across Great Lakes states; Western pines: western states	Very light and soft woods with moderate resistance to decay and termites, but high resistance to warping. Somewhat weak and flexible; moderate nail-holding ability. Shrinkage-prone. Very easy to work.	Framing, exterior siding (if treated), interior paneling and trim, flooring, cabinetry, shelving.
Pine, southern yellow (longleaf, slash, shortleaf, loblolly)	Southeastern U.S. from Maryland to Florida; Atlantic Coast to East Texas	Like Douglas-fir, very strong and stiff, hard, good nail-holding ability. Moderately easy to work. Resistant to decay and termites only if pressure-treated with preservatives.	Framing, posts and beams, subflooring, interior paneling and trim, decks (if treated).
Redwood	Northwestern California, extreme southwestern Oregon	Heartwood known for its durability and resistance to decay, disease, termites. Moderately light with limited structural strength (but strong for its weight). Good workability, but brittle; splits easily. Medium nail-holding ability.	Posts and beams, exterior siding and trim, interior paneling and trim, decks, fences, saunas.
Spruce (Engelmann, eastern)	Englemann: Cascades and Rocky Mountains; Eastern: Maine through Wisconsin, Canada	Lightweight and soft with little decay-resistance. Does resist warping, splitting. Average strength and stiffness; good nail-holding ability; easy to work.	Framing, flooring, interior finish work.

look through the stacks yourself to choose your boards; many lumberyards will allow this, if you leave the stacks neatly piled afterward. Here's what to look for:

Vertical or flat grain: As illustrated below, quarter-sawn lumber—lumber that is cut nearly perpendicular to the annual growth ring—results in vertical grain, with grain lines running the length of the piece. Pieces that are flat-sawn—cut tangential to the growth rings—have a marbled appearance referred to as flat grain. Whenever you can, choose quarter-sawn lumber; it's less likely to warp or shrink noticeably.

Heartwood or sapwood: Heartwood is the wood nearest the center of a living tree. The wood next to the bark, containing the growth cells, is referred to as sapwood. Heartwood is denser and resists decay more efficiently. For this reason, many building codes require that lumber within 6 inches of the ground be heartwood sawn from species naturally resistant to decay, such as redwood, cedar, or cypress. (Or you may choose to use less durable woods that have been pressure-treated with preservatives—see page 49.) Heartwood and sapwood are usually different in color (heartwood is usually darker), and for finish work, you may prefer one over the other.

Defects: Examine lumber for defects such as board warpage. Lift each piece and sight down the face and edges. Refer to the chart at right for information on the most common kinds of weathering and milling defects. Also be on the lookout for problems such as rotting, staining, insect holes, and pitch pockets (sap reservoirs below the surface).

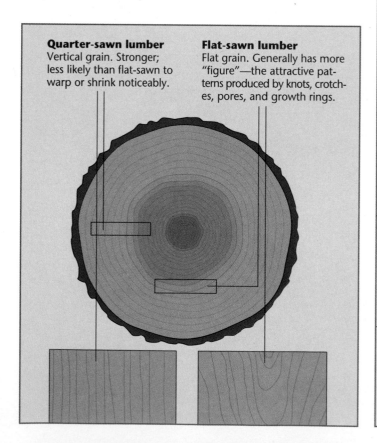

Quarter-sawn lumber
Vertical grain. Stronger; less likely than flat-sawn to warp or shrink noticeably.

Flat-sawn lumber
Flat grain. Generally has more "figure"—the attractive patterns produced by knots, crotches, pores, and growth rings.

COMMON LUMBER DEFECTS

Defect	Description	What to do
Crook	Warp along the edge line; also known as crown.	Straighten with a circular saw and a clamped-on guide.
Bow	Warp on the face of a board from end to end.	Cut the piece into smaller, unbowed pieces, or remove the bow by planing the face.
Cup	Hollow across the face of a board.	Dry the piece until both faces have equal moisture content, or cut the piece to eliminate the cupped part.
Twist	Multiple bends in a board.	Cut off the twisted part, or plane the face to remove the twist.
Knot or knothole	A tight knot is not usually a problem; a loose or dead knot, surrounded by a dark ring, may fall out later, or may already have left a hole.	Cut off the part with a knot or knothole; remove any loose knots before machining the lumber. Sound knots may be kept if a knotty look is desired.
Check	Crack along the wood's annual growth rings, not passing through the entire thickness of the wood.	Cut off the checked portion.
Split	Crack going all the way through the piece of wood, commonly at the ends.	Cut off the split part of the board.
Shake	Separation of grain between the growth rings, often extending along the board's face, and sometimes below its surface.	Cut off the shake.
Wane	Missing wood or untrimmed bark along the edge or corner of the piece.	Cut off the affected part.

SHEET PRODUCTS

Manufactured plywood, hardboard, and particleboard have enabled lumber mills to make good use of marginal or waste lumber and milling by-products. These sheet products offer several advantages over solid lumber; they're strong in all directions (except particleboard), they resist warping, are easy to work with, and economical. Construction uses for sheet products in their unfinished state include wall and roof sheathing, subflooring, and underlayment for floor coverings. You'll also find them used quite commonly in finish carpentry applications such as cabinetry, countertops, closets, and shelving.

Often, sheet products are imprinted or surfaced with decorative grooves or patterns intended to enhance their appearance for use as exterior siding or interior paneling. For more details on these products, refer to the section on interior paneling and trim *(page 39)*, and siding materials *(page 43)*.

PLYWOOD

To make plywood, a sharp blade peels thin wood layers (veneers) from a log; these veneers are then glued together, with each layer's grain running perpendicular to adjacent veneers, giving plywood strength in all directions.

Carpenters use plywood extensively, both for finish work (such as cabinets, countertops, furniture, and shelving) and as a structural "skin" (sheathing and subflooring, for instance) over house framing.

The difference between interior and exterior grades of plywoods lies in the type of glue used to make them, and in the quality of inner veneers. (Exterior grades are made with weatherproof glue and better veneers.) Standard plywood size is 4 feet by 8 feet, though you can find sheets as long as 10 feet. Some lumberyards sell half or quarter sheets.

Like solid lumber, plywoods are divided into softwoods and hardwoods, according to the nature of their face and back veneers only.

Softwood plywood: Though softwood plywood may be manufactured from up to 70 species, Douglas-fir and southern pine are the most common. The different species are classified into five groups depending on their strength and stiffness; Group 1 is the strongest.

The look of a panel's face and back dictates its grade. Letters N and A through D designate the different grades. You may have trouble finding the top-of-the-line N grade, which has to be special-ordered. Grades A to D have more defects and repairs; generally, an A face is suitable for natural finishes, a B face for stains, and a repaired C face (C-Plugged) for a surface that is to be painted.

Several different face/back grade combinations are available, though most lumberyards don't stock all of them. If only one side of a panel is going to be visible,

A/C (exterior) and A/D (interior) panels will provide good value for your money. When appearance is not a factor, you can save money by looking for "shop" plywood, defective panels that don't meet grading standards. Marine plywood, an exterior type with high-quality inner veneers, performs best for areas in constant contact with moisture, although it's expensive.

Look for a stamp on the back or edge of each panel indicating characteristics such as the face and back grades, glue type, and group number; an example is illustrated on page 38.

The most common thicknesses of standard softwood plywood range from 1/4 to 3/4 inch in 1/8-inch increments.

Performance-rated plywood: These softwood panels are rated for strength in such applications as wall or roof sheathing and subflooring. Panel thicknesses run from 1/4 inch up to 1 1/8 inches; the tongue-and-groove edges available in some types eliminate the need for edge support. The three classifications of exposure durability are: Exterior (the only type for continuous exposure to the elements), and Exposure 1 and 2 (both for protected applications; 1 can tolerate moisture).

The grading stamps on performance-rated panels *(page 38)* supply you with some extra information. Panels that are intended for all-purpose sheathing have two numbers separated by a slash. The left-hand number, for roofing, indicates the maximum allowable spacing "on-center" (O.C.) between rafters that support the panel. The second number gives the maximum spacing between floor joists when the panel is used for single-layer floors. Both are given in inches. Panels designed only for subflooring are printed with one number, such as "24 O.C." Be sure to clear all these span ratings with your local building officials before you build.

Hardwood plywood: While more expensive than softwood types, hardwood plywoods nonetheless provide a lower-priced alternative to solid hardwoods for interior applications. The panel is categorized by the

---

 ASK A PRO

HOW CAN I ESTIMATE MY PLYWOOD NEEDS?
First, brush up on the procedures for your particular application. (For guidelines on subflooring, wall sheathing, and roof decking, see pages 63, 75, and 81, respectively.) With that done, sketch the standard 4x8-foot panels over the framing system you have planned; then count them. You may need to order plywood by the square foot; if so, divide the square footage by 32 to arrive at the number of panels needed.

type of veneer used on its face; popular domestic faces include ash, birch, black walnut, cherry, maple, and oak, and several imported woods are also available.

Generally, hardwood plywood is chosen by its appearance, although there is a grading system, with the AA face-grade being the highest. This grade is recommended for paneling, doors, and cabinets. A is also used where the best appearance is a factor. B will display the wood species' natural look. C, D, and E have more repairs and color differences. The back grades range from 1 to 4, with 1 having the fewest defects.

HARDBOARD

Hardboard is harder, more solid and less costly than plywood; both sides may be smooth, although the back is often textured. You'll usually see hardboard only in $1/8$- and $1/4$-inch thicknesses. To make hardboard—commonly sold in 4x8 sheets—chips of waste wood are rendered into fibers; these fibers are then glued together under pressure.

There are two main types of hardboard: standard and tempered. The latter has higher strength and moisture resistance. Standard, unfinished hardboard is used for floor underlayment, cabinet backs, sliding doors, and drawer bottoms. You'll usually see perforated hardboard, best known by its trade name, Pegboard™, up on the wall for tool storage.

Fiberboard, less dense than hardboard—but sold in thicker sheets—is readily available as MDF (medium-density fiberboard). This product can be used as an alternative to solid wood, and some of its applications include cabinets, doors, door jambs and casings, and baseboards and trim.

Hardboard and fiberboard products are no more difficult to cut and shape than any other type of stock, but the glue used in their manufacture is very abrasive; carbide-tipped blades and bits are recommended. For fastening, drill a pilot hole first.

PARTICLEBOARD AND ORIENTED-STRAND BOARD

Particleboard, composed of chips and particles of waste wood glued together under heat and pressure, has a less uniform appearance than hardboard. It's sold in the same standard 4x8 sheet, ¼ to 2 inches thick. Typical uses include floor underlayment, shelving, cabinets, countertops, and core stock for plastic lamination. Oriented-strand board (OSB) is composed of larger flakes than particleboard and has a rougher surface. It is most suitable for wall or roof sheathing or subflooring. If you plan to use either type for structural applications, be sure to check the local building codes first.

You can use standard carpentry tools to work particleboard and OSB, but carbide-tipped saw blades and router bits are required. To fasten, always start with a pilot hole.

PLAY IT SAFE

WORKING WITH SHEET MATERIALS

Wear respiratory protection and work in a well-ventilated area when you're cutting sheet products. Ensure that there are no sparks or open flames nearby. When purchasing MDF or particleboard, look for panels that are certified as low in formaldehyde emissions.

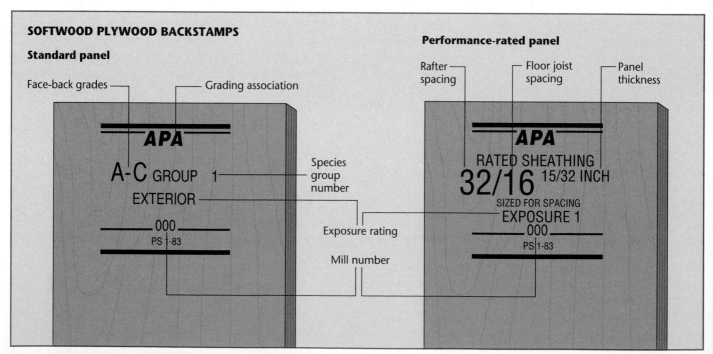

SOFTWOOD PLYWOOD BACKSTAMPS

Standard panel

Face-back grades — Grading association

APA

A-C GROUP 1 — Species group number

EXTERIOR

000

PS 1-83

Performance-rated panel

Rafter spacing — Floor joist spacing — Panel thickness

APA

RATED SHEATHING

32/16 15/32 INCH

SIZED FOR SPACING

EXPOSURE 1

000

PS 1-83

Exposure rating

Mill number

Stamps courtesy of the American Plywood Association.

INTERIOR PANELING AND TRIM

The wide spectrum of interior paneling provides many dramatic possibilities for giving your walls the look you want. There are two main types of paneling: solid board and sheet. Board paneling encompasses the many species and millings of both softwoods and hardwoods. Sheet paneling includes plywood, hardboard, gypsum wallboard, and some less common materials, all usually available in 4x8 panels in a range of natural, grooved, prefinished, and printed sheets.

Moldings provide a "finished," custom look to your paneling, hiding any inaccuracies in joints between materials, but more importantly, they allow for expansion of materials without cracking.

Solid board paneling: This includes any paneling made up of solid pieces of lumber positioned side by side. Standard, square-edged lumber may be used—1x4s, 1x6s, etc. But usually the boards' edges are specially milled to overlap or interlock. The three basic millings are shown at right.

The thickness of paneling boards ranges from $3/8$ to $7/8$ inch, but the most common thicknesses are $1/2$ and $3/4$ inch (1-inch nominal size). Board widths fall between 3 and 10 inches; but these are nominal sizes—the chart on page 33 gives you the true widths of a variety of sizes of surfaced lumber. Actual paneling widths may vary somewhat, depending on the milling. Standard boards are found in lengths from 6 to 16 feet.

You have many woods to choose from. Hardwood boards are milled from such species as birch, cherry, mahogany, maple, oak, pecan, teak, and walnut. Common softwoods include cedar, cypress, fir, hemlock, pine, redwood, and spruce. The grade of wood you select will depend on the look you want, either clear or knotty. Boards may be surfaced either smooth or "resawn" (rough). Another option is "barnwood," made from softwoods such as redwood or cedar. Some barnwood is simulated; but some is actually weathered boards salvaged from unpainted barns and shacks. Boards designed for exterior siding are another option.

Kiln-dried boards tend not to shrink or cup much, but in any case, it's ideal to "condition" the boards by stacking them in the room to be paneled for a full 7 to 10 days prior to installation. This allows the paneling to fully adapt to the room temperature and humidity, reducing buckling after installation.

To estimate the amount of solid board paneling you'll need, first calculate the square footage to be covered by multiplying height by length. From this figure, subtract the area of all the openings. Then decide on the pattern of application (*page 107*), as well as board width and type of edge-milling. Keep in mind that a board's actual width is less than its nominal size; you may also need to subtract the width of the edge-milling. Your dealer can help you calculate coverage.

Plywood sheet paneling: Generally, any of the standard unfinished plywood sheets described on pages 37-38 may be used for wall paneling. Look for softwood and hardwood types without defects. Prefinished and vinyl-faced decorative styles are also available, and resin-coated panels are especially designed for painting. Plywood comes with different face textures, ranging from highly polished to resawn; many types feature decorative grooves or shiplap edges. In addition to the standard 4x8 sheets, you can also find some types in 4x9 or 4x10 dimensions.

The standard thicknesses of interior sheet paneling are $1/4$ inch or $5/16$ inch. Avoid thinner panels, as these are difficult to work with and require a backing. Exterior plywood sidings—ideal for the rustic, rough-sawn look—come primarily in two thicknesses, $3/8$ inch and $5/8$ inch. The former is ample for interiors.

Estimate the materials you require using this method that applies to any type of sheet paneling: If the wall you're covering has a standard 8-foot height, measure the length of the wall in feet and divide by the width of your panel. Round the figure off to the next highest number; the result is the number of panels needed. Unless a very large part of the wall is windows and doors, don't bother deducting materials for them.

Hardboard sheet paneling: Hardboard makes a tough, pliable, and water-resistant paneling. Sold in 4x8 sheets, it ranges in thickness from $3/16$ to $3/8$ inch; $1/4$ inch is standard. The most common surface finishes for hardboard are imitation wood; generally grooved to look like solid board paneling, wood imitations come in highly polished, resawn, or coarser brushed textures. You also can find panels embossed with a pattern.

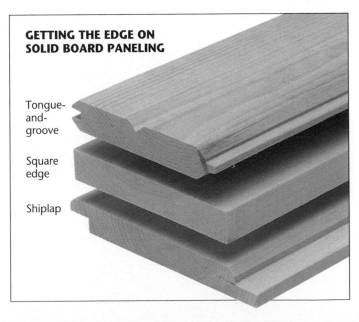

GETTING THE EDGE ON SOLID BOARD PANELING

Tongue-and-groove

Square edge

Shiplap

For installation around tubs and showers, use hardboard with a vinyl or plastic-laminated finish that sheds water and is easily cleaned; the plastic-laminated type is most durable. In utility areas, standard or perforated hardboard makes economical, paintable paneling.

Gypsum wallboard sheet paneling: Compressed gypsum dust sandwiched between a smooth, paintable paper face and a heavier paper backing is the most common wall and ceiling material. It is used as inexpensive finish panels or as backing for other materials.

Joints between these panels are concealed *(page 104)*, then the panels may be painted, wallpapered, or coated with a textured surface treatment. Factory-decorated, vinyl-faced varieties are available as finished panels.

Wallboard panels are 4 feet wide; lengths vary from the standard 8 feet up to 14 feet. Common thicknesses are $1/2$ inch for a backing material for other paneling or for final wall coverings, $3/8$ inch if you're going over pre-existing surfaces, or $5/8$ inch to meet fire code requirements (for example, where walls border a garage space). Choose a water-resistant type, identified by green paper covers, in the bathroom or kitchen sink area, or wherever moisture may collect.

Moldings and trim: Even in the most basic room, moldings have their place along the base of walls and around door and window frames.

Wood moldings come in many standard patterns and sizes, commonly ranging from 3 to 20 feet. You can buy them natural, prefinished, or vinyl-wrapped with decorative printing. The natural or stained type are normally continuous, clear lengths, while the painted and vinyl-wrapped ones are often shorter lengths finger-jointed at their ends to make longer pieces. Ponderosa pine is the most popular molding stock. Many dealers carry a wide variety of wood-grain-printed plastic, vinyl, or aluminum moldings and color-matched nails.

When ordering moldings, remember that thickness of the piece is specified first, width second, and length last. Both thickness and width are measured at their widest point.

Many of the standard molding patterns and their common applications over joints between wall, ceiling, and floor coverings are shown below, but you can also choose strips or boards—for example, clear redwood 1x4s or 1x6s—for handsome, bold trim over either solid board or sheet paneling.

MOLDING AND TRIM POSSIBILITIES

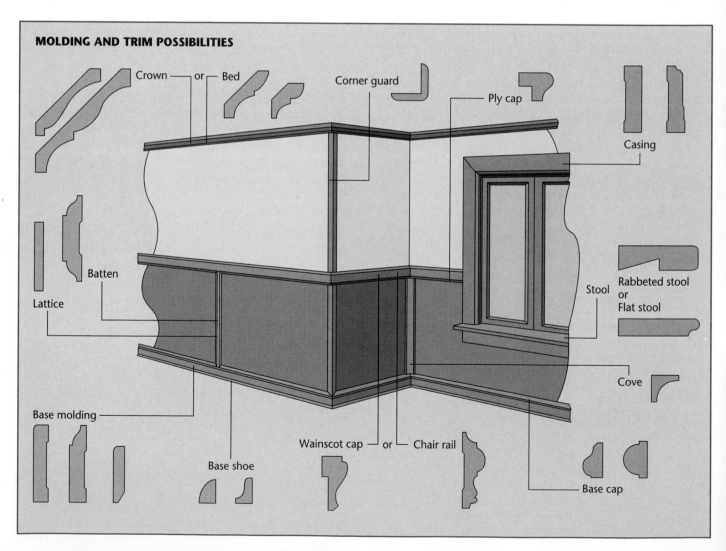

ROOFING MATERIALS

Asphalt, wood, and tile—the most common choices for rooftop protection—find competition today from aluminum, galvanized steel, and slate. Flat or very low-sloping roofs may have surfaces of tar and gravel, or polyurethane foam (contractor-applied only) that provides insulation as well as weather-proofing.

For a direct comparison of the roofing materials most commonly available, refer to the chart on page 42. You'll find materials to meet nearly every budget and architectural style. Here are some additional terms and factors to consider:

Hidden roofing components: Roofing materials are not fastened directly to rafters. Decking—the nailing base that's attached to roof rafters—may be either solid (plywood sheathing or boards) or open (usually spaced 1x4s). Underlayment, in the form of asphalt-impregnated roofing felt, lies atop the decking. Flashings, most commonly made from malleable, 24- or 26-gauge sheet metal, provide essential protection at interfaces such as valleys, chimneys, drip edges, skylights, and vents. For details on these components, see page 81.

Roof slope: The slope, or pitch, of a roof refers to the vertical rise measured against a standard horizontal distance of 12 inches. The term "4 in 12," means that the roof rises 4 inches vertically for every 12 horizontal inches. As a rule, do-it-yourselfers shouldn't attempt to work on roofs with slopes steeper than 6 in 12.

Figuring out material needs: Roofing materials are often sold by the square, a term indicating the amount of roofing material needed to cover 100 square feet of roof (allowing for overlap). To estimate the amount of materials, calculate the number of squares in the roof surface. For a gable roof with unbroken planes, first figure the surface area of each of the roof's rectangles (multiply the length by the width). Next, total up the amounts and divide by 100, rounding off to the next higher figure. For more complex roof designs, roughly figure the areas of additional rectangles or triangles.

Buying roofing materials: The slope of your roof and local building codes will quickly eliminate the materials that aren't suitable for your project. Compare the remaining materials in terms of cost versus durability (premium-quality asphalt shingles may be less expensive than standard asphalt shingles on a cost-per-year basis); warranties (some provide only material replacement, others also cover labor); ease of application; availability (shipping or delivery may inflate the price of some materials); and appearance.

The Underwriters' Laboratory has tested all types of roofing materials for fire resistance. Look for the UL symbol; materials are rated Class A (those with the most fire-retardant qualities), Class B, and Class C. Because of their flammable nature, materials such as untreated wood shingles or shakes receive no rating.

It's a backbreaking job to load materials onto the roof. Ask when you're ordering to have them delivered up there directly—especially if you're putting down shingles or shakes over open sheathing *(page 82)*. Have materials delivered just before it's time to install them, and spread out bundles to distribute the weight load. If materials must be kept on site for some time, store them indoors in a dry place, away from extreme temperatures. Materials left outdoors should be stacked off the ground on 2x4s and covered with plastic; avoid direct sunlight for shingles with glue strips, as they could stick together.

Measuring roof slope

TOOLKIT
- Carpenter's level
- Tape measure or ruler

Using a level
Mark a line on the level 12" from the end, then rest that end on the roof, raising or lowering the opposite end to obtain a level reading. Then, with the tape measure or ruler, measure the distance between the roof and the 12" mark on the level *(left)*. This distance is your slope.

COMPARATIVE GUIDE TO ROOFING MATERIALS

Material	Weight per square (Pounds)	Durability	Fire rating	Recommended minimum slope	Characteristics
Asphalt shingles (felt base)	240-345	12-20 years, depending on sun's intensity	C	4 in 12 down to 2 in 12 with additional underlayment	Available in wide range of colors, textures, Standard and Premium weights; easy to apply and repair; low maintenance; economical. But, less durable and fire-resistant, though equal in cost to fiberglass base shingles.
Asphalt shingles (fiberglass base)	220-430	15-25 years, depending on sun's intensity	A	4 in 12 down to 2 in 12 with additional underlayment	Durable and highly fire-resistant; available in wide range of colors, textures, Standard and Premium weights; easy to apply and repair; low maintenance. But, brittle when applied in temperatures below 50°F.
Wood shingles and shakes	144-350	10-15 years, depending on slope, heat, humidity	None, untreated; C, if treated with retardant; B, with use of retardant and foil underlayment	4 in 12 down to 3 in 12 with additional underlayment	Appealing natural appearance with strong shadow lines; durable. Use #1 ("Blue Label") shingles for roofing. (For more on shingles and shake types, turn to page 85.) Flammable unless treated with retardants; treated wood expensive; time-consuming application.
Tile (concrete and clay)	900-1000	50+ years	A	4 in 12 down to 3 in 12 with additional underlayment	Extremely durable; fireproof; comes in flat, curved, and ribbed shapes; moderate color range. Costly to ship; hard to install; needs strong framing to support weight; cracks easily if walked on.
Slate	900-1000	50+ years	A	4 in 12	Attractive, traditional appearance; does not deteriorate; fireproof; comes in several colors. Expensive to buy and ship; hard to install; requires strong framing to support weight; may get brittle with age.
Aluminum shingles	50	25+ years	C or better	4 in 12	Light; fire-resistant; resemble wood shakes; moderate range of colors. Can be damaged by heavy hail, falling branches.
Metal panels (aluminum or steel)	45-75	20+ years	C or better	1 in 12	Aluminum: lightweight; durable; maintenance-free if prepainted; sheds snow. Steel: strong; durable; fire-resistant; sheds snow. Contraction and expansion can cause leaks at nail holes; noisy in rain.
Asphalt roll roofing	90-180	5-10 years (depends on water runoff at low slope)	C or A	1 in 12	Economical, easy to apply, but drab appearance.
Asphalt ("tar") and gravel	250-650	10-20 years, depending on sun's intensity	A	1/4 in 12	Membrane roof; most waterproof of all. Must be professionally applied; built-up and single-ply; hard to locate leaks; black surfaces absorb heat (white gravel helps reflect sun's rays).
Sprayed polyurethane foam	20 for 1" thickness	Life of building with proper maintenance	A	1/4 in 12	Continuous membrane produces watertight surface; good insulation value; lightweight; durable when protective coating is maintained. Must be professionally applied; quality depends on skill of applicator; deteriorates under sunlight if not properly coated (and periodically re-coated).

SIDING MATERIALS

Where the protection of your house is concerned, siding is every bit as important as a good roof. But siding offers more than protection. The color, texture, and pattern create the "look" of your house.

The range of wood-based siding materials includes traditional solid boards, exterior plywood, hardboard, and shakes and shingles. In addition, there are sidings of aluminum, steel, and vinyl. The chart below and on page 44 offers a closer look at all these materials; other favorites—brick, imitation stone and brick, and stucco—are beyond the scope of basic carpentry. Remember that the relative cost of a particular type of siding varies widely from region to region. Also, when you're shopping for solid board or exterior plywood, keep an eye out for the same general characteristics and grading scales by which you'd judge standard lumber *(page 33)* or plywood *(page 37)*.

Because many siding products cannot be fastened directly to wall studs, your costs may include sheathing, building paper, and flashing. Sheathing is required under some siding to increase rigidity, provide a solid nailing base, and to add structural strength. Building paper adds an extra protective layer over sheathing. Flashing keeps water away from door and window frames, and from seams between plywood or hardboard panels. For more details on all these components, see the section beginning on page 74.

To estimate the amount of materials needed, divide the surfaces to be covered into rectangles (walls) and triangles (gable ends). Round off measurements to the nearest foot. To determine the area of a rectangle, multiply height by length. To figure the area of a gable end triangle, simply multiply one-half the length of the span —base—by the rise—height. To avoid climbing a ladder to measure the height of your walls, measure the width of one board or the length of a shingle exposure, and multiply this by the number of boards or courses from top to bottom.

Add together all the areas that you've computed and then subtract the areas of all openings. Add 10% for waste, plus another 15% if your house has steep triangles at the gables or any features that will require extensive cutting. Most plywood sidings are sold by the sheet; for other treatments, convert figures to square, lineal, or board feet. Don't forget the overlap in some styles of siding—your dealer should be able to help.

COMMON DO-IT-YOURSELF SIDINGS

Material	Types and characteristics	Maintenance	Installation	Merits and drawbacks
Solid boards	Available in many species; redwood and cedar have natural decay-resistance. Milled in variety of patterns. Applied horizontally, vertically, or diagonally *(see chart, page 77)*. Nominal dimensions are 1" thick, 4" to 12" wide, random lengths to 16'. Bevel patterns slightly thinner; battens may be narrower. Sold untreated, pretreated with water repellent, primed, painted, or stained. Good for 30 years to life of building, depending on periodic maintenance.	Treat ends with water repellent before installation. Needs painting or opaque staining every 4-6 years, transparent staining every 3-5 years, or finishing with water repellent every 2 years.	Difficulty varies with installation pattern. Most are manageable with basic carpentry skills and tools.	Natural material; broad range of styles and patterns. Easy to handle and work. Takes wide range of finishes. But, burns, prone to split, crack, warp, and peel (if painted). Species other than redwood and cedar heartwoods susceptible to termite damage when in direct contact with soil, and to decay if not properly finished.
Exterior plywood	Typical siding species are Douglas-fir and southern pine. Face veneer determines designation. Textures range from rough to smooth overlay for painting. Typical pattern has vertical grooves, like solid board siding. Sheets are 4' wide, 8' to 10' long; applied vertically or horizontally. Lap boards are 6" to 12" wide, 16' long. Thicknesses of both: 3/8" to 5/8". Sold untreated, pretreated with water repellent, primed, painted, or stained. Good for 30 years to life of building, depending on maintenance.	Before using, seal all edges with water repellent, stain sealer, or exterior house paint primer. Restain or repaint every 5 years.	Sheets go up quickly. Manageable with basic carpentry skills and tools.	Many styles and patterns. Easy to apply. Can also serve as sheathing, adding structural support and strength; provides some insulation. Less expensive than wood boards, offers same look, but burns, and may "check" (show small surface cracks) or delaminate from excessive moisture. Susceptible to termite damage when in contact with soil, and to water rot if not properly finished.

COMMON DO-IT-YOURSELF SIDINGS (continued)

Material	Types and characteristics	Maintenance	Installation	Merits and drawbacks
Hardboard	Available smooth or in textures including rough-sawn board, stucco, and others. Sheets are 4' wide, 8' to 10' long; usually applied vertically. Lap boards are 6" to 12" wide, 16' long. Thicknesses of both: $7/16$" and $1/2$". Sold primed, primed and painted, or opaque stained. Good for 30 years to life of building, depending on maintenance. Commonly available factory-primed (topcoat to be added); guaranteed to 5 years.	Before using, seal all edges with water repellent, stain sealer, or exterior house paint primer. Paint or stain unprimed and preprimed hardboard within 60 days of installation; repaint or re-stain every 5 years.	Sheets go up quickly. Manageable with basic carpentry skills and tools.	Uniform in appearance, without typical defects found in wood. Easy to apply. Many surface textures and designs available. Takes finishes well. Does not have plywood's strength or nail-holding ability. Susceptible to termite damage when in direct contact with soil, and to water rot and buckling if not well finished. Cannot take transparent finishes.
Cedar shingles and shakes	Mostly western red cedar; some are eastern white cedar. Shingles distinguished by grade: #1 ("Blue Label") the best; #2 ("Red Label") acceptable as underlayment when double-coursing. Available in many specialty patterns. Shakes come in different textures. Also sold as "sidewall shingles," specialty products that are grooved, sanded, or squared. Shingle and shake widths are random, from 4" to 14". Lengths: 16" (shingles only), 18", and 24". Shakes are thicker than shingles, with butts $1/2$" or $3/4$" thick. Both come prebonded on labor-saving 4' and 8' panels. Primarily unpainted; also available prestained or painted. Good for 20 to 40 years, depending on heat, humidity, and maintenance.	In hot, humid climates, apply fungicide/mildew retardant every 3 years. In dry climates, preserve resiliency with oil finish every 5 years. There are also specially treated shingles and shakes available that require no maintenance.	Time-consuming because of small pieces; also come prebonded on 4' plywood panels. Manageable with basic skills and tools plus a roofer's hatchet.	Rustic look of real wood; easy to handle, work, and repair. Adapt well to rounded walls and intricate architectural styles. Burns, but fire-resistant and fireproof shingles now available. Prone to rot, splinter, crack, and curl; may be pried loose by wind. Change color with age unless treated.
Vinyl	Extruded from polyvinyl chloride (PVC) in white and some colors; smooth and wood-grain types available. Horizontal panels simulate single 8" wide lap boards; vertical panels look like single 4" wide boards with battens. Other styles: single panels that simulate two 4", 5", or 6" wide lap boards, or three 4" wide boards. Standard length: 12'6". Last 40 years or more.	None except annual hosing off.	Manageable with basic carpentry skills and tools, plus zipper tool, snap-lock punch, and aviation shears or circular saw.	Won't rot, rust, peel, or blister. Doesn't burn, but will melt. Resists denting and scratches do not show. But, only white and pastel colors available; can only be painted by a professional. Sun may cause long-range fading and deterioration. Brittle when cold.
Aluminum	Rolled form panels in wide range of factory-baked colors, textures. Types and dimensions same as vinyl. Good for 40 years to life of building.	Needs annual hosing. Clean stains with non-abrasive detergent. Refinish as recommended by manufacturer.	Manageable with basic skills and tools, plus aviation shears or a circular saw and a tool for bending trim. Use aluminum nails.	Won't rot, rust, or blister. Fireproof and impervious to termites. Lightweight and easy to handle. Dents and scratches easily. May oxidize or discolor; may corrode near salt water.
Steel	Styles include horizontal panels that simulate two 4" or 5" lap boards (or a single 8"), and vertical panels in 12" or 16" widths. Available in a wide range of colors. Lasts the life of the building.	May need an occasional hosing. Clean with non-abrasive detergent. Can be repainted, following manufacturer's instructions.	Manageable with basic skills, but requires steel shears or tin snips for cutting. Use galvanized nails.	Does not expand or warp in heat. Not brittle in cold. Rigid—can span uneven parts of wall. Impervious to hail, fire, and termites. May rust if scratched. More expensive than vinyl, but lasts much longer.

FASTENERS

Nails, screws, bolts, and adhesives are used by the carpenter to assemble all the other materials covered in this chapter. The fastest way to join two pieces is to nail them together, so nails are the most popular fastener for most jobs. When the project demands extra strength and a finer appearance, carpenters usually turn to screws or adhesives, or both together. If strength alone is the issue, oversize lag screws or bolts provide the answer.

Fortunately, for special problems there are special fasteners, such as metal framing connectors to avoid toenailing, and fasteners for materials like gypsum wallboard, plaster, masonry, or concrete. To estimate metal framing connectors, start by counting the number of posts, beams, joists, or rafters with which you'll use the connectors. Once a basic pattern is set, the number of bolts and screws needed are obvious. Nails, on the other hand, are difficult to estimate. Probably the best approach is to assess your planned nailing pattern for a given unit, count up the number of nails for that unit, and multiply by the total units—then add 10 to 15 percent. If you're going to need more than a couple of boxes, your best buy is bulk nails.

NAILS AND SCREWS

Screws are more expensive and time-consuming to drive than nails, but they create stronger joints—especially when combined with glue. The kinds of screws most commonly used in wood are shown below.

Nails are sold in 1-, 5- and 50-pound boxes, or loose in bins. The common types are shown on page 46; carpenters generally choose one of the basic nail types—common, box, spiral, finishing, or casing—and then add special-use nails (check building supply stores for these). Nails may be identified by "penny" size (abbreviated as "d"), which once referred to the cost of 100 nails. Now the term indicates a nail's length.

Use hot-dipped galvanized, electroplated galvanized, aluminum, or stainless steel nails on a house exterior. The best hot-dipped nail will rust in time, particularly at the exposed nailhead, where the coating is battered by your hammer. Stainless steel or aluminum nails won't rust, but they're expensive and hard to find. Coated nails or nails with special shafts have extra holding power.

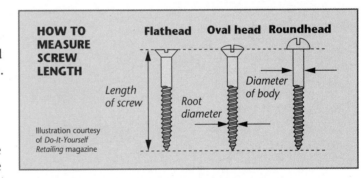

HOW TO MEASURE SCREW LENGTH

Flathead Oval head Roundhead

Length of screw

Root diameter

Diameter of body

Illustration courtesy of *Do-It-Yourself Retailing* magazine

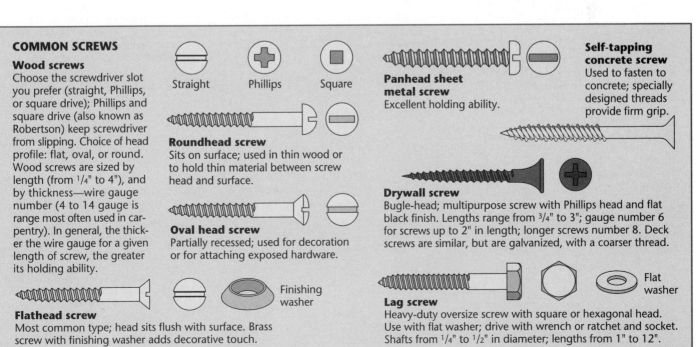

COMMON SCREWS

Wood screws
Choose the screwdriver slot you prefer (straight, Phillips, or square drive); Phillips and square drive (also known as Robertson) keep screwdriver from slipping. Choice of head profile: flat, oval, or round. Wood screws are sized by length (from 1/4" to 4"), and by thickness—wire gauge number (4 to 14 gauge is range most often used in carpentry). In general, the thicker the wire gauge for a given length of screw, the greater its holding ability.

Straight   Phillips   Square

Roundhead screw
Sits on surface; used in thin wood or to hold thin material between screw head and surface.

Oval head screw
Partially recessed; used for decoration or for attaching exposed hardware.

Finishing washer

Flathead screw
Most common type; head sits flush with surface. Brass screw with finishing washer adds decorative touch.

Panhead sheet metal screw
Excellent holding ability.

Self-tapping concrete screw
Used to fasten to concrete; specially designed threads provide firm grip.

Drywall screw
Bugle-head; multipurpose screw with Phillips head and flat black finish. Lengths range from 3/4" to 3"; gauge number 6 for screws up to 2" in length; longer screws number 8. Deck screws are similar, but are galvanized, with a coarser thread.

Flat washer

Lag screw
Heavy-duty oversize screw with square or hexagonal head. Use with flat washer; drive with wrench or ratchet and socket. Shafts from 1/4" to 1/2" in diameter; lengths from 1" to 12".

A NAIL FOR ALL REASONS

Common nail
For heavy construction. Extra-thick shank for greater strength. Wide, thick head spreads load and resists pull-through.

Spiral nail
Rotates slightly as driven in to provide extra grip. Commonly used in framing.

Box nail
Similar to common nail in shape and use, but with slimmer shank. Less likely to split wood, but easier to bend. Available 1" to 5" long.

Finishing nail
Used when nailhead shouldn't show. Drive it nearly flush, then sink rounded head with nailset. Available in 1" to 4" lengths.

Casing nail
Like finishing nail, but with thicker shank and more angular head; use for heavier work, such as adding casings around doors. May be hard to find; available in 2" to 5" lengths.

Duplex nail
Double-headed nail used for temporary work (like nailing wall bracing or constructing concrete forms). Drive lower head tight against surface; pull nail out by upper head.

Fluted-shank masonry nail
Case-hardened for extra strength; useful for securing sole plates for stud walls to concrete, or for fastening furring strips to masonry. Always wear eye protection when driving these—shards can break off.

Flooring nail
Spiral or screw shank provides strong grip to stop boards from squeaking. Available with casing head as shown, or with countersink head.

Cement-coated nail
Vinyl, glue, or resin coating melts as nail is driven in, then hardens to provide stronger grip; extra grip is only temporary.

Underlay nail
Sharp rings grip tightly in softer woods.

Roofing nail
Wide head gives maximum holding power. Varies greatly in size and shape; buy type recommended by manufacturer of your roofing material. Galvanized to resist rusting.

Drywall nail
Typically ring-shanked for extra holding power; may be coated instead. Used to hang gypsum wallboard. 1 1/4" to 1 5/8" long. Head slightly beveled on underside and hollowed on top, making it easier to sink nails below wallboard surface.

Colored finishing nails
Used for attaching wall paneling to studs; come in different colors to match paneling.

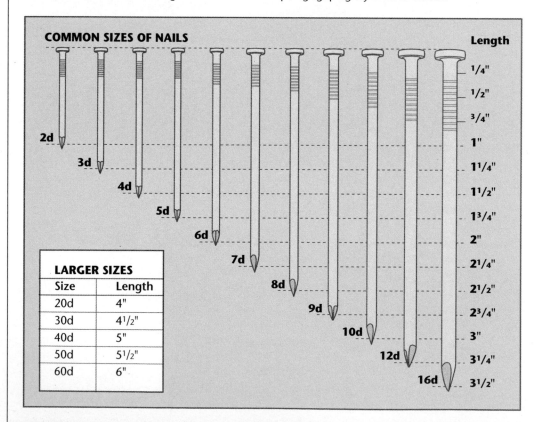

COMMON SIZES OF NAILS

Length
- 1/4"
- 1/2"
- 3/4"
- 1"
- 1 1/4"
- 1 1/2"
- 1 3/4"
- 2"
- 2 1/4"
- 2 1/2"
- 2 3/4"
- 3"
- 3 1/4"
- 3 1/2"

2d, 3d, 4d, 5d, 6d, 7d, 8d, 9d, 10d, 12d, 16d

LARGER SIZES

Size	Length
20d	4"
30d	4 1/2"
40d	5"
50d	5 1/2"
60d	6"

Brads
Resemble miniature finishing nails. Useful for securing moldings to cabinets and walls, or for joining delicate wood edges.

Fence staple
U-shaped galvanized staple used to hold wire fencing to wood posts.

Electric wire staple
Flat-headed. Designed to secure nonmetallic cable to wood framing, but handy wherever you need large staple.

BOLTS, GLUE, SPECIALTY FASTENERS, AND CONNECTORS

In addition to nails and screws, there are four other types of fasteners that are used for special materials or to provide extra strength:

Adhesives: The strength, water resistance, ability to fill gaps, and setting time of adhesives vary *(see right)*.

Bolts: The most common bolts, nuts, and washers are shown below. A bolt's threaded shaft goes right through the materials and is tightened down with a nut. Bolts are stronger than nails or screws because the head and nut hold the material from both sides.

Bolts are classified by diameter (1/8 to 1 inch) and length (3/8 inch and up). To give the nut a firm bite, pick a bolt 1/2 to 1 inch longer than the combined thicknesses of the pieces to be joined plus the washer. If you can't find a long enough bolt, cut threaded rod—a bolt shaft without a head—to the desired length, and add a nut and washer at each end; however, these are not as strong as a normal bolt.

Metal framing connectors: These galvanized steel fasteners provide much stronger joints between framing members than nails alone. Special joist hanger nails are used for nailing connectors to 2-by lumber. For connections to larger pieces, use nails that are specified by the manufacturer. For outdoor applications, use galvanized or stainless steel nails, if available.

You'll find the framing connectors shown on page 48 at almost any lumberyard, available in sizes to fit either rough or surfaced lumber.

Wall and masonry fasteners: Plaster, gypsum wallboard, concrete, and masonry all lack the resilience to hold common fasteners. To hang shelves, picture frames, or mirrors, use one of the devices shown on page 48. For gypsum or plaster walls, fasteners depend on a spreading frame that distributes weight more widely than a nail or screw. To secure fixtures or ledger strips to a masonry wall or to anchor a new stud wall to an existing concrete slab, use a masonry fastener.

THE BEST GLUE FOR THE JOB

When using glues, always follow any safety instructions on the product label.

• **White (polyvinyl) glue.** This standard household glue works well on wood if the pieces to be joined are firmly clamped. Apply it straight from the bottle, and wipe the excess off with a damp rag. White glue isn't waterproof, but it resists grease and solvents; it will soften if used near high heat.

• **Yellow (aliphatic resin) glue.** Often labeled "carpenter's glue," this is a good choice for an all-around adhesive. Though similar to white glue, aliphatic resin has a higher resistance to moisture and heat, sets up faster, and is stronger. It can also be applied at temperatures as low as 60° F.

• **Resorcinol glue.** Waterproof resorcinol is used in building boats and outdoor structures, and indoors in wet, humid areas. It leaves a dark stain that may show through paint, so be neat if you want a fine finish.

• **Contact cement.** This adhesive is applied to both surfaces. When each is dry, the glue bonds on contact and needs no clamps. Contact cement is frequently used to attach wood veneers or plastic laminate to wood surfaces. You must be careful, though: since the initial bond is permanent, you must align parts exactly. The older type is highly flammable and noxious; buy the newer, water-base type if you can.

• **Paneling adhesive.** Solvent or water-base paneling adhesive is typically packaged in 11-ounce cartridges and is applied with a caulking gun *(page 28)*. Use it to fasten plywood and hardboard wall paneling, gypsum wallboard, and subflooring materials to framing members.

BOLTS, NUTS, AND WASHERS

Machine bolt
Hexagonal head driven with wrench.

Carriage bolt
Self-anchoring head digs into the wood as nut is tightened.

Stove bolt
Slotted for screwdrivers.

Flat washer
Most bolts need washer at each end. Self-anchoring bolts, such as carriage bolts, require only one washer, inside nut.

Wing nut
Quickly tightened or loosened by hand.

T-nut
Driven flush into bottom material, preventing it from rotating. Weaker than other nuts.

Hex nut
Standard type of nut.

Nylon-insert locknut
Holds bolt tightly in place without marring wood.

Acorn nut
Decorative nut, used where appearance counts.

Lock washer
Help keeps nut from working loose.

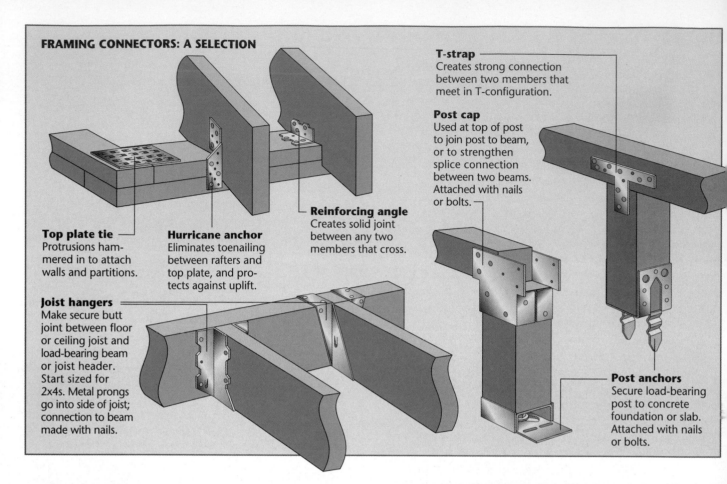

FRAMING CONNECTORS: A SELECTION

T-strap
Creates strong connection between two members that meet in T-configuration.

Post cap
Used at top of post to join post to beam, or to strengthen splice connection between two beams. Attached with nails or bolts.

Reinforcing angle
Creates solid joint between any two members that cross.

Top plate tie
Protrusions hammered in to attach walls and partitions.

Hurricane anchor
Eliminates toenailing between rafters and top plate, and protects against uplift.

Joist hangers
Make secure butt joint between floor or ceiling joist and load-bearing beam or joist header. Start sized for 2x4s. Metal prongs go into side of joist; connection to beam made with nails.

Post anchors
Secure load-bearing post to concrete foundation or slab. Attached with nails or bolts.

Installing wall and masonry fasteners

Installing a spreading anchor
This is used for gypsum or plaster walls. Drill a hole, using the bit size indicated on the package. Slip the screw through the object to be attached, and thread it into the sleeve. Push sleeve into wall and tighten screw; the sleeve expands against back side of wall *(right)*.

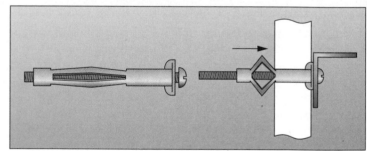

Installing a toggle bolt
Used for gypsum or plaster walls. Drill a hole large enough for the compressed toggles. Pass the screw through the fixture to be mounted and attach the toggles. Slide the toggles through the hole *(near left, above)*—they're spring-loaded and will open once through the wall (the screw must be long enough to go all the way through the wall). Tighten the screw to pull toggles up against the back side of the wall.

Installing a metal shield
This is the fastener to use for masonry. Drill a hole the diameter of the sleeve, and slightly longer, then tap the sleeve in. Slip the lag screw through the fixture to be attached, and tighten it into the sleeve *(far right)*.

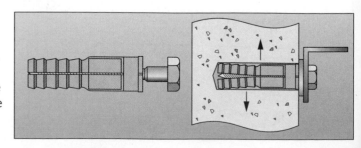

SEALING PRODUCTS

A house protects its inhabitants from rain, snow, wind, cold, and summer sun, but the structure itself must be able to withstand weather damage over time, and that's where sealing products play a role. Wood preservatives help fight wood decay; they're especially important where wood touches the ground or standing water. Caulking compounds fill exterior cracks or seams that let in moisture, drafts, and insects. Effective insulation stops warm air from escaping in winter and slows down the accumulation of heat from outside in summer.

These two pages present the materials with which a carpenter can keep weather out and comfort in.

Wood preservatives: These products extend the life of lumber by increasing its resistance to the decay caused by fungi, mold, and wood-eating insects.

Pressure treatment, the most effective method of application, forces chemical preservatives deep into wood fibers; in this way, lumber from species such as southern pine or Douglas-fir can be made as durable as the hardier types —redwood, cedar, or cypress.

Pressure-treated lumber is widely available; if it's not available in your region, you can special-order it from a building supplier. Depending on the amount of chemical injected, the wood may be labeled "22, ground-contact use," or "L.P. 2, above-ground use." All pressure-treated lumber should be handled with care *(see page 34)*. Preservatives can also be applied with a brush or by immersion, but the long-term results are less satisfactory.

Because many of these materials are considered toxic, you should read the manufacturer's precautions carefully before applying them. For a discussion of basic safety equipment and procedures, see page 5.

Because it's nontoxic to plants and animals, **Copper naphthenate** is especially useful for treating garden structures. Applied by brushing, the dark green tinge it leaves on treated wood can be covered with two coats of paint. **Waterborne salt preservatives** are clean and odorless when applied to wood, but leave a light yellow, green, or brownish tinge. Their main limitation is that they must be applied by pressure treatment. The following two types are highly toxic and require a license for home application: **Creosote** is both a water repellent and a preservative. Because it has a heavy odor and cannot be painted, its role in residential construction is generally limited to below grade (below ground level). **Pentachlorophenol** is an oil-borne preservative that is as effective as creosote, except for below-grade use. It's commonly found in commercial water-repellent preservatives. In their clear form, these compounds provide the most effective treatment for woods left in their natural hues.

Caulking compounds: These vary in both price and composition—as a rule, you get what you pay for. For most caulking jobs, the 11-ounce cartridge and the caulking gun *(page 28)* are simplest to use. Make sure the surface is clean, dry, and free from oil and old caulking material before you apply any caulk. Check the manufacturer's instructions for any special requirements.

The best products are **Elastomeric caulks**, because they effectively seal most types of crack or joint, adhere to most materials, and will outlast ordinary caulks by many years. The generic types in this category include polysulfides, polyurethanes, and silicones. These products have some drawbacks other than cost. Silicone rubber is awkward to smooth out, and won't accept paint. Polysulfide can't be used on porous surfaces unless a primer is applied first. **Latex** and **butyl-rubber caulks** are medium-priced, all-purpose caulks that offer average performance. The acrylic latex caulks outperform nonacrylic latexes. Both are easy to apply and clean up with water. Butyl-rubber caulk, more flexible and durable than acrylic latexes, can be used on any type of surface or material. It has a tendency to shrink slightly while curing. **Oil-base caulks** are the lowest-priced and lowest-performance caulks on the market. Limit their use to stable interior seams and cracks.

Insulation: A well-insulated house can drastically reduce heating bills. However, insulation material can irritate your skin, eyes, nose, and lungs, and some studies indicate that fiberglass may be a carcinogen. To protect yourself when working with insulation material, always wear gloves, respiratory protection, goggles, long pants, and a long-sleeved shirt with tape around the wrists. See page 96 for details on installation.

You'll need to determine how much insulation is enough. Insulation materials are rated by their resistance to heat flow; these ratings are called "R-values." The higher the R-value a material has, the better it will insulate. To estimate the necessary amount of insulation for each area, first find the square footage of the walls, floors, and ceilings. Next compute the square footage of the doors and windows, and other areas to be excluded; subtract this figure from the first. If studs or joists are spaced on 16-inch centers, as a rule of thumb, multiply the net square footage by 0.85 to allow for the area taken up by these framing members. If studs or joists are on 24-inch centers, multiply by 0.88. The resulting figure is the total square footage of insulation needed for that area. Each bag of insulation you buy should be labeled with its square-foot coverage.

In all but the driest climates, it's necessary to install a vapor barrier on the warm side to prevent humid house air from condensing inside insulated walls, floors, and roofing materials. Blankets and batts are commonly sold with a vapor barrier of foil or kraft paper: if your insulation doesn't have this protection, cover it with polyethylene sheeting, foil-backed wallboard, or building paper.

One very popular type of insulation is made from mineral wool—fiberglass or rock wool. This is most commonly available in large rolls known as **blankets** or precut 4- or 8-foot lengths, called **batts**. Both are sized to fit in the space between adjacent wall studs, rafters, or joists. **Loose fill insulation** can be poured where access is limited. This product is ideal for unfinished attics, although some types can be blown into walls covered on both sides. Vermiculite and rock wool are the most common hand-poured materials; cellulose is sometimes hand-poured, but machine-blown installation is more efficient. **Rigid foam insulation boards** come in 4x8, 4x4, or 2x8 panels. Some types can double as nonstructural exterior sheathing for light frame construction with corner bracing; others are used for exterior insulation for foundations.

RECOMMENDED TOTAL R-VALUES FOR EXISTING HOUSES IN EIGHT INSULATION ZONES
(Based on the assumption that no structural modifications are needed to accommodate the added insulation.)

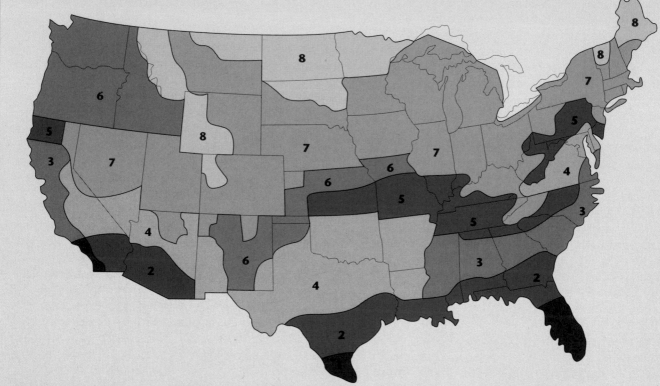

Component	Floors over unheated crawl spaces, basements	Exterior walls (wood frame) Δ	Crawl space walls ¤	Ceilings below ventilated attics	
Insulation Zone	ALL FUEL TYPES			Electric resistance	Heat pump, oil, gas
1	—	11	11	30	(19)
2	—	11	19	30	—
3	19	11	19	38	(30)
4	19	11	19	38	(30)
5	19	11	19	38	—
6	19	11	19	38	—
7	19	11	19	49	(38)
8	19	11	19	49	—

Δ R-value of full wall insulation (3½ inches thick) will depend on material. Range is R-11 to R-13. For new construction R-19 is best for exterior walls. Jamming an R-13 batt in a 3½-inch cavity will not yield R-19.

¤ Insulate crawl space walls only if dry all year, floor above is not insulated, and all ventilation to space is blocked. A vapor barrier (e.g., 4- or 6-mil polyethylene film) should be installed on the ground to reduce moisture migration into the crawl

Courtesy of the North American Insulation Manufacturers Association

ROUGH CARPENTRY

You'll often hear carpenters talk of "rough" and "finish" work. Rough carpentry means framing the house floors, walls, and roof, and adding siding and roofing materials; the more refined "finish" carpentry, which includes all the finishing touches, such as installing doors, windows, and trim is covered in the last chapter. This chapter will illustrate the basic building components and how they fit together, showing how hundreds of boards and thousands of nails are assembled in a simple, logical system to form a house frame.

Three distinct house framing styles are shown on the following pages: platform, balloon, and post and beam. After this overview, we go on to show the procedures involved in platform framing in more detail. Starting with the foundation footings, you can follow the complete sequence you'd take to build it yourself, finishing up with exterior siding and roofing. Whether you're replacing crumbling wall paneling or raising a new structure from the ground up, this chapter will help prepare you for the task. You can learn about the entire building process and apply those basic procedures to your own plans. If you're adding only a few improvements, turn directly to the appropriate sections.

Refer to the chapter beginning on page 4 for information on tools and how to use them. Be sure to follow the safety procedures outlined on pages 5 to 7, and always use caution when working with power tools.

This seemingly abstract arrangement of boards is in fact a carefully planned roof frame composed of bearing walls, ceiling joists, rafters, and purlins. In this chapter you'll learn what these—and many other—terms mean, and how all the pieces that make up a house fit together.

THREE TYPES OF FRAMING

On the next four pages, we peel away the outer skin of three basic house framing styles to show how each is constructed. Platform framing (covered in detail in this chapter) is today's standard, while balloon framing is common in older homes. Post-and-beam is gaining popularity for its simplicity and its architectural flair.

PLATFORM FRAMING

Platform framing (sometimes called "western") is the simplest, safest house-building method in practice today, and the most common. It is identified by joists alone on the mudsill *(page 58)*. The "platform" consists of the foundation and floor structure; the walls are built up starting from the subfloor. If the house is taller than one story, additional layers of floor platforms and walls are stacked on top of the first floor walls. The structure is completed with ceiling and roof framing. The walls, ceiling, and roof are composed almost entirely of 2-by dimension lumber, and are usually held together by nails, sometimes supplemented by metal framing con-

nectors. The wall framing job begins with the exterior stud walls, formed by vertical studs and a horizontal sole and top plate. These walls are fastened to the subfloor and joists below through their sole plates. A layer of ceiling joists follows. The interior bearing wall supports the joists above as the girder did below *(page 58)*.

Framing for a straightforward gable roof consists of evenly spaced rafters that meet at a ridgeboard and are tied together with collar beams; gable studs make up the open end. A popular alternative to standard roof framing uses triangular trusses, which combine ceiling joists, rafters, and diagonal bracing into single, factory-made units.

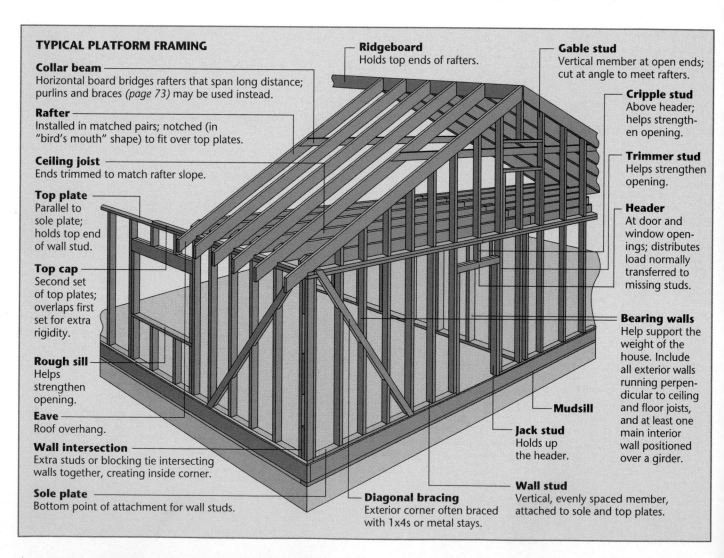

TYPICAL PLATFORM FRAMING

Collar beam —
Horizontal board bridges rafters that span long distance; purlins and braces *(page 73)* may be used instead.

Rafter —
Installed in matched pairs; notched (in "bird's mouth" shape) to fit over top plates.

Ceiling joist —
Ends trimmed to match rafter slope.

Top plate
Parallel to sole plate; holds top end of wall stud.

Top cap
Second set of top plates; overlaps first set for extra rigidity.

Rough sill
Helps strengthen opening.

Eave —
Roof overhang.

Wall intersection —
Extra studs or blocking tie intersecting walls together, creating inside corner.

Sole plate —
Bottom point of attachment for wall studs.

Ridgeboard
Holds top ends of rafters.

Gable stud
Vertical member at open ends; cut at angle to meet rafters.

Cripple stud
Above header; helps strengthen opening.

Trimmer stud
Helps strengthen opening.

Header
At door and window openings; distributes load normally transferred to missing studs.

Bearing walls
Help support the weight of the house. Include all exterior walls running perpendicular to ceiling and floor joists, and at least one main interior wall positioned over a girder.

Mudsill

Jack stud
Holds up the header.

Wall stud
Vertical, evenly spaced member, attached to sole and top plates.

Diagonal bracing
Exterior corner often braced with 1x4s or metal stays.

BALLOON FRAMING

Standard practice until about 1930, this is still used in some two-story houses, especially those with stucco, brick, or other masonry exteriors. If you're planning a remodeling project that involves cutting into wall framing, you'll need to know if your house has a balloon frame. To check, look in your basement or crawl space for paired joists and studs resting on the mudsill.

Like the platform frame, the backbone of a balloon-framed house includes footings and foundation walls, floor joists, subfloor, wall studs, ceiling joists, and rafters. Wall sheathing and roof decking complete the structural skin. The chief difference between the platform frame and the balloon frame is that, in the latter, the bearing wall studs extend in one piece from the mudsill on top of the foundation wall to the doubled top plate two stories above.

Balloon framing has some advantages over platform framing when constructing a two-story house. The one-piece studs create a more stable surface for masonry sidings and wall coverings, and wall shrinkage and settling are more uniform because the studs are continuous. In addition, skilled carpenters can erect the walls in less time than is required for platform framing. However, one real drawback is the hazard of working at heights without the solid subfloor of platform framing; another is the difficulty these days of finding quality 18- to 20-foot studs.

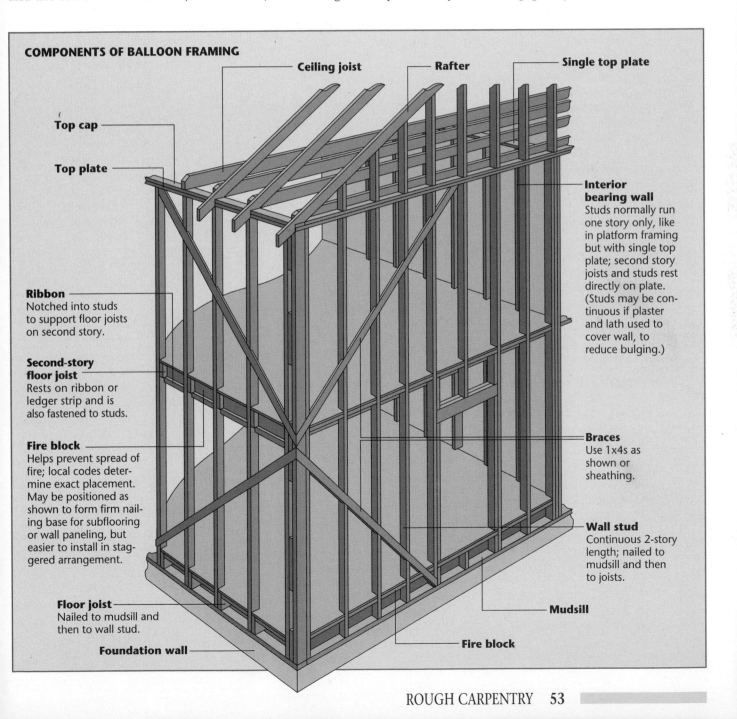

COMPONENTS OF BALLOON FRAMING

Ceiling joist

Rafter

Single top plate

Top cap

Top plate

Interior bearing wall
Studs normally run one story only, like in platform framing but with single top plate; second story joists and studs rest directly on plate. (Studs may be continuous if plaster and lath used to cover wall, to reduce bulging.)

Ribbon
Notched into studs to support floor joists on second story.

Second-story floor joist
Rests on ribbon or ledger strip and is also fastened to studs.

Braces
Use 1x4s as shown or sheathing.

Fire block
Helps prevent spread of fire; local codes determine exact placement. May be positioned as shown to form firm nailing base for subflooring or wall paneling, but easier to install in staggered arrangement.

Wall stud
Continuous 2-story length; nailed to mudsill and then to joists.

Floor joist
Nailed to mudsill and then to wall stud.

Mudsill

Foundation wall

Fire block

POST-AND-BEAM FRAMING

The post-and-beam design is an updated version of traditional timber and pole framing styles, which utilized heavy structural members at greater intervals instead of light, closely spaced 2-by dimension lumber. Post-and-beam (more accurately post, beam, and plank) framing not only lends variety to architectural styles but can also help keep both material and labor costs lower than standard construction. You can recognize this type of framing by looking for the bottom ends of posts sitting on the sole plate, with lighter framing members in between the posts. Also, inside the house you'll usually

see exposed structural members on the walls or ceiling, spaced 4 to 8 feet apart.

The basic frame consists of sturdy posts that hold up the beams, which in turn support the planks that tie the structure together and form the floor, ceiling, and roof deck. The open beam ceiling is a trademark of the design, showing off the clean, bold lines of the planks and beams; and the wide, non-weight-bearing spaces between the posts permit large expanses of glass. Posts and beams may be solid lumber, glue-laminated members, or 2-by sections nailed and glued together.

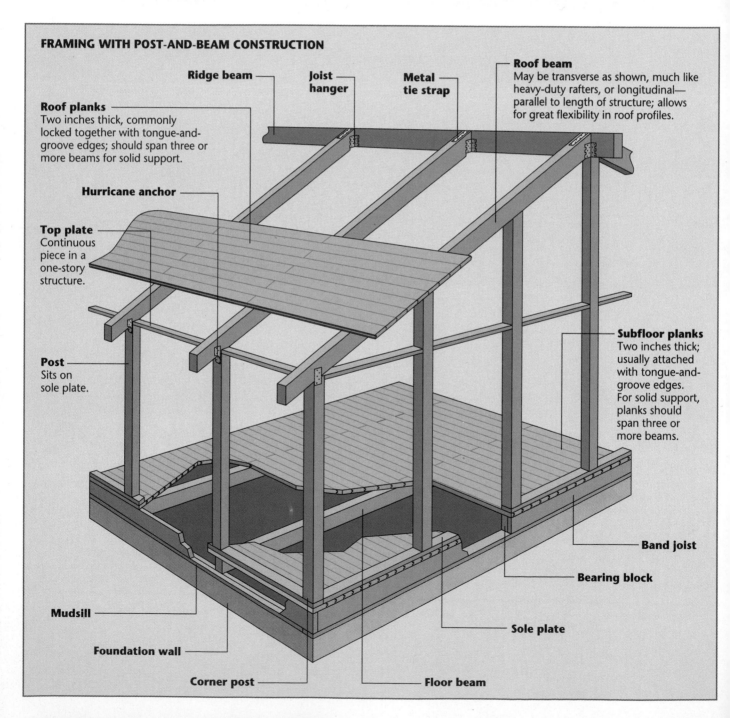

FRAMING WITH POST-AND-BEAM CONSTRUCTION

Ridge beam

Joist hanger

Metal tie strap

Roof beam
May be transverse as shown, much like heavy-duty rafters, or longitudinal—parallel to length of structure; allows for great flexibility in roof profiles.

Roof planks
Two inches thick, commonly locked together with tongue-and-groove edges; should span three or more beams for solid support.

Hurricane anchor

Top plate
Continuous piece in a one-story structure.

Subfloor planks
Two inches thick; usually attached with tongue-and-groove edges. For solid support, planks should span three or more beams.

Post
Sits on sole plate.

Band joist

Bearing block

Mudsill

Sole plate

Foundation wall

Corner post

Floor beam

This system has some disadvantages. The massive posts and beams are difficult—and potentially dangerous—for do-it-yourselfers to manipulate. Also, because each member carries a large load, the house design must be precisely engineered and framing connections carefully made. Metal framing connectors or tie straps are needed, rather than ordinary nails (these unattractive fasteners can usually be concealed). Overhead electrical and plumbing lines can be hidden by installing "spacer blocks" between doubled beams and covering the gap at the bottom with trim, to form inner passageways for the lines.

Once the frame is constructed, the walls must be filled in; light dimension lumber installed between posts provides a framework for exterior and interior paneling, insulation, and electrical or plumbing lines. Headers are not required if you opt for large amounts of glass or many doors, since these wall sections bear no weight. To complete a post-and-beam structure, roofing materials are laid atop the planks. When roof planks serve as the ceiling below, you can insulate by laying rigid board insulation over the deck and then installing plywood sheathing. Turn to page 74 for more roofing and siding details.

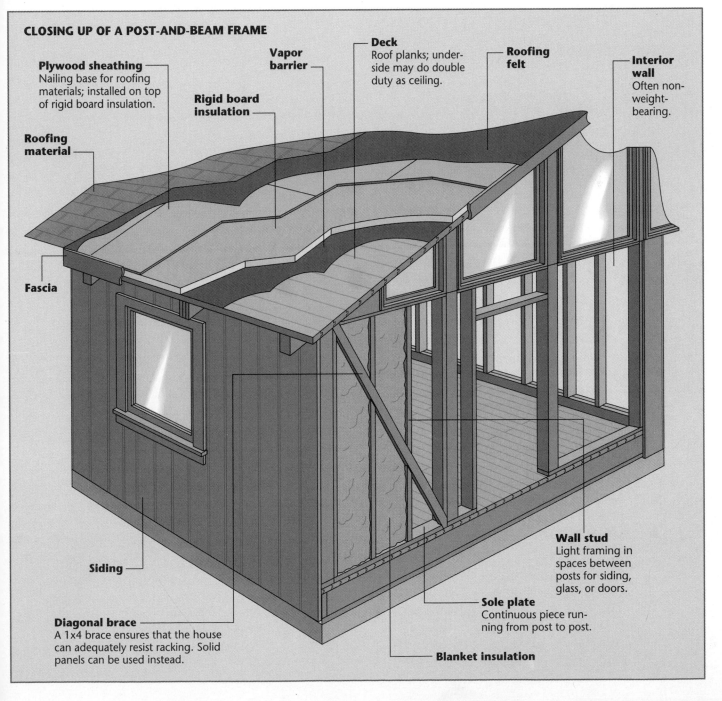

CLOSING UP OF A POST-AND-BEAM FRAME

Plywood sheathing — Nailing base for roofing materials; installed on top of rigid board insulation.

Rigid board insulation —

Roofing material —

Roofing felt —

Vapor barrier —

Deck — Roof planks; underside may do double duty as ceiling.

Interior wall — Often non-weight-bearing.

Fascia —

Siding —

Diagonal brace — A 1x4 brace ensures that the house can adequately resist racking. Solid panels can be used instead.

Blanket insulation —

Sole plate — Continuous piece running from post to post.

Wall stud — Light framing in spaces between posts for siding, glass, or doors.

Before plunging into a project, investigate local restrictions and building codes; decide whether or not you need help; select and purchase materials; and think through the exact sequence of building steps.

☑ **Check the deed and zoning restrictions.** Your deed may restrict the style of architecture or materials that can be used, or even colors of exterior paint. It may also specify where an addition can be placed, and may restrict building of garages or second stories. Zoning ordinances define the type of occupancy, sewage regulations, and use of municipal water. They also regulate the maximum percentage of land coverage; front, side, and back property setbacks; the heights of fences and utility buildings; and window placement in relation to adjacent houses.

☑ **Research the building codes.** Most government building departments have adopted one of the various national model codes: the Uniform Building Code in western states; the Standard Building Code in southern states; and the Building Officials and Code Administrator's Building Code (BOCA) in the East and Midwest. State, county, or local building departments may adopt only part of one of these codes, rewriting or adding specifications for their own needs. Your project's design and materials must measure up to your particular local code.

A condensed version endorsed by all model codes is available in the booklet *One and Two Family Dwelling Code*, from the Council of American Building Officials (CABO). It also lists relevant plumbing, mechanical, and electrical codes.

☑ **Acquire building permits.** According to most codes, you need a permit for almost every structural job, but in actual practice, there's a little more leeway. Though codes vary, they're seldom concerned with cabinetry, paneling, painting, and other projects that don't alter the basic structure.

If you're doing all the work yourself, discuss your ideas with the building inspector and ask whether you'll need a building permit. If so, you may have to describe the planned work and give the lot, block, tract, street address, or assessor's parcel number of the location; indicate use or occupancy; state the valuation; and submit two to four sets of building plans. In earthquake and slide areas you may also be required to file a geologist's report. You may have to take out an electrical and plumbing permit as well.

☑ **Hire help.** If you're building a sizable structure or beginning a major remodeling job, you may need to hire some help. Workers must be covered by worker's compensation insurance to cover possible job-related injuries. If they're hired by a licensed contractor, they're covered by that contractor's policies. However, for those you pay directly, you must carry the insurance.

For an extensive project, you may also need to register with state and federal governments as an employer, withhold and remit income taxes and disability insurance, and pay social security and unemployment costs.

Subcontractors can prove invaluable when there are specialized tasks to be done. They can offer expert and efficient work in trenching, foundations, plumbing and heating, electrical work, and so forth. They'll know how to use the specialized tools that make the job go faster with fewer risks.

If you decide to work with subcontractors, then you're the boss. On a large job, this can be a huge task—coordinating the work, arranging for permits and inspections, scheduling deliveries, and paying the subcontractors. Consider hiring a general contractor to oversee part—or even all—of the project. Work out an agreement that allows you to perform the jobs you wish to do yourself; itemize points in a contract that you both sign. You also might establish penalties for work that is completed behind schedule, and determine such details as who is responsible for hauling away garbage.

☑ **Buy materials.** Once you've estimated your materials (see Chapter 2 for tips), make a shopping list that is complete down to the last nail. To cut the costs of materials, order as many materials as possible at a single time from a single supplier; choose your supplier on the basis of competitive bids; and order materials in regularly available, standard dimensions and in quantities 5 to 10 percent greater than your estimated needs. If part of the construction is being done by a licensed contractor, he or she may arrange to purchase materials at a professional discount. Be on the lookout for materials that have been salvaged from dismantled structures. In some areas, wreckers specialize in the sale of such salvage. Contractors with large projects nearing completion are also good sources of salvage. Make sure you check local codes before using salvaged materials.

If you're having trouble preparing a detailed materials list, take your plans with you to the lumberyard; often the people there can help you.

☑ **Make a schedule.** Think through in advance the exact sequence of procedures. Allow extra time—and money. Plan work days so you're not caught by night or bad weather when you've just opened up your home's exterior for a new window or skylight. Consider how long you may need to have power and water supplies turned off.

READING PLANS

Though few nonprofessionals have the knowledge or skills to draw up a really accurate set of blueprints, understanding them is essential for anyone planning to take on much of the work. Reading house plans isn't that difficult. For any complex project, you'll most likely be referring to a number of scale drawings, as shown below, where the floor plan, elevation, and section views combine to show the full picture of a proposed one-room addition. (To the right of the drawings is a key to the standard architectural symbols used.) These scale drawings will include some or all of the following:

Plot plan: This overview shows the relationship of the building or improvement to property lines, topography, easements, and the like.

Floor plan: This classic bird's-eye view of the structure's layout shows dimensions and positions of walls, windows, doors, and other features. If the space isn't complicated, the plan may include plumbing and electrical layouts as well.

Foundation and framing plans: These specialized drawings, shown from the same vantage point as the floor plan, feature foundation layout or framing members—floor, wall, or roof. They allow you to visualize quickly structural details and to estimate your needs.

Elevations: These are straight-on views of single interior or exterior walls that help explain the floor plan. They often specify dimensions and materials, in addition to pointing out special design features.

Sections and details: These are added whenever standard views or scales can't show fine points. Sections are planes sliced vertically or horizontally through the building to indicate, for example, windows or foundation footings. Large-scale details—normally side views—show trim, fastenings, and dimensions in great detail.

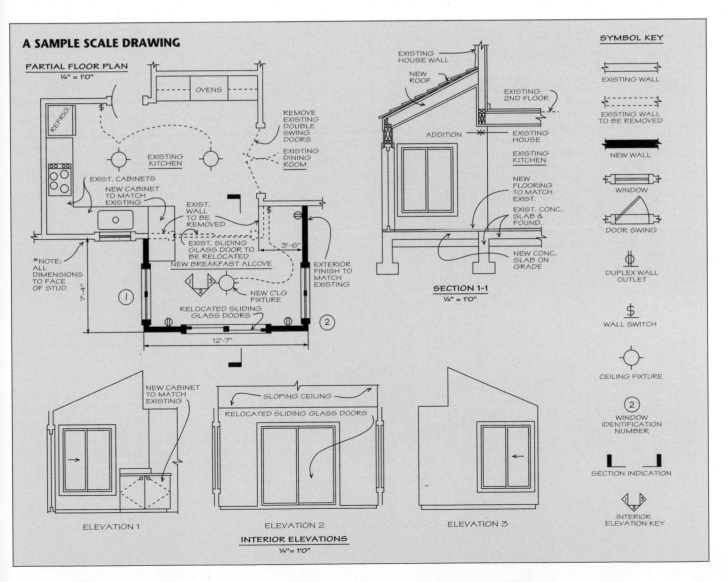

FLOOR FRAMING

loor framing, though structurally simple, must be precise; if the basic platform is not exactly level and square, imperfections will continue throughout the entire construction process. The following pages will show you the major components of floor framing, and guide you through the steps involved in building and installing mudsills, girders and posts, floor joists, floor openings, and subflooring.

Foundations begin with wide concrete pads, or footings. The foundation walls (or posts) rest on the footings. Depending on the depth of the excavation, these perimeter walls create a full 8-foot basement or a shallower crawl space. All-wood foundations are built from treated framing plywood.

In frost-free areas, a variation on this design is the concrete slab foundation. The continuous slab doubles as both foundation and subfloor, though footings are still required around perimeters and below interior bearing walls. In this type, the walls are attached directly to the slab. For concrete slab foundations, begin assembling exterior walls (page 64) once the foundation has cured. Otherwise, begin the four-phase process of framing the floor as follows:

1. Install mudsills along the tops of foundation walls.
2. Assemble any girders and supporting posts that span the interior of the crawl space or basement. (A structure wider than about 16 feet needs a girder.)
3. Install floor joists, band joists and blocking or bridging between joists, which make up a frame for the subfloor. At this point, below-the-floor work (plumbing, heating, wiring, or insulation) should be complete.
4. Lay a subfloor on top of the joists. The floor deck, nailed directly to the tops of the joists, completes the floor system. Though traditional solid board decking is still used, plywood has become the material of choice because of its structural rigidity and ease of installation.

PLATFORM FRAMING: GETTING TO THE BOTTOM OF IT

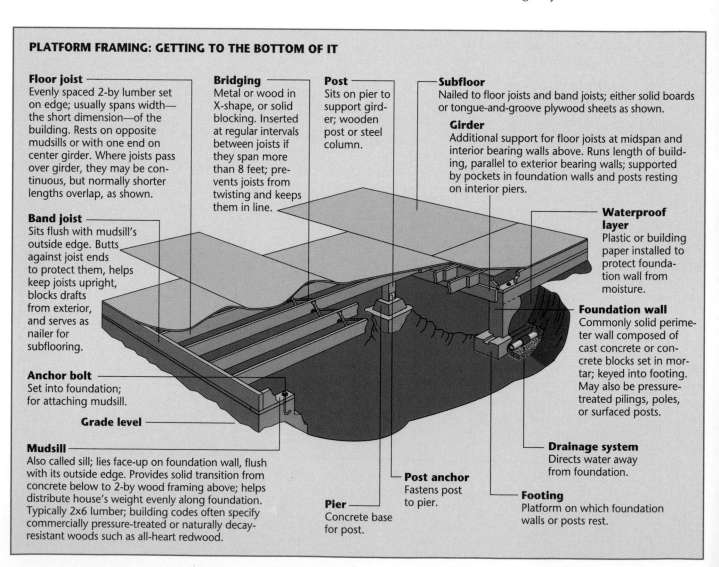

Floor joist
Evenly spaced 2-by lumber set on edge; usually spans width—the short dimension—of the building. Rests on opposite mudsills or with one end on center girder. Where joists pass over girder, they may be continuous, but normally shorter lengths overlap, as shown.

Band joist
Sits flush with mudsill's outside edge. Butts against joist ends to protect them, helps keep joists upright, blocks drafts from exterior, and serves as nailer for subflooring.

Anchor bolt
Set into foundation; for attaching mudsill.

Grade level

Mudsill
Also called sill; lies face-up on foundation wall, flush with its outside edge. Provides solid transition from concrete below to 2-by wood framing above; helps distribute house's weight evenly along foundation. Typically 2x6 lumber; building codes often specify commercially pressure-treated or naturally decay-resistant woods such as all-heart redwood.

Bridging
Metal or wood in X-shape, or solid blocking. Inserted at regular intervals between joists if they span more than 8 feet; prevents joists from twisting and keeps them in line.

Post
Sits on pier to support girder; wooden post or steel column.

Pier
Concrete base for post.

Post anchor
Fastens post to pier.

Subfloor
Nailed to floor joists and band joists; either solid boards or tongue-and-groove plywood sheets as shown.

Girder
Additional support for floor joists at midspan and interior bearing walls above. Runs length of building, parallel to exterior bearing walls; supported by pockets in foundation walls and posts resting on interior piers.

Waterproof layer
Plastic or building paper installed to protect foundation wall from moisture.

Foundation wall
Commonly solid perimeter wall composed of cast concrete or concrete blocks set in mortar; keyed into footing. May also be pressure-treated pilings, poles, or surfaced posts.

Drainage system
Directs water away from foundation.

Footing
Platform on which foundation walls or posts rest.

Installing mudsills

TOOLKIT
- Tape measure
- Chalk line
- Combination or try square
- Drill and bit slightly bigger than anchor bolt
- Wrench
- Water level

1 ▶ Checking the foundation for square

Even the best foundation walls may be slightly askew in the corners or a trifle long on one side; rather than follow these flaws, it's important to lay the sills square. To check for square on a regular rectangular or square shape, measure the diagonals between opposite corners as shown at right; the lengths of AD and BC must match exactly. Also check the lengths of the foundation walls against your planned dimensions.

If your measurements don't agree, mark the offending corners (for example, "long ½ inch" or "short ¼ inch") to establish the correct corners. Then measure the sill's width and mark this distance in from each edge at the corners—adding or subtracting for any discrepancies. Snap a chalk line between each pair of marks to indicate the inside edge of each sill, keeping the sill flush with the outside edge of the foundation wall.

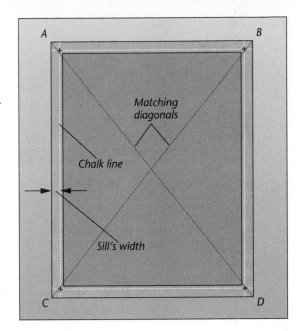

2 ▶ Drilling holes in the sills for anchor bolts

Choose the longest, straightest sill material you can find. Hold the first piece against the anchor bolts embedded in the foundation wall and use a square to transfer the location of each bolt to the sill *(left)*. To locate the bolt hole on the sill's width, measure the distance from the chalk line to the center of each bolt; mark this on the sill. Remove the sill and drill slightly oversize holes (about ¾" for a standard ½" diameter anchor bolt) through the sill. Repeat this procedure for each length of sill material you'll use.

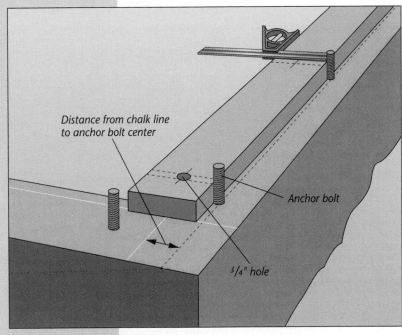

3 ▶ Installing the sills

If you're in termite country, install a termite barrier between the foundation wall and the sill. Termite barriers must be a minimum of 26-gauge galvanized iron or another acceptable metal. In any case, before installing the sill, protect the gap between it and the foundation wall with fiberglass sill sealer.

To install a sill, position it on the anchor bolts, install washers, and run the nuts down fingertight. Recheck the diagonals, make final adjustments, and tighten the nuts. Now, using a water level, check the sills for level all around the perimeter. You can correct a sloping sill later by inserting shims (tapering lengths of cedar shingles) every 4' or so between the sill and band joist—or outer joist—along the problem wall.

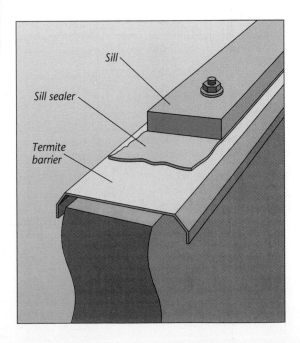

POSTS AND GIRDERS

Posts are either solid lumber, built-up lumber, concrete-filled steel columns (known as Lally tubes), or concrete (cast in cylindrical cardboard forms). The standard solid lumber post sits on a concrete pier or a metal post anchor embedded in the footing.

Girders may be steel beams, solid lumber, or "built-up" lengths of 2-by dimension lumber nailed together. A built-up girder is the simplest type to handle, since it's assembled while it rests on the foundation walls near its final destination.

The design of posts and girders is interrelated: the depth and thickness of the girder is determined by its span, the size and placement of posts below, footing displacement, and the load of the structure above—all specified by the local building code. In many areas, wood posts and girders within 12 inches of the ground must be pressure-treated or naturally decay-resistant.

The simplest way to assemble a post-and-girder structure is to position the posts first and then lay the girder right on top, as shown below.

Installing posts and girders

TOOLKIT
- Tape measure
- Water or line level
- Saw
- Hammer
- Carpenter's level
- Screwdriver (optional)

1 Installing the posts

To figure out post heights, string a line of mason's twine across the top of the mudsills, as shown below, designating the center of the girder. Use a water or line level to make sure that the twine is level. Now measure the distance between each pier or post anchor and the twine; subtract the depth of the girder and cut the posts to length. Temporarily brace any posts higher than 12" by driving 1x4 or 2x4 stakes into the ground, then tacking a 1x3 or 1x4 brace to each stake with a couple of duplex nails, as shown; add a brace to one other side to prevent the post from tipping sideways. Center each post below the string and check it for plumb, using a carpenter's level on adjacent sides; adjust the braces if necessary. Fasten the post to the post anchor; if post caps are to be used, set them in place now. (Remove the braces after the girder is installed, or when they get in the way.)

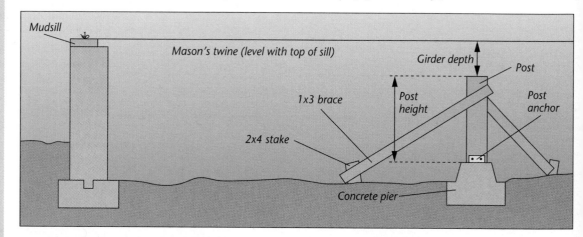

Mudsill

Mason's twine (level with top of sill)

Girder depth

Post

Post anchor

1x3 brace

Post height

2x4 stake

Concrete pier

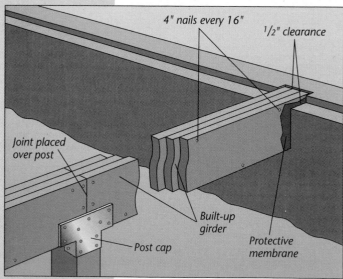

4" nails every 16"

1/2" clearance

Joint placed over post

Built-up girder

Post cap

Protective membrane

2 Installing the girders

A typical built-up girder consists of three thicknesses of 2-by lumber. Nail the pieces together with 4" nails spaced 16" apart along the top and bottom edges, alternating the nails on opposite sides. If you must use shorter lengths to assemble a long girder, stagger the joints between successive layers so joints are located over a post. Be sure the crowns on the pieces are aligned on the same side; the crown is the high side of an edgeline warp or crook (page 36).

Line the pocket in the foundation wall with sill sealer. Then with your helpers, place the girder crown-side up on top of the posts, with its ends resting in the foundation wall pockets (left); there should be 1/2" clearance between the back and sides of the pocket and the girder. If you have to raise a girder level with the sill, use metal shims, which won't compress or rot. Toenail the girder to each post with 3" nails; or, if you're using metal post caps, nail or screw them to the girder.

FLOOR JOISTS

Common joist sizes are 2x6, 2x8, 2x10, and 2x12. The size you choose depends on the distance spanned, the load to be carried, the lumber species and grade you're planning to use, and the spacing between joists. Framing members are evenly spaced, and the distance between them is usually specified in inches "on center" (O.C.)— the measurement from the center of one member to the center of the next. On page 62 you'll find a chart that lists maximum spans for several common species and grades. Be sure to check the code requirements in your area.

Nail the floor joists both to band joists and to the sills (by toenailing) at opposite sides of the building. Where joists cross a girder, they may continue, butt together (as long as reinforcing gussets are nailed to each side of the joint), or overlap. Where joists overlap, nail them first to each other, then to the girder. Overlapping allows you to buy and use shorter joists.

Joists are doubled below a concentrated load—such as a cast-iron bathtub, around floor openings, and below interior partition walls. Where plumbing lines run up through a partition, doubled joists are often spaced apart with blocks, as shown below, to allow access to plumbing and wiring. As with all the other framing components, floor joists are subject to particular types of load-bearing stresses; check that you are using the right materials for the job.

Installing floor joists

TOOLKIT
• Tape measure
• Chalk line
• Hammer
• Saw

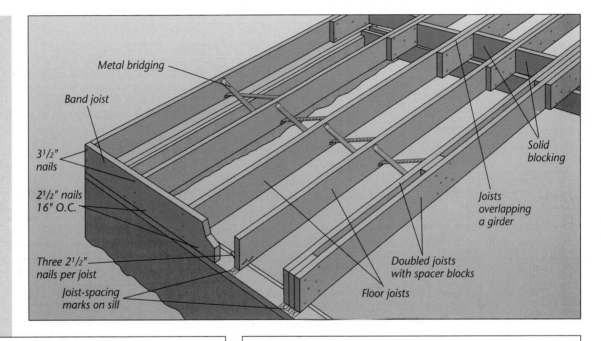

Metal bridging

Band joist

$3^1/2$" nails

$2^1/2$" nails 16" O.C.

Three $2^1/2$" nails per joist

Joist-spacing marks on sill

Solid blocking

Joists overlapping a girder

Doubled joists with spacer blocks

Floor joists

1 Laying out the joists
First, mark the joist spacing on one sill, as shown above. Starting at an outside corner, mark the $1^1/2$" thickness of the first joist, or stringer, with a line and an X. For the standard 16" joist centers, hook your tape measure over the sill's end and measure off $15^1/4$" and $16^3/4$"; then mark another set of lines and an X between. From these lines, continue in even 16" intervals to the far end of the sill. When you're doubling joists, mark another line to one side, but stick with the basic 16" spacing. Don't worry if the last interval is smaller than 16".

Once the layout is complete, transfer the same spacing to the opposite mudsill or the girder. An exception to this is if you're overlapping joists—the layout on the opposite sill must be offset $1^1/2$" to allow for the overlap. Mark the outline of the first joist at $13^3/4$" and $15^1/4$" from the end; then mark every 16" as before.

2 Securing the joists
Use dry lumber that is as straight as possible for joists and band joists. Sighting along each joist, find the crown and mark that side; install joists crown-side up. If you need to level the band joist, insert shims between it and the mudsill.

Begin by toenailing the band joist flush with the sill, using $2^1/2$" nails every 16". (You can attach several joists to the band joist first, then pull it flush with the sill and toenail— the weight of the joists will help keep the band joist from moving.) Cut the floor joists to length, butting them against the band joist; face-nail them with three $3^1/2$" nails. Once the joists are in place, also toenail each to the sill with three $2^1/2$" nails. At the far end, nail the band joist to the joist ends and then toenail it to the sill. Where joist ends rest on a girder, the joists should overlap a minimum of 4". Tie the joists together with 3" nails and toenail them to the girder.

FLOOR JOIST SPANS (Design criteria: Strength 10 lbs. per sq. ft. dead load plus 40 lbs. per sq. ft. live load).

Species or group	Grade	Span (feet and inches)							
		2x6		2x8		2x10		2x12	
		16" O.C.	24" O.C.	16" O.C.	24" O.C.	16" O.C.	24" O.C.	16" O.C.	24" O.C.
Douglas-fir-Larch	1 & Btr	10-2	8-10	13-4	11-8	17-0	14-5	20-5	16-8
	1	9-11	8-8	13-1	11-0	16-5	13-5	19-1	15-7
	2	9-9	8-1	12-7	10-3	15-5	12-7	17-10	14-7
	3	7-6	6-2	9-6	7-9	11-8	9-6	13-6	11-0
Douglas-fir (South)	1	9-1	7-11	12-0	10-5	15-3	12-9	18-1	14-9
	2	8-10	7-9	11-8	10-0	14-11	12-2	17-4	14-2
	3	7-4	6-0	9-3	7-7	11-4	9-3	13-2	10-9
Hem-Fir	1 & Btr	9-6	8-3	12-7	11-0	16-0	13-9	19-6	16-0
	1	9-6	8-3	12-7	10-9	16-0	13-1	18-7	15-2
	2	9-1	7-11	12-0	10-2	15-2	12-5	17-7	14-4
	3	7-6	6-2	9-6	7-9	11-8	9-6	13-6	11-0
Spruce-Pine-Fir (South)	1	8-10	7-8	11-8	10-2	14-11	12-5	17-7	14-4
	2	8-7	7-6	11-4	9-6	14-3	11-8	16-6	13-6
	3	6-11	5-8	8-9	7-2	10-9	8-9	12-5	10-2
Western woods	1	8-7	7-0	10-10	8-10	13-3	10-10	15-5	12-7
	2	8-4	7-0	10-10	8-10	13-3	10-10	15-5	12-7
	3	6-6	5-4	8-3	6-9	10-1	8-3	11-8	9-6

Chart courtesy Western Wood Products Association

ASK A PRO

SHOULD I USE BLOCKING OR BRIDGING FOR FLOOR JOISTS?

Solid blocking, 1x3 or 1x4 cross-bridging, or manufactured metal bridging will keep joists from rotating along their mid-spans. As a rule of thumb, install blocking or bridging at 8-foot intervals; if your span is less than 16 feet, split the distance. Metal bridging, the simplest to install, requires no nails; simply hammer the spiked ends into adjacent joist faces. To lay out a run of bridging, measure the desired distance in from both ends of the sill and snap a chalk line across the joists.

(To make a working platform, span the joists with a board near the line.) Attach the tops of the bridging along the chalk line; leave a slight gap between adjacent pieces. When the subfloor is down, hammer the bottoms into place from the crawl space or basement. Install solid wood blocks—the same dimension stock as the joists—between joists at the girder. Snap a center line, and nail the blocks to the joists with four 2¹/₂" nails at each end; stagger every second block.

Framing a floor opening

TOOLKIT
• Tape measure
• Hammer
• Saw

Assembling the framing

Floor openings require special framing—add trimmers, headers, and tail joists around any opening you're planning. If the opening is more than 4' wide, use double headers. Use joist hangers to attach headers longer than 6' to the trimmers, and tail joists longer than 12' to the headers. When assembling the framing, temporarily omit the full-length joist on each side to allow yourself nailing room. Install the initial trimmer joist on each side of the opening. Next, attach the first headers with three 3¹/₂" nails on each end. Cut the tail joists to length and nail them with 3¹/₂" nails too. Now add second headers inside the first, nailing them through the trimmers as before, and face-nail them to the first headers. Finally, double the trimmers, nailing them together along top and bottom edges with 3¹/₂" nails.

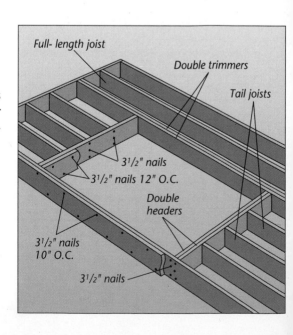

Full-length joist

Double trimmers

Tail joists

3¹/₂" nails

3¹/₂" nails 12" O.C.

Double headers

3¹/₂" nails 10" O.C.

3¹/₂" nails

LAYING THE SUBFLOOR

Most floor decks consist of two layers. The first layer, or sub-floor, is 7/16-inch to 1 1/8-inch plywood—rated Sheathing, C-Plugged, or similar grade. A thinner, smoother second layer, or underlayment, goes on just before the finish floor, creating a smooth surface. Increasingly popular, though, are combination subfloor-underlayment panels. Ranging in thickness from 19/32-inch to 1 1/8 inches, these panels are available with tongue-and-groove edges that eliminate the need for edge support between joists. Additional underlayment is usually unnecessary.

Installing a subfloor

TOOLKIT
• Tape measure
• Chalk line
• Hammer
For combination sub-floor-underlayment:
• Sledgehammer

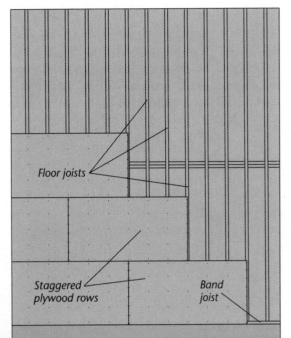

Floor joists

Staggered plywood rows

Band joist

Installing a plywood subfloor
Panels are laid perpendicular to joists, with their ends centered on joists. You don't need to support panel edges if the joints of the underlayment above will be staggered or if you plan to install 25/32" wood strip flooring. For a 16" joist spacing, 7/16" sheathing is normally the minimum thickness; for 24" joist centers, 3/4" thick sheathing is required.

To install the subfloor, measure in 48" from the outside edge of the band joist at both ends and snap a chalk line across the joists. Lay the first row of plywood with edges flush to this line, and ends centered on joists. Panel ends in adjacent rows must be staggered: begin every second row with a half sheet, as shown at left. When laying out the subfloor, simply tack the panels in place as you go, so that you can make adjustments if necessary. Later, snap a chalk line across joist centers and nail into the joist. Use 2" nails for panels up to 1/2" thick, and 2 1/2" nails for thicker panels. Space nails 6" apart at panel ends and 10" apart at intermediate joists.

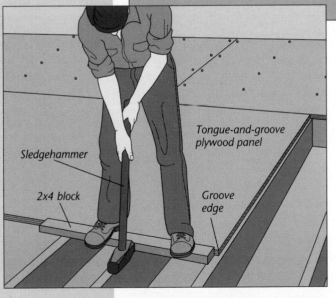

Tongue-and-groove plywood panel

Sledgehammer

Groove edge

2x4 block

  ASK A PRO

HOW DO I NAIL THE PANELS WHERE JOISTS OVERLAP?
Where the floor joists overlap, their spacing changes. To finish nailing one row of panels, "scab on" (nail) 2x4 blocking to the new joists, as shown. Then, offset the next row so the panel edges will be centered on the new joists.

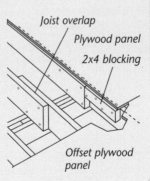

Joist overlap

Plywood panel

2x4 blocking

Offset plywood panel

Installing combination subfloor-underlayment
Combination panels are laid out in the same way as standard subfloors, but working with tongue-and-groove edges calls for a special technique. Begin the first row by positioning the tongue to the outside, over the band joist. To fit the tongues of the second row into the grooves of the first, use a sledgehammer to hit a 2x4 wood block up and down the groove edge *(above, left)*, seating the tongue. When tacking the sheets, don't nail the groove edge or you'll have trouble fitting the next panel's tongue. For an even sturdier deck, use both nails and an elastomeric construction adhesive. Gluing enables you to use fewer nails—space them 12" apart, both at panel ends and at intermediate supports. Use 2" ring-shank nails for panels up to 3/4" thick, and 2 1/2" nails for thicker panels.

WALL FRAMING

With a solid subfloor underneath, framing the walls involves these steps: assembling the wall components while they lie on the floor deck; raising each wall section into position, checking it for plumb and bracing it securely; and fastening individual wall sections to the floor framing and to each other. For new construction, assemble and raise the exterior side walls first, tie in the end walls, then add interior partition walls. Framing for any wall includes a sole plate, evenly spaced wall studs, and a top plate; horizontal fire blocks between studs may also be required. Walls with doorways or window openings need extra studs, as well as headers to span the opening.

Traditionally, walls were built from 2x4 studs and plates, with studs placed on 16-inch centers. In recent years, the growing concern with energy-efficient structures has led to higher R-value recommendations *(page 50)* than are possible with insulated 2x4 walls. Many builders respond by framing exterior walls with 2x6s, which means they can place the studs on 24-inch centers. Whichever design you choose, basic wall construction is the same.

Walls are classified as either bearing or nonbearing. A bearing wall helps support the weight of the house; a nonbearing wall does not. All exterior walls running perpendicular to floor and ceiling joists are bearing; they support joists and rafters at their ends or at midspan. Normally, at least one main interior wall—situated over a girder or interior foundation wall—is also bearing. Design requirements for interior nonbearing walls—often called "partitions" are less strict; partitions built from 2x4s on 24-inch centers are the norm. The framing for an opening, particularly the header, may be lighter.

The standard ceiling height for interior spaces is 8 feet. Because ceiling materials encroach on this height, you'll have trouble installing 4x8-foot gypsum wallboard or sheet paneling unless you frame the walls slightly higher—8 feet $^3/_4$ inch is standard. When you subtract the thickness of the sole plate and doubled top plates, this leaves a length of 7 feet $8^1/_4$ inches ($92^1/_4$ inches) for the wall studs. Lumberyards frequently stock precut studs in this length.

Assembling a basic wall

TOOLKIT
• Saw
• Combination square
• Tape measure
• Framing square (optional)
• Hammer
• Chalk line

1 Laying out the wall

First, cut both the sole and top plates to length. If you need more than one piece for each, locate the joints at stud centers; offset any joints between top and sole plates at least 4'. Now lay the top plate against the sole plate on the deck, and beginning at one end, measure in $1^1/_2$"—the thickness of a stud—from one end and draw a line across both plates with pencil and combination square for the end studs. If your studs are on 16" centers, start once more from that end; measure and draw lines at $15^1/_4$" and $16^3/_4$" (or $23^1/_4$" and $24^3/_4$" for 24"-centers). From these lines, continue marking lines at 16" (or 24") intervals until you reach the far end of both plates *(below)*—most good tape measures have marks every 16" for stud placement, with all studs evenly spaced 16" on center.

You may find that an easier method is to use a framing square; you can use the tongue's thickness ($1^1/_2$") to scribe one side of the studs, and its length (16") to position them. Note that you don't have to mark both sides of the studs, as shown in the illustration. Most carpenters mark one side consistently, and put a rough "X" on the side of the line where the stud goes.

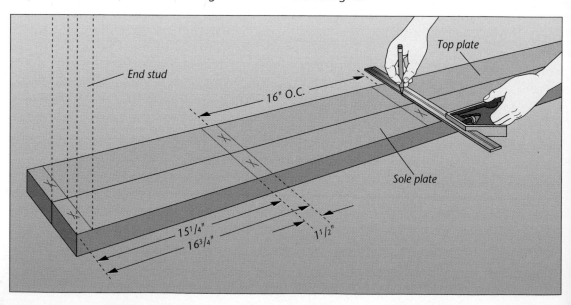

End stud

16" O.C.

Top plate

Sole plate

$15^1/_4$"
$16^3/_4$"

$1^1/_2$"

Fire block (optional) — Top plate — Stud markings — Wall stud — Sole plate — 3¹/₂" nail

2 Assembling the pieces

Unless you're using precut studs, measure and cut the wall studs to exact length. Spread the plates apart on the deck and turn them on edge, stud markings inward. Place the studs between the lines and face-nail them through each plate with two 3¹/₂" nails. If fire blocks are required, center them 4' above the bottom of the sole plate. Snap a chalk line across the studs and stagger alternate blocks slightly so you can face-nail through the studs into the fire block, rather than toenailing.

For a door or window, check the manufacturer's "rough opening" dimensions and mark the center line of the opening on the plates. Or, measure the unit and add an extra ³/₈" on sides and top for windows, or ¹/₂" at top and sides for doors. This space lets you level and plumb the unit with shims.

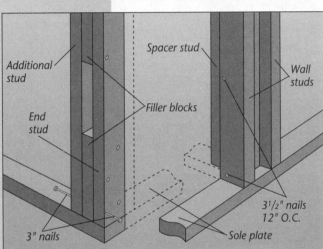

Additional stud — Spacer stud — Wall studs — Filler blocks — End stud — 3¹/₂" nails 12" O.C. — 3" nails — Sole plate

3 Framing corners

Where walls meet, you need extra studs. After a long exterior wall is assembled, add extra studs at both ends; space them away from end studs with filler blocks (far left). Nail through both studs into each block with three 3" nails. Where an interior (partition) wall ties in—meets the exterior walls—add 3 studs (near left), or 2 studs and filler blocks. Nail the outside studs to the spacer with 3¹/₂" nails. It's easier to do this once the interior wall is raised.

If walls will be covered with plywood siding or sheathing or diagonally laid solid lumber (page 75), you may not need to brace exterior walls. Any other materials require diagonal bracing—let-in 1x4s or steel straps—at all corners and every 25' along a wall. Notch (for 1x4s) or groove (for ribbed straps) wall framing for the bracing; fasten both types to each stud or plate with two 2¹/₂" nails.

Installing rough door framing

TOOLKIT
• Tape measure
• Hammer
• Saw

1 Installing king and trimmer studs

You'll need king studs, trimmers, a header (made up of 2 boards and a spacer) and cripple studs. Measure half the rough opening width in each direction from the center line, and draw a line to mark the inside edge of each trimmer stud. Mark off both trimmer studs and king studs on the 2 plates, then nail the king studs to the plate. Next, cut and install the trimmer studs: Trimmer height equals the rough opening height plus the thickness of the finish floor and underlayment (page 89). Subtract the 1¹/₂" thickness of the sole plate and cut the trimmers to this length. Nail them to the king studs with 3" nails in a staggered pattern (right).

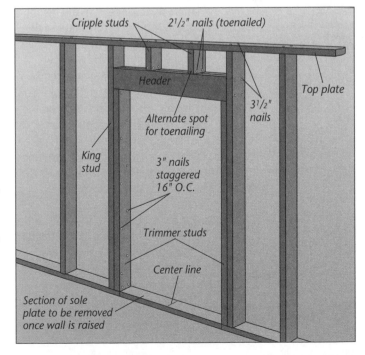

Cripple studs — 2¹/₂" nails (toenailed) — Header — Top plate — 3¹/₂" nails — Alternate spot for toenailing — King stud — 3" nails staggered 16" O.C. — Trimmer studs — Center line — Section of sole plate to be removed once wall is raised

2 Making and installing headers

Bearing wall headers for 2x4 walls are typically composed of matching lengths of 2-by lumber turned on edge, with a 1/2" plywood spacer sandwiched between them. The exact depth of the required header depends on the width of your opening—and on your local building code; common header sizes are listed in the chart below.

To assemble a header, cut 2-bys and plywood to the length between king studs. Nail the pieces together with 3 1/2" nails spaced 16" apart along both top and bottom edges *(below left)*. For 2x6 walls, make a 5 1/2" thick header by using thicker lumber for the spacers. A partition wall header may also be a single 2x4 or 2x6 laid flat across the opening. Place the header snugly on top of the trimmers and nail it through the king studs with 3 1/2" nails. Measure and cut cripple studs to length; if possible, use the same 16" spacing as standard studs. Nail the cripples through the top plate with 3 1/2" nails; then toenail the bottoms to the header with 2 1/2" nails.

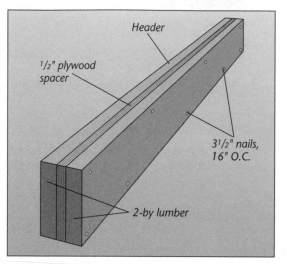

Header

1/2" plywood spacer

3 1/2" nails, 16" O.C.

2-by lumber

MINIMUM HEADER SIZES

Opening width	Header size
Up to 4'0"	4x4 or two 2x4s on edge
4'0" to 6'0"	4x6 or two 2x6s on edge
6'0" to 8'0"	4x8 or two 2x8s on edge
8'0" to 10'0"	4x10 or two 2x10s on edge
10'0" to 12'0"	4x12 or two 2x12s on edge

Note: Sizes are for 2x4 stud walls in single-story structures. If there's a second story above, choose the next larger header size.

Rough window framing

TOOLKIT
- Tape measure
- Hammer
- Saw

Installing a rough sill and cripples

To begin window framing, place king studs as described for door framing; nail king studs to both plates. Ideally, the tops of all doors and windows should be the same height (typically 6'8"), so that the bottom edges of the headers match. Measure the height from the top of the sole plate to the bottom of any installed door header. Mark this height on the window opening's king studs. Working down from the mark, subtract the height of the rough opening. This indicates the top of the rough sill. Subtract another 1 1/2" for the sill's thickness and make another mark. The remaining distance to the top of the sole plate equals the height of the lower cripple studs.

After cutting lower studs to length, nail the outside pair to the king studs with 3" nails. Cut the sill and attach it to king studs with 3 1/2" nails. Add remaining lower cripples and the trimmer studs on each side. Finally, install the header and upper cripple studs as described for door framing.

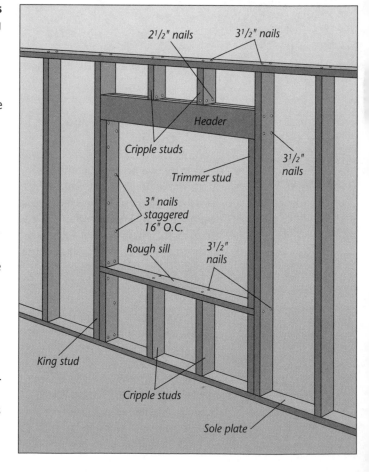

2 1/2" nails

3 1/2" nails

Header

Cripple studs

3 1/2" nails

Trimmer stud

3" nails staggered 16" O.C.

Rough sill

3 1/2" nails

King stud

Cripple studs

Sole plate

Installing the walls

TOOLKIT

• Chalk line
• Hammer
• Saw
• Carpenter's level
• Drill and wrench
  if wall is to be
  attached to a
  concrete slab
• Tape measure

1 ▶ Raising a wall

Snap a straight chalk line on the subfloor, indicating the sole plate's inside edge. Slide the wall along the floor deck until the sole plate lies near the edge of the deck; to prevent the sole plate from slipping off the platform, nail scrap blocks to the band joist, as shown at right. Cut several 1x4 braces and 2x4 blocks. To raise a wall, you need at least three workers: one on each end and another in the middle. Holding the wall by its top plate, raise the plate in unison, "walking" your hands down the wall *(right)* until it's in the upright position. With one person supporting each end, the third worker then taps the sole plate into line and tacks it to the subfloor with a few duplex nails. To brace the wall, tack three 1x4 braces to wall studs—one near each end and another in the middle *(below)*. Nail the lower ends to the sides of 2x4 blocks. By eye, check the wall for plumb, and then nail the blocks to the deck.

Scrap blocks to stop sole plate

Block

Carpenter's level

2x4 block

1x4 brace

Straight board

Block

2 ▶ Plumbing a wall

Using a carpenter's level, check the wall for plumb along both end studs on adjacent faces. Where the wall is out of plumb, loosen that brace, align the wall, and nail the brace once more. If an end stud is warped, bridge the warp with a straight board and two small blocks attached, as shown at left. When both ends are plumb, adjust the middle.

When building on a concrete slab, attach a wall's sole plate directly to preset anchor bolts—much like a standard mudsill *(page 59)*. Drill holes in the sole plate for each bolt, assemble the wall, then raise and brace it as described above—nail the braces to stakes outside the slab—and finally secure the washers and nuts on the bolts.

3 Anchoring the walls

Before you anchor the first wall permanently, raise, brace, and plumb the remaining exterior walls. Install side (long) walls first, then add end walls and any projections. Now measure the diagonals from corner to corner across the deck. Adjust the walls as necessary until the diagonals match. When everything is aligned, nail each wall through the sole plate into the joists, band joist, or stringer, spacing 3 1/2" nails every 16". Don't nail the sole plate within a doorway—that section will be cut away when the door is installed *(page 90)*. Plumb the corners, then nail through the end walls into the corner posts in the side walls with 3" nails staggered every 12".

4 Adding interior walls

Before raising an interior wall, snap another chalk line on the floor deck to indicate the correct layout. Interior walls are raised, braced, and plumbed just like exterior walls. Where they intersect exterior walls, nail through the end studs into the exterior studs with 3" nails staggered every 12". When all the walls are anchored, nail a second set of top plates—the "top cap"—onto the first, offsetting all joints below by at least 4'. At corners and intersections, overlap the joints below. Space 3 1/2" nails every 16", and use two nails at joints and intersections. Leave all braces in place until the ceiling joists and rafters are installed.

TOOLKIT
- Stud finder (optional)
- Hammer
- Tape measure
- Chalk line
- Plumb bob
- Saw
- For masonry floor: drill with masonry bit
- Carpenter's level

1 Plotting the location

Unlike walls for new structures, a partition for an existing house—to separate one living space from another or to subdivide a room—is usually built right in place. (To install framing for an opening, see pages 65-66.)

The new wall should be anchored securely to the floor, to the ceiling joists, and to wall framing on at least one side. To locate existing wall studs, try knocking along the wall until the sound changes from hollow to solid. If you have wallboard, you can use a commercial stud finder, though you'll find that the nails that hold wallboard to the studs are often visible on close inspection. Find studs behind plaster walls by driving a small test nail just above the baseboard.

To locate the ceiling joists, you can use the same methods or else, from the attic or crawl space above, drive small nails down through the ceiling on both sides of a joist to serve as reference points. Adjacent joists and studs will be evenly spaced, usually 16" or 24" on center from those you've located.

2 Positioning the sole plate

A wall running perpendicular to the joists will be the easiest to attach. If wall and joists will run parallel, though, try to center the wall under a single joist; otherwise you'll need to install nailing blocks every 2' between two parallel joists, as shown below right. If the side of the new wall falls between existing studs, remove wall materials and install additional nailing blocks.

On the ceiling, mark both ends of the center line of the new wall. Measure 1³/₄" (half the width of a 2x4 top plate) on both sides of each mark; snap parallel lines between corresponding marks with a chalk line. To position the sole plate, hang a plumb bob from each end of the lines you just marked and mark these new points on the floor. Snap two more chalk lines to connect the floor points. Cut both sole plate and top plate to the desired length. Lay the sole plate between the lines on the floor and nail it in place with 3" nails spaced every 16". If you're planning a doorway, don't nail through that section of the plate; it will be cut out later. With masonry floors, use a masonry bit to drill holes through the sole plate and into the floor every 2' or 3', then insert expanding anchors.

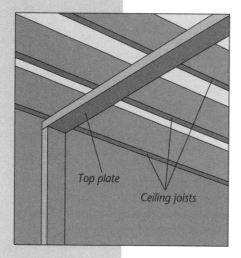

Top plate

Ceiling joists

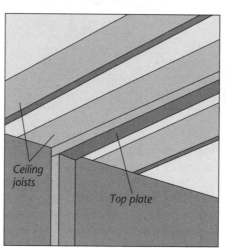

Ceiling joists

Top plate

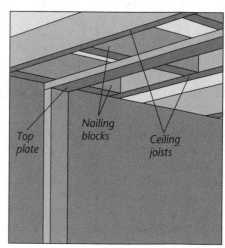

Top plate

Nailing blocks

Ceiling joists

3 Fastening the top plate

Lay the top plate against the sole plate and mark the stud positions *(page 64)*. If local codes permit, use 24" spacing to save lumber; adjust the initial placement of lines to 23¹/₄" and 24³/₄". Then, with two helpers, lift the top plate into position between the lines marked on the ceiling; nail it to perpendicular joists *(above, left)*, to one parallel joist *(above, middle)*, or to nailing blocks *(above, right)*. Measure and cut the studs to exact length, one by one. Attach one end stud (or both) to existing studs or to nailing blocks between studs. It's best to cut and install one stud before starting on the next one. To install, lift the stud into place, line it up on the marks, and check plumb using a carpenter's level. Toenail the stud to both the top plate and the sole plate with 2¹/₂" nails. Some building codes require horizontal fire blocks between the studs *(page 65)*.

CEILING AND ROOF FRAMING

Though visually different, most roof configurations are variations on the basic gable roof, which consists of evenly spaced pairs of common rafters running from the top plates to a central ridgeboard at the peak.

Unless you're working with premade trusses, the framing sequence includes installing ceiling joists; measuring, cutting, and assembling rafters; and finishing with gable studs, barge rafters, and collar beams. Ceiling joists support the load of the ceiling materials below, and help to permanently brace exterior walls against the thrust of the rafters above. Think of ceiling joists as lighter versions of floor joists (page 61); in fact, sometimes they are floor joists for rooms above. Like floor joists, they normally span the structure's short dimension, but rest on opposite exterior walls or on top of an interior bearing wall at one end.

Typically made from 2x4s, 2x6s, or 2x8s, ceiling joists are spaced 16 or 24 inches apart on center (O.C.). The size of the joists depends on several factors: lumber species and grade, the span, the spacing between joists, the type of ceiling below, and how much traffic or storage you anticipate in the attic or crawl space above. Consult the building code for your area; it will contain specialized span charts, allowing you to choose the exact size of joist for your combined requirements.

Rafters are usually 2x4s, 2x6s, or 2x8s, installed on either 16- or 24-inch centers. As with joists, the correct rafter size depends on span, spacing, and the load to be carried. In addition, consider the roof's slope; your local building department will have all the variables worked out. At the peak, rafter pairs butt against a central ridgeboard—either 1-by or 2-by lumber. Choose a ridgeboard that is one width larger than the rafters; for example, if you have 2x6 rafters, use an 8-inch-wide (nominal size) ridgeboard. When you lay out a rafter, measure, mark, and cut one rafter perfectly, and then use that as a pattern for the rest; you can use the "stepping off" method or the "rafter table" method, explained on the following pages.

Before beginning, check the walls for square once more by measuring diagonals from corner to corner across the top plates. Safety is the major concern when framing a roof. Always take time to plan the proper operating sequence before you start.

Installing ceiling joists

TOOLKIT
- Tape measure and combination square, or framing square
- Saw
- Hammer

1 ▶ Laying out the joists
The positions of ceiling joists are laid out along the top plates with a tape measure and combination square (page 64) or with a 16" long framing square. It's safest to stand on a firm ladder while you mark the spacings. Lay the rafters out at the same time; if their spacings are the same, place rafters and joists next to one another, so that when the rafters are installed, they can be nailed to the joists. If spacings are different—24" and 16" O.C.—space them so they'll meet every 48". Many carpenters position a joist just inside the top plate on each end wall to provide a solid nailing base for ceiling materials at the edge. Plan to butt long spans together, as shown in step 2.

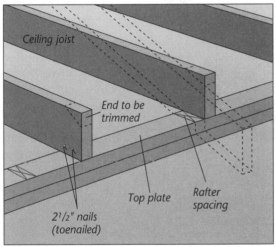

◀ 2 Installing the joists
Cut all the joists to length, then pull them up into position and nail them down. This takes two carpenters working from ladders at opposite ends. Toenail the joists to each plate with three 2½" nails. If the joists butt together at the center, nail each to the plate or beam and tie them together with 2-by blocking (left).

When a partition wall's top plate falls between parallel joists, install nailing blocks every 2' (opposite), and toenail through the blocks into the plate. Frame a ceiling opening in the same manner as you would a floor opening (page 62).

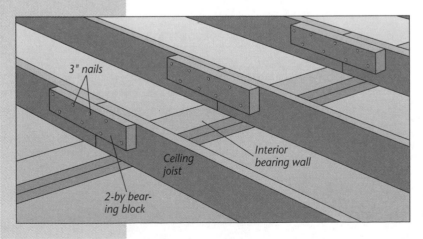

Basic roofing terms that you'll need to understand include span, run, and rise *(below)*. Note that the outline of the run, the rise, and a rafter's top edge form a right triangle. Then remember the Pythagorean theorem for right triangles: $A^2 + B^2 = C^2$. If run and rise—A and B below—are known, then the length of C—the rafter—can be quickly calculat-ed. The slope (pitch) of a roof is usually simplified in terms of unit rise and unit run. Unit run is always 12 inches; unit rise equals slope in those 12 inches. You'll hear a roof described as—for example—"5 in 12." This means that the roof rises 5 inches vertically for every 12 inches of run. Refer to page 52 for the definitions of the basic framing members.

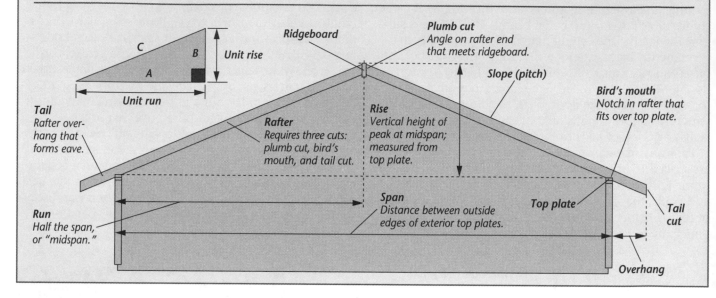

Ridgeboard

Plumb cut
Angle on rafter end that meets ridgeboard.

Slope (pitch)

Bird's mouth
Notch in rafter that fits over top plate.

Tail
Rafter over-hang that forms eave.

Rafter
Requires three cuts: plumb cut, bird's mouth, and tail cut.

Rise
Vertical height of peak at midspan; measured from top plate.

C B **Unit rise**
A
Unit run

Run
Half the span, or "midspan."

Span
Distance between outside edges of exterior top plates.

Top plate

Tail cut

Overhang

Laying out a rafter by stepping off

TOOLKIT
• Framing square
• Square gauges

1 Using a framing square
To "step off" a rafter, choose a straight piece of lumber for your pattern; if there's a crown *(page 36)*, place the crown side away from you (the rafters will be installed crown-side up). Now, align the framing square so that the figure for unit run—12—and the figure representing unit rise (5 in the example below) on the outside of the body and tongue, respectively, meet the rafter's edge. To mark the plumb cut, trace a pencil line along the tongue. Then draw a line along the body. Move the framing square down the rafter until the 5 figure on the tongue intersects the line you drew along the body at the rafter edge; line the body up with the 12 figure and the 12 figure with the rafter's edge again and draw another line along the body. Continue stepping off increments in the same way. If you're measuring a run of 10', for instance, step off 10 times. Square gauges *(page 9)* are useful here.

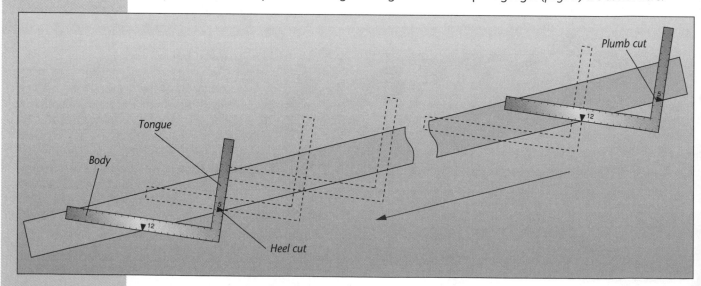

Plumb cut

Tongue

Body

Heel cut

2 Marking the bird's mouth

Align the square again and draw a new line along the tongue; this line is the heel cut of the bird's mouth. To lay out the horizontal seat cut of the bird's mouth, measure up 1½" from the bottom end of the heel line. Slide the square back toward the top of the rafter, keeping the figures lined up, until the edge of the body intersects the 1½" mark *(below)*. Draw the seat cut line along the body. If your actual run is an odd increment like 10'8", extend the line along the body on your 10th step with the square, then make a mark at 20"—8 extra inches. Slide the square down the rafter until the tongue aligns with this mark; draw a heel cut. For an overhang, step the overhang off from the heel cut. The rafter tail can be cut plumb, level, or perpendicular to the rafter.

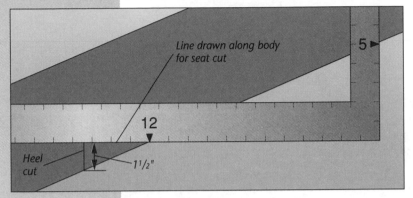

Line drawn along body
for seat cut

5

12

Heel
cut

1½"

3 Accounting for the ridgeboard

The total rafter distance you have laid out represents the theoretical length—just as if there were no ridgeboard at the peak. You must now go back and subtract one-half of the thickness of the ridgeboard—³/₈" for a 1-by ridgeboard, ³/₄" for a 2-by ridgeboard—and then draw a parallel line inside the original plumb cut line.

ASK A PRO

HOW DO I USE THE TABLES ON MY FRAMING SQUARE?

Below each inch mark on the body's face side is a column of six or seven figures. The inch marks on the body serve as an index to unit rise; in our example, we'd check the column under the 5-inch figure. The top set of numbers represents the "length common rafters per foot run." Thus, for every 12 inches of unit run and 5 inches of rise, the rafter length will be 13 inches. Multiplying this by the 10 feet of run in our example gives you 130 inches—or 10 feet, 10 inches.

(NOTE: The charts on your square may differ from those discussed; consult the instruction booklet.)

To lay out the rafter, draw the plumb cut at the top by aligning the square as described in step 1. Now measure the actual distance (10 feet, 10 inches) along the rafter edge to the heel cut. Lay out the heel and seat cuts, as described earlier, and add on the tail's length. Subtract half the thickness of the ridgeboard from the theoretical length you've laid out.

Assembling a gable roof

TOOLKIT
- Circular saw
- Crosscut saw
- Chisel (optional)
- Tape measure
- Hammer
- Carpenter's level
- Plumb bob

1 Making the cuts

Although plumb and tail cuts are straightforward, a bird's mouth requires special care. Beginning with a circular saw, cut along the heel and seat cut lines only to the point where they intersect. Finish the corner with a crosscut saw held upright. If a rough edge remains, clean it out with a sharp chisel.

2 Preparing the rafters and ridgeboard

After your first rafter is laid out and cut, make a duplicate so you'll have a pair. To check your work, get some helpers and place the rafters up on the ceiling joists. For solid footing, tack plywood sheets on the joists. Attach a scrap block of the same material you'll use for the ridgeboard to one rafter's plumb cut. Then raise both rafters into position; they should be snug against the top plate at both ends and flush with the ridgeboard scrap. If so, take them down and cut the remaining rafters.

Measure and cut the ridgeboard to length, transferring the rafter spacing marks to its sides. If your structure is too long for a single ridgeboard, the joint should fall between a rafter pair. For a gable overhang (rake), the ridgeboard must extend the appropriate distance beyond the end rafters.

3 Installing the end rafters

To begin raising a roof, nail two upright 2x4s flush against the wall's top plate, as shown below. Prop each rafter against the top plate near its intended mark; when you need a rafter, pull it up into position. Align the first end rafter flush with the end wall's plate. It takes two people to raise a large rafter: the first lines the rafter up with the end of the plate; the second raises it into position, making sure the bird's mouth is snug on the top plate, and then toenails the rafter to the plate with three 2½" nails, or with a metal framing connector. Finally, tack the rafter to the 2x4 brace.

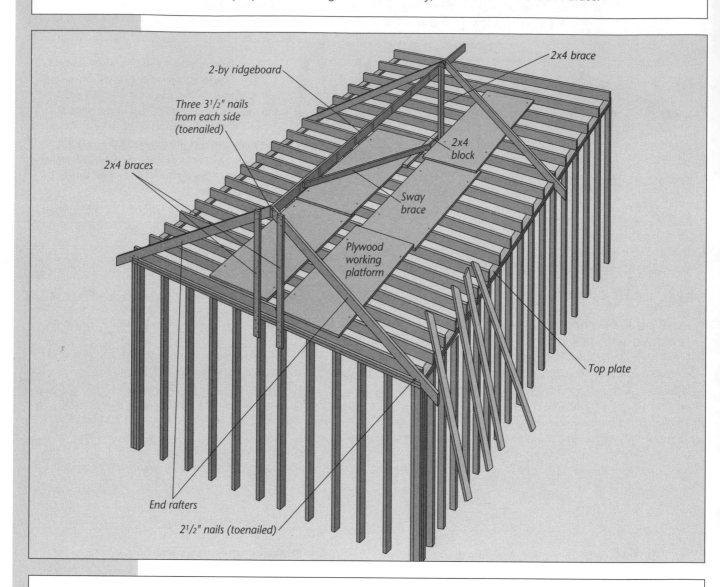

2-by ridgeboard

Three 3½" nails from each side (toenailed)

2x4 braces

2x4 brace

2x4 block

Sway brace

Plywood working platform

Top plate

End rafters

2½" nails (toenailed)

4 Raising and bracing the ridgeboard

While a helper supports the far end of the ridgeboard, raise it into position, align it with the top of the first rafter, and nail it to the rafter with three 2½" (for a 1-by ridgeboard) or 3½" (for a 2-by) nails. If the ridgeboard is a single piece, repeat the procedure at the other gable end. If it's in two pieces, brace it at the far end, so the ridge is level; then attach one rafter at the first spacing back from the end. Now go back and install the matching rafters, toenailing them to the ridgeboard from the opposite side. Then check your work: the end rafters should be flush with the end of the wall, and the ridgeboard must be both level and centered over the midspan—check with a carpenter's level and plumb bob.

To brace the ridgeboard, nail a sway brace running diagonally from the ridgeboard to a 2x4 block nailed across the joists. Add the other rafters to the run in pairs, fastening each to the top plate and then to the ridgeboard. To add a second ridgeboard, proceed as before from the other direction; the boards' junction must be covered by two rafters.

Where rafters meet ceiling joists, tie them together with three 3" nails; cut the joist ends to match the rafter slope.

Filling in gable ends; framing overhangs

TOOLKIT
- Tape measure
- Carpenter's level
- T-bevel, saw
- Hammer
- Chalk line

1 Adding gable studs

With the rafters in place, start at the point directly below the peak, centering a stud spacing on this spot. Now move toward both ends of the plate, laying out stud spacings on 16" centers. The first stud fits securely between the ridgeboard and top plate. To lay out the remaining studs, position one on its mark, flush against the back of the end rafter, and check it for plumb. Trace the rafter angle onto the edge of the stud. Then mark an adjacent stud. The difference in length between these studs is called the common difference, and will be consistent between each adjacent stud in the row. Cut the studs in pairs at the correct angle, using a T-bevel to transfer the angle. Toenail each stud to the plate and rafter with 3" nails. If your plans call for a gable end vent, frame the opening with horizontal 2x4s, bridging the studs as shown on page 52.

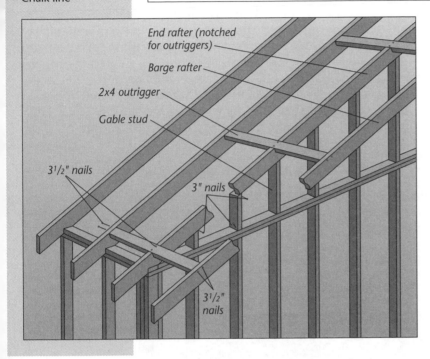

End rafter (notched for outriggers)

Barge rafter

2x4 outrigger

Gable stud

3¹/₂" nails

3" nails

3¹/₂" nails

2 Adding outriggers

To form a roof overhang at the gable end (rake), add outriggers and a pair of barge rafters to the ridgeboard extending past the end walls. Outriggers are 2x4s laid flat and positioned perpendicular to the rafters. Spaced every 4' down from the ridgeboard, they begin at the first rafters in from the end rafters; end rafters are notched so that the outriggers sit flush with the roof plane. Nail outriggers to the first pair of rafters and then into end rafters at notches, using 3¹/₂" nails. Leave them slightly longer than the ridgeboard; snap a chalk line 1¹/₂" in from the end of the ridgeboard and cut the outriggers off. Position barge rafters as shown at left, nailing them to the ridgeboard and into the ends of the outriggers. NOTE: Exercise caution—the gable overhang is the most dangerous area to work on the entire roof.

Installing a collar beam or a purlin

TOOLKIT
- Tape measure
- Carpenter's level (for collar beams)
- Saw
- Hammer

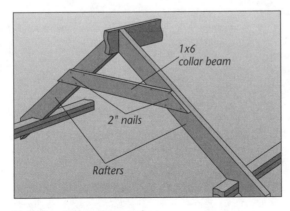

1x6 collar beam

2" nails

Rafters

Reinforcing rafter pairs

Roof structures with long spans or without ceiling joists may be tied together with collar beams or ties, which bridge every pair of rafters. To install a collar beam, measure down a third to a half the length of each matching rafter. Hold a 1x6 board against the marks, check that it's level, and trace the rafter angles on the back. Cut the collar beam on these lines and nail it to each rafter with 2" nails (above).

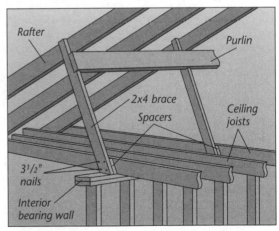

Rafter

Purlin

2x4 brace

Spacers

Ceiling joists

3¹/₂" nails

Interior bearing wall

Bracing rafters

When rafters exceed the maximum allowable span, they must be supported at midspan by horizontal purlins and braces (above). As a rule, choose a purlin the same size as the rafters. The braces must sit on top of a bearing wall and may be nailed directly to the plate or to ceiling joists with 3¹/₂" nails.

APPLYING THE EXTERIOR SKIN

Once the house is framed, the finishing touches include securing windows and exterior doors to their framed openings, and adding door sills and thresholds. Then the finish siding and roofing materials go on to enclose the framing and protect it from the elements. Exterior finish work is done next, including trim at house corners, fascia boards, or enclosed soffits *(page 78)* below the eaves. Adding exterior window and door casings as needed completes the exterior, as shown below.

Siding materials will close up the exterior walls of your new structure, or refurbish your present one—usually just a matter of nailing the siding to the wall studs or the existing surface. Some materials require a backing layer of wall sheathing; others, such as plywood sheet siding, may not.

Two major siding materials—solid boards and plywood sheets—are discussed in detail in this section. Two popular alternatives, hardboard and plywood lap boards,

are installed similarly. For tips on working with wood shingles or shakes, see page 85. Sidings such as aluminum, vinyl, steel, and stucco require special techniques or tools; get information from the manufacturer.

Roofs *(page 81)* require a deck of sheathing over the rafters. A layer of roofing felt then goes on the deck along with protective flashings at spots that are especially vulnerable to moisture penetration. If your present roof is made of asphalt, and both the roof and its sheathing are in fairly good condition, you can probably lay a new roof directly on top of your old one. You can also lay a new roof over wood shingles, though many professional roofers advise against reroofing over either wood shingle or shake roofs. Whatever the material, if you're dealing with a badly worn surface or rotted sheathing, or if your home has already had the maximum number of reroofings permitted by code, you'll have to tear the old roof off.

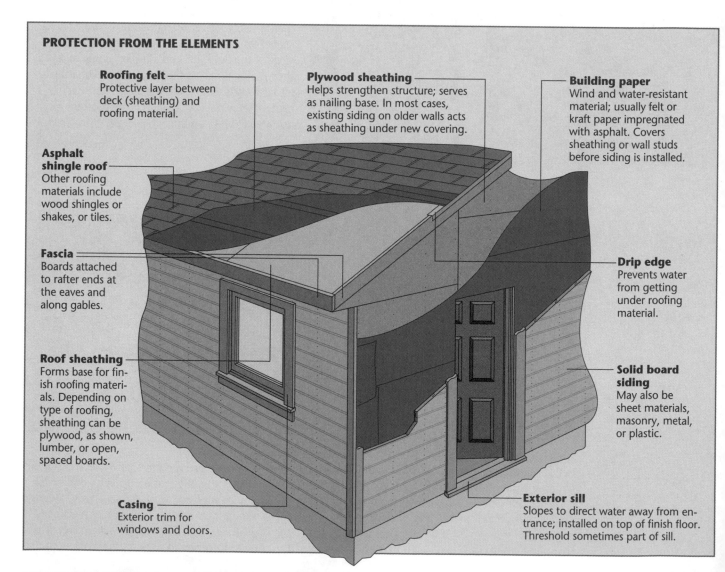

PROTECTION FROM THE ELEMENTS

Roofing felt
Protective layer between deck (sheathing) and roofing material.

Plywood sheathing
Helps strengthen structure; serves as nailing base. In most cases, existing siding on older walls acts as sheathing under new covering.

Building paper
Wind and water-resistant material; usually felt or kraft paper impregnated with asphalt. Covers sheathing or wall studs before siding is installed.

Asphalt shingle roof
Other roofing materials include wood shingles or shakes, or tiles.

Fascia
Boards attached to rafter ends at the eaves and along gables.

Drip edge
Prevents water from getting under roofing material.

Roof sheathing
Forms base for finish roofing materials. Depending on type of roofing, sheathing can be plywood, as shown, lumber, or open, spaced boards.

Solid board siding
May also be sheet materials, masonry, metal, or plastic.

Casing
Exterior trim for windows and doors.

Exterior sill
Slopes to direct water away from entrance; installed on top of finish floor. Threshold sometimes part of sill.

SIDING

The first step toward installing any type of siding is wall preparation. In new construction, the wall studs are exposed and you can begin the preparation steps outlined on page 76. However, if the wall is already covered with a layer of siding, you may have to add furring strips or remove the old siding.

Structural sheathing, generally applied only to new structures, is used under some siding materials to increase their rigidity, help brace the structure, serve as a solid base for nailing, and improve insulation. In most cases, the existing siding on older walls acts as sheathing under a new covering. Check local building codes to determine whether structural sheathing is required with the type of siding you've chosen.

Several types of structural sheathing are commonly used, including plywood, exterior fiberboard, and exterior gypsum board. Plywood is most popular because the large panels are easy to apply and usually afford enough lateral strength to eliminate the need for bracing during the framing of a house. The chart below compares the main types of sheathing and basic application techniques. Nail all types directly to wall studs. As a rule, choose rustproof common nails that will penetrate at least one inch into the studs.

Rigid foam insulation boards (page 50) are often applied as sheathing, but they are not structural. If structural sheathing is required, it can be applied on top of the foam boards.

Building paper, a wind and water-resistant material (usually felt or kraft paper impregnated with asphalt), is applied between the sheathing or studs and the siding. It comes in rolls 36 to 40 inches wide, long enough to cover 200 to 500 square feet—allowing for overlap. Some local codes require the use of building paper. You may also want to choose it if your siding will be subjected to heavy winds or to wind-driven rain or snow. It's also a good idea to apply it if the siding to be used consists of narrow boards or shingles that present many places for wind and water to penetrate. A newer option is housewrap, a material that is wrapped around the frame of the house to prevent drafts and to retain heat.

 ASK A PRO

SHOULD I REMOVE OLD SIDING?

Avoid this job if at all possible. It's almost certain to be a lot of messy work, and it will expose your house to the weather. On the other hand, there may be no alternative if you want to install insulation batts or blankets inside existing walls. You also have no choice if your present siding is aluminum, vinyl, or steel, or if the siding that's on the house—whatever the material—is in extremely bad condition.

A COMPARISON OF WALL SHEATHINGS

Qualities	Types			
	Exterior plywood	Exterior fiberboard	Exterior gypsum board	Foam boards
Direction of application	Vertical or horizontal	Horizontal	Vertical or horizontal	Vertical
Panel sizes and types	$1/16$", $1/8$", $1/2$", or $15/32$" thickness in panels of 4'x8'; square edge.	$1/2$", $25/32$" thicknesses in 2'x8' panels; tongue-and-groove or shiplap.	$1/2$" thickness, 2'x8' panels. Tongue-and-groove.	4'x8', 4'x9'
Rigidity	Good	Fair	Good	Poor
Insulative value	Low	Good	Low	High
Nailing	Nail every 6" along panel's edge and every 12" into center supports.	Use roofing nails 3" apart along edges, 6" apart intermediately.	Drywall nails every 4" around edges and every 8" intermediately.	12" O.C. 8" O.C. around perimeter.
Diagonal bracing required on wall	No	Yes, with standard types	In some areas	Yes
General notes	Use performance-rated or exterior grade; apply panel ends spaced $1/16$" apart and edges $1/8$" apart.	Easy to handle and apply. Don't nail within $5/8$" of edges. Only a special type will serve as sole nailing base for siding.	Not a nailing base for siding.	Not structural; does not provide extra rigidity or a nailing base.

Preparing a wall for siding

TOOLKIT
- Utility knife
- Stapler (optional)
- Hammer
- Chalk line
- Shovel (optional)

For masonry walls:
- Drill and masonry bit (optional)

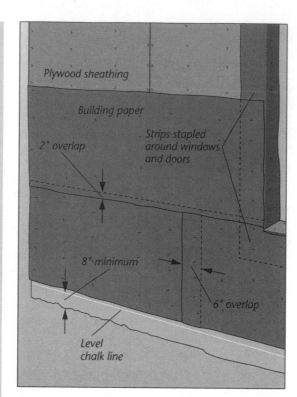

Plywood sheathing

Building paper

2" overlap

Strips stapled around windows and doors

8" minimum

6" overlap

Level chalk line

1 Applying building paper, marking the base line, and grading

Apply building paper in horizontal strips, starting at the bottom of each wall and working up, as shown at left. Overlap 2" at the horizontal joints, 6" at vertical joints; wrap the paper 12" around each corner. Cut building paper with a utility knife, and staple or nail it (with roofing nails) to studs or sheathing, using just enough fasteners to hold it in place—at a later stage the siding nails will fasten it permanently.

For any type of siding, snap a level chalk line at least 8" above grade (ground level) to align the siding's lowest edge along the base of each wall. Whenever new siding is going over old, set the line 1" below the lower edge of the existing siding. If necessary, excavate the surrounding soil anywhere it interferes with this 8" clearance, sloping the grade away from the house so that water won't pool at the foundation. You can "step" the siding—adjusting the base line up or down—to conform to a hillside or an irregular grade.

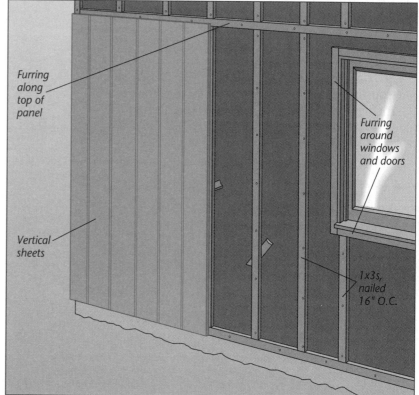

Furring along top of panel

Furring around windows and doors

Vertical sheets

1x3s, nailed 16" O.C.

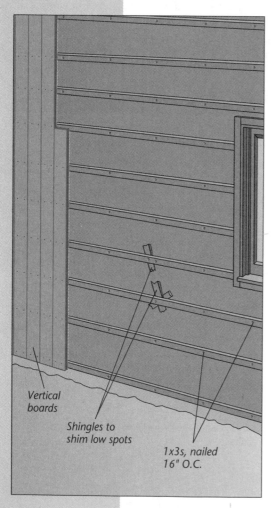

Vertical boards

Shingles to shim low spots

1x3s, nailed 16" O.C.

2 Preparing a grid for nailing

If present siding is bumpy, or made of masonry, provide a base of furring strips—a gridwork of 1x3 boards, placed to provide nailing support for siding at intervals. The two layouts shown—for vertical boards (left) or sheets (above)—can be adapted to most purposes. Nail through the strips every 12" with nails that penetrate studs at least 1". If walls are masonry, use concrete nails or masonry anchors to fasten the strips.

INSTALLING SOLID BOARD SIDING

For the sake of simplicity, all solid board siding patterns have been grouped into a single category. For proper installation, however, you must treat each basic pattern individually. Consult the chart below to learn whether a particular pattern is applied vertically or horizontally, as well as the type of backing it requires, the size of nail to use, and the correct nailing technique.

Before you begin nailing up siding boards, figure out how you want to treat the corners *(page 78, step 3)*. When planning your layout, try to get board rows to fall evenly around windows, doors, and other openings; with horizontal siding, a slight adjustment to the base line may

do it. If you must butt board ends, stagger these joints as much as possible between successive rows.

Solid board siding needs rustproof nails. Spiral or ring-shank nails offer the best holding power; they work especially well in applying new siding over an existing wall covering. The nail sizes in the chart are for new construction; if siding over an existing wall, choose nails that penetrate studs at least 1 inch. Use finishing nails if you plan to countersink and fill over nailheads. If your boards are thin or dry, drill nail holes, especially at board ends. Blunting the tips of nails with a hammer is another way to help keep them from splitting boards.

SPECS ON SOLID BOARD SIDING

Siding type	Direction of application	Nail size (new construction)	Nailing tips
Board on board (unmilled)	Vertical	2¹/₂" for underboards; 3" for overboards	For new construction, sheathing may be required. Otherwise, install blocks between studs, or furring strips (on centers recommended by code). Face-nail underboards once per bearing vertically; face-nail overboards twice, 3" to 4" apart, at center. Minimum overlap 1".
Board and batten (unmilled)	Vertical	2¹/₂" for underboards; 2¹/₂" or 3" for battens	For new construction, sheathing may be required. Otherwise, install blocks between studs, or furring strips (on centers recommended by code). Space underboards ¹/₂" apart. Face-nail boards once every 24" vertically. Minimum overlap 1".
Clapboard (unmilled)	Horizontal	3"	Face-nail 1" from overlapping edge (just above preceding course) once per bearing. Minimum overlap 1". First board requires starter strip for correct angle.
Bevel	Horizontal	2¹/₂" for ³/₄" thick board; 2" for thinner board	Face-nail once per bearing, 1" from lower edge. Allow expansion clearance of ¹/₈". Minimum overlap 1". First board requires starter strip for correct angle.
Shiplap, channel rustic	Horizontal or vertical	2¹/₂" for 1" thick board; 2" for thinner board	For vertical application, install blocks between studs, or furring strips (on centers recommended by code) in new construction. Face-nail once per bearing for 6" widths, twice (about 1" from overlapping edges) for wider styles.
Tongue-and-groove	Vertical, horizontal, or diagonal; can mix widths	2¹/₂" (finishing nails for blind-nailing, otherwise spiral or ring-shank nails)	For vertical or diagonal application, install blocks between studs, or furring strips (on centers recommended by code) in new construction. Blind-nail 4" to 6" widths through tongue with finishing nails, once per bearing. Face-nail wider boards with two spiral or ring-shank nails per bearing.

Installing solid boards

TOOLKIT
- Hammer and saw
- Level and plane (vertical siding)
- T-bevel
- Caulking gun
- Chalk line and tape measure (closed soffit)

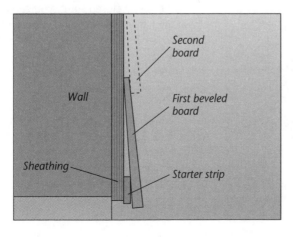

Wall

Second board

First beveled board

Sheathing

Starter strip

1 Nailing the first board
With horizontal siding, the first board goes at the bottom. Beveled and clapboard types require a starter strip beneath the board's lower edge, along the base of the wall, to push it out to match the angle of the other boards *(left)*.

For vertical wood siding, begin at one corner of the house. Align one edge of the first board with the corner and check its other edge for plumb. If it isn't plumb, adjust it as necessary; then trim the outside edge with a plane or saw until it fits the corner. Be sure the board's lower end is flush with your base line; then nail it in place.

2 Installing successive boards

To lay out horizontal board siding, you'll need a story pole. Make this from a 1x3 that's as long as the height of your tallest wall (unless that wall is more than one story). Starting at one end, mark the pole at intervals equaling the width of the siding boards, taking the overlap into account; it will indicate the bottom of each board. Holding or tacking the story pole flush with the base line, transfer the marks to each corner and to the trim at each window and door casing. Apply the siding boards from bottom to top. Unless the type of siding is overlapped or spaced, fit the boards tightly together. To match the slope of a roofline, measure the angle with a T-bevel. Transfer the angle to each board end, then cut. Where boards will be end-joined, brush a sealant on the ends before installation and be sure to make the joint square and snug. To fit shiplap or tongue-and-groove boards around windows and doors, first rip the board to the proper width. Then miter the back edge that will butt against the frame; this will make it easier to push the board into place and will make it look like an exact fit from the outside.

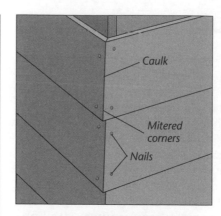

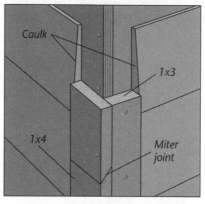

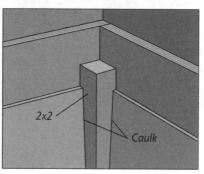

3 Covering a corner

Where siding boards meet at a corner, choose one of the three methods shown at left for moisture protection and a neat appearance. For an outside corner *(top and center)*, miter the board ends, or attach 1x3 and 1x4 boards to the corner for the board ends to butt against. (To join these vertical boards end to end, miter the joint at a 45° angle, with the board ends sloping toward the faces as shown, to ensure proper water runoff).

A typical treatment for inside corners uses a 2x2 piece of stock for the board ends to butt against *(bottom)*.

For any of these three corner treatments, caulk the joints.

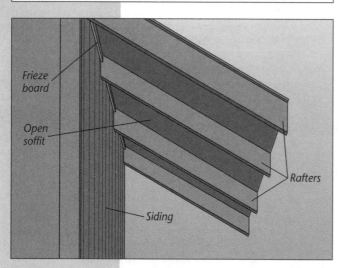

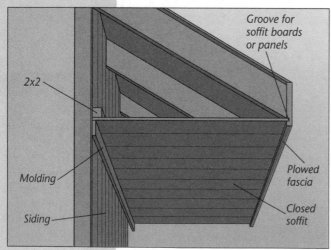

4 Finishing the soffit

Soffits (sometimes called cornices) are often left open when solid board siding is used—the boards extend to the tops of the rafters, and are notched where they intersect a rafter *(left, above)*. Install a frieze board—molding or a narrow trim board—along the top edge.

If you prefer a closed soffit, you can buy or make a plowed fascia board—a board with a routed groove near one edge for holding soffit boards or panel—and nail it over the rafter ends *(left, below)*. To complete the closed soffit, mark a point at both ends of the wall, level with the top of the groove in the fascia board. Snap a chalk line between the two marks; then nail a 2x2 above the chalk line. Measure the distance from the interior of the groove to the wall. Cut the soffit boards to fit, install them in the plowed fascia, and nail them to the bottom of the 2x2. Hide the nails with molding, fastening it with galvanized finishing nails set below the surface.

INSTALLING PLYWOOD SIDING

Plywood's large panel size (4x8, 9, or 10 feet), its strong laminated construction, and its variety of surface styles make it a popular siding material. Not only can it be applied rapidly, but it can eliminate the need for bracing on the wall's frame.

Plywood siding applied directly to studs without sheathing must be at least 3/8 inch thick for studs on 16-inch centers, and at least 1/2 inch thick for studs on 24-inch centers. Panels as thin as 5/16 inch may be applied over wall sheathing or firm older walls. Be sure to specify exterior-grade plywood.

Plywood panels may be mounted either vertically or horizontally. If you choose the horizontal pattern, stagger vertical end joints and nail the long, horizontal edges into fire blocks or other nailing supports to make sure the joints are protected (see next page). Vertical installation is the most common method, since it minimizes the number of horizontal joints.

Nailing: Use rustproof nails, not finishing nails. For re-siding over wood boards or sheathing, use hot-dipped galvanized ring-shank nails. Nails should be long enough to penetrate studs or other backing by 1 1/2 inches. For new siding nailed directly to studs, use 2-inch nails for 3/8-inch or 1/2-inch panels, and 2 1/2-inch nails for 5/8-inch panels. Nail every 6 inches around the perimeter of each sheet, and every 12 inches along intermediate supports. Be careful not to dimple the wood surface with the last hammer blow.

Installing plywood sheet siding

TOOLKIT
- Tape measure
- Chalk line
- Saw
- Carpenter's level
- Hammer
- Caulking gun
- Carpenter's square (optional)

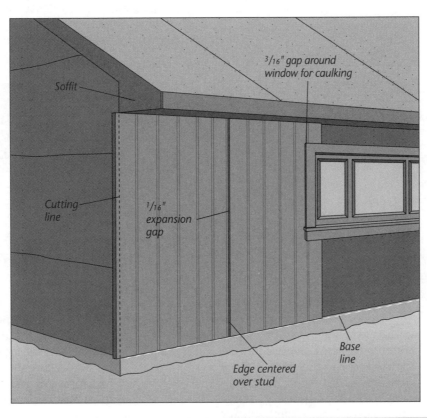

Soffit

3/16" gap around window for caulking

Cutting line

1/16" expansion gap

Edge centered over stud

Base line

1 **Cutting to length**
Before you begin putting up panels, you'll need to determine their correct lengths; they should reach from the base chalk line to the soffit *(left)*. Should the distance from base line to soffit be longer than the plywood sheets, you'll need to join panels end to end. Use one of the methods shown below for protecting horizontal seams. In any case, brush all panel edges with a sealant before installation.

2 **Putting up the first sheet**
To begin your installation, position the first sheet at an outside corner, its bottom edge flush with the base line. Use a carpenter's level to check that the vertical edges are plumb. If the corner itself isn't plumb, you'll need to trim the plywood edge to align with it. The inside vertical edge must be centered over a stud, furring strip, or other firm backing. Hold or tack the sheet in place, flush with the base line, and trace along the outermost points of the existing siding or framing from top to bottom. Take the panel down and cut along this line. Nail the trimmed panel in place.

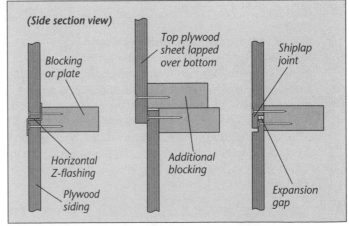

(Side section view)

Blocking or plate

Horizontal Z-flashing

Plywood siding

Top plywood sheet lapped over bottom

Additional blocking

Shiplap joint

Expansion gap

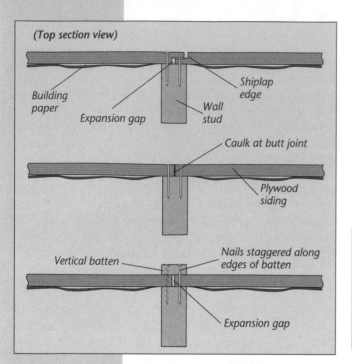

(Top section view)

Building paper

Expansion gap

Shiplap edge

Wall stud

Caulk at butt joint

Plywood siding

Vertical batten

Nails staggered along edges of batten

Expansion gap

3 Putting up successive sheets

The next sheet butts against the first sheet, often with an overlapping shiplap vertical edge *(left, top)*. Leave a $^1/_{16}$" expansion gap at all joints (in humid climates, leave $^1/_8$"). Sheets must join over studs, blocking, or other sturdy backing. Be careful not to nail through the laps.

If your plywood doesn't have a shiplap edge, caulk along vertical edges and butt them loosely, leaving about $^1/_{16}$" for expansion *(middle)*. Cover the joints with 1x2 strips called battens *(bottom)* unless there's building paper behind each joint.

ASK A PRO

WHAT IF I CHOOSE A HORIZONTAL PATTERN?

For a horizontal pattern, stagger vertical end joints and nail the long, horizontal edges into fire blocks or other nailing supports. Protect horizontal seams with metal Z-flashing, by overlapping, or by choosing panels with shiplap edges—as shown on the previous page.

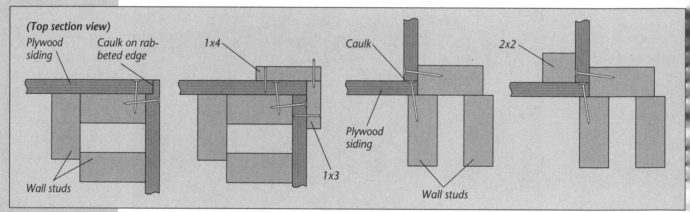

(Top section view)

Plywood siding

Caulk on rabbeted edge

1x4

Caulk

2x2

Plywood siding

Wall studs

1x3

Wall studs

4 Dealing with corners

Plywood siding requires special corner construction to ensure a weathertight joint. Outside corners can either be rabbeted together and caulked *(above, far left)*, or covered by a 1x3 and 1x4 trim board *(above left)*.

Inside corners are generally just caulked and butted together *(above right)*, although you can also supply a vertical corner trim board, such as a 2x2 *(above, far right)*. If the plywood is milled with grooves, the grooves under corner boards might let dirt and water penetrate. To prevent this, nail the vertical trim boards directly to the corner studs or siding, caulk along the edges, and butt the plywood against them.

5 Creating window and door openings

When you're cutting out these large areas, remember the carpenter's maxim, "Measure twice, cut once." To make fitting easier, include an extra $^3/_{16}$" gap around all openings. If possible, center the seams between sheets over or under the opening. Lay out the cuts with a carpenter's square or chalk line, then make the cuts. If you're using a saber saw for cutting corners and curves, cut the sheets on the back side to avoid splintering the face, since these saws cut on the upstroke. (When you're laying out the lines, beware: the sheet will be flipped over when installed.)

6 Installing soffits

On plywood-sided houses, soffits are usually closed, since an open soffit requires very exacting cuts to fit snugly around rafters. Consider running a plowed fascia board along the rafter tails and lengths of siding along the soffit, as detailed on page 78.

PUTTING A ROOF OVER YOUR HEAD

Before you start roofing you'll need a smooth deck on top of the rafters followed by underlayment and then by flashings to protect the roof from moisture.

On the following pages, you'll find instructions for roofing with common materials—asphalt shingles, wood shingles and shakes. The type of roof sheathing or decking will depend on the roofing material: Asphalt shingles go over a solid deck of plywood sheathing or boards, with an underlayment of 15-pound roofing felt. Wood shakes are often laid on solid decking, though in many instances they're placed on spaced 1x4 boards. Wood shingles are typically laid on spaced decking.

Flashings protect your roof at vulnerable points—valleys, vents, chimneys, skylights, and eaves—anywhere water can seep through. They're usually made of malleable 28-gauge galvanized sheet metal. On asphalt shingle roofs, valleys and vents may also be flashed with mineral-surface roll roofing. Plastics or aluminum are used too, and copper may be preferred for chimney flashing. Buy preformed flashings or make your own.

Installing plywood decking and underlayment

TOOLKIT
• Hammer
• Tape measure
• Chalk line
For underlayment:
• Utility knife
• Staple gun (optional)

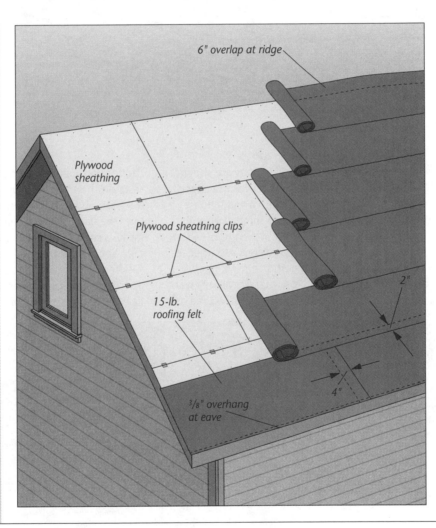

6" overlap at ridge

Plywood sheathing

Plywood sheathing clips

15-lb. roofing felt

3/8" overhang at eave

2"

4"

1 Installing the sheets
Though some codes permit plywood as thin as 5/16" on roofs with 12" spans, or 3/8" on 24" spans, either 1/2" or 5/8" sheathing will offer a sturdier nailing base. (Lighter panels may call for tongue-and-groove edges, plywood sheathing clips, or solid blocking for support.)

Stagger the panels horizontally *(left)*, with the ends centered on rafters. To allow for expansion, leave 1/16" between adjoining panels, and 1/8" between edges (double this in a very humid area). Space nails every 6" along the vertical ends of each panel, and every 12" at intermediate supports. Use 2" nails for 1/2" sheets, and 2 1/2" nails for thicker sheets.

2 Rolling out the underlayment
To evenly align rows of underlayment, measure the roof carefully and, if underlayment is not pre-marked, snap horizontal chalk lines before you begin. Snap the first line 33 5/8" above the eave (this allows for a 3/8" overhang). Then, providing for a 2" overlap between strips of felt, snap each succeeding chalk line at 34". To apply the felt, start at the eave and lay the strips horizontally along the roof, working toward the ridge. Felt should be trimmed flush at the rake (gable end) and overlapped 6" at any valleys, hips, and ridges. Where two strips meet in a vertical line, overlap them by 4" *(above)*. Drive just enough staples or nails to hold the felt in place (generally, one for every square yard of felt).

Installing open decking

TOOLKIT
- Hammer
- Saw
- Tape measure

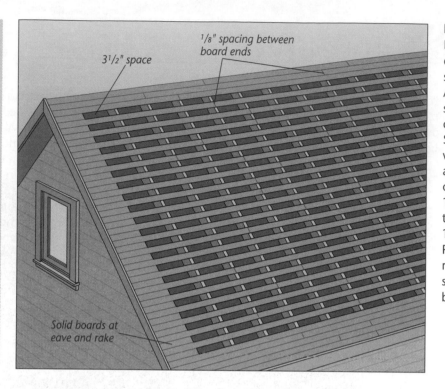

3¹/₂" space

¹/₈" spacing between board ends

Solid boards at eave and rake

Placing the boards

For this type of spaced decking *(left)*, use well-seasoned 1x4 boards. At overhangs, there should be continuous decking without gaps. Start your installation with solid rows of 1x4s at the eaves and rake overhangs. Then lay 1x4s horizontally along the roof, using another 1x4 as a spacing guide. Fasten each board to the rafters, allowing a ¹/₈" spacing where boards butt together.

Adding roof flashings

Flashings for five trouble spots

The common locations for flashings are shown below, but check building codes for the exact requirements in your area. For valleys, choose between an open finish where shingles are cut away to expose the valley, or a woven finish where asphalt shingles overlap the valley. Along eaves, install drip edge underneath the roofing felt; along rakes, install it on top. You'll probably want to install vent pipe flashings at the same time as the roofing materials, since part of the flashing rests on the shingles. Apply plastic cement under the base of the flashing, and lay the top shingles over the flashing, as shown. For chimney flashing, install a solid base along the bottom with overlapping step flashing up the sides, and a continuous saddle flashing at the top. You may want to add a second layer, or cap flashing to the first. For vertical walls, use step flashing.

Roofing felt

Shingle line

Roofing felt

Drip edge
Required at eaves and rakes.

Vertical wall
Use step flashing where roof meets wall.

Vent pipe flashing

Valley flashing
Must be very sturdy; valleys conduct more water to gutters than any of the roof planes. Open, as shown, or woven.

Chimney base flashing

Step flashing   Saddle flashing

APPLYING ASPHALT SHINGLES

Asphalt shingles come in a wide variety of colors, and most have self-sealing mastic that welds one shingle tab to another by the heat of the sun after the shingles are installed. The standard asphalt shingle is 12 by 36 inches with three integral tabs *(right)*. After overlapping courses are applied, the lower 5 inches of each shingle will generally be exposed to the weather. A narrow starter row runs the length of the eave to form a base for the first full course of shingles. The instructions presented here represent a typical installation; follow the package directions for the shingles that you buy.

Nailing: Use 12-gauge galvanized roofing nails with $3/8$-inch-diameter heads: $1^{1}/4$-inch-long for a new roof, $1^{1}/2$-inch-long for roofing over old asphalt, or $1^{3}/4$-inch-long for roofing over an old wood roof.

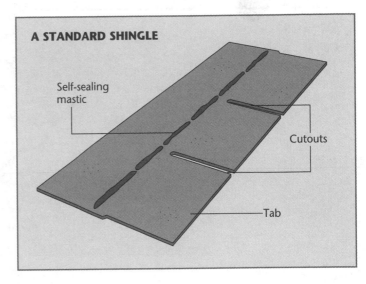

A STANDARD SHINGLE

Self-sealing mastic

Cutouts

Tab

Laying the starter course and first course

TOOLKIT
- Tape measure
- Utility knife
- Carpenter's square or straightedge
- Hammer

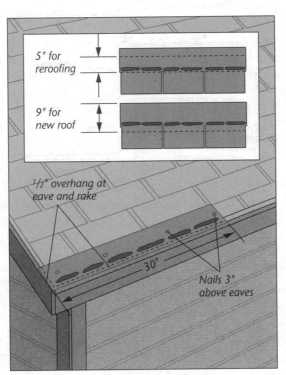

5" for reroofing

9" for new roof

$1/2$" overhang at eave and rake

30"

Nails 3" above eaves

Laying the starter course

If you're reroofing, a 5" wide starter course will correspond to the exposure of the lowest course of old shingles. Use a utility knife and carpenter's square to cut 5" off the tabs and 2" from the top edges of 12" wide shingles: Score the shingle's back, then bend it to break. For a new roof use a 7" strip of asphalt roll roofing, or cut 3" off the tabs of the 12" wide shingles *(inset, left)*.

Install the starter course along the eave, starting at the left rake. Shorten the first shingle by 6" to offset the cutouts. Allowing a $1/2$" overhang at both eave and rake, and $1/16$" spacing between shingles, fasten the shingles to the deck 3" above the eave, using 4 nails 1" and 12" in from each end *(left)*. For roll roofing, space nails 12" apart.

Laying the first course

When reroofing, you'll need a 10" wide course to cover the two 5" exposures of the first two courses of old shingles. Cut 2" off the top edges of as many shingles as were necessary for the starter course. For a new roof, use full-width shingles.

Allowing the same $1/2$" overhang at the rake and eave, and $1/16$" between shingles, offset the tabs of the first course shingles by 6", then nail them over the starter course, using 4 nails per shingle. Space these nails $5^{5}/8$" above the butt line, 1" and 12" in from each end *(inset, right)*, or as directed by the manufacturer.

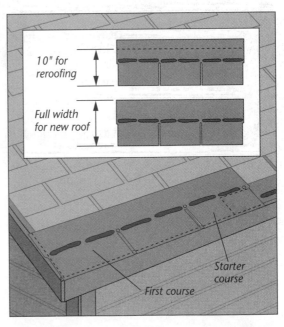

10" for reroofing

Full width for new roof

Starter course

First course

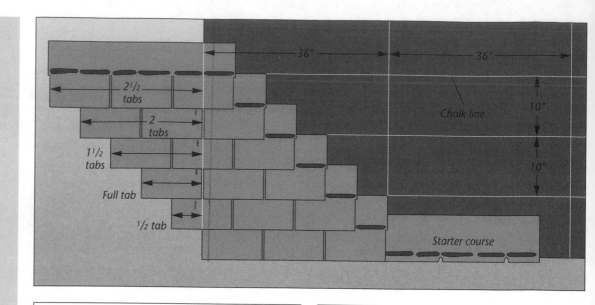

Laying successive courses

TOOLKIT
• Chalk line
• Tape measure
• Roofer's hatchet (optional)
• Hammer
• Utility knife

Labels on illustration: 2½ tabs, 2 tabs, 1½ tabs, Full tab, ½ tab, 36", 36", Chalk line, 10", 10", Starter course

1 Aligning the shingles

Your main concern when you lay the second and successive courses is proper alignment of the shingles—both horizontal and vertical. Aligning shingles horizontally is simply a matter of snapping chalk lines across the deck (new roof) or placing new shingles against the butts of old ones (reroofing). If you're using chalk, snap lines every 10" from the bottom of the first course, as shown above. Then, as you move toward the ridge, the upper edge of every other course of shingles should line up against the chalk lines. You could also use a roofer's hatchet (page 86). Before you start your second row of shingles, also snap vertical chalk lines from the roof ridge to one end of every shingle along the first course.

2 Installing the shingles

With standard three-tab shingles, you can produce different patterns by adjusting the length of the first shingle of each course. Centered alignment, shown above, is the most common and offers the most uniform appearance. Cutouts or shingle edges must line up—within ¼"—with cutouts or edges two rows above and below. Line up each successive row staggered by half a tab to the left. Lay each shingle just below the cutout line of the previous one. Mark the end shingle, allowing for overhang; then remove and trim it (save the pieces for the other edge of the roof). Replace the end shingle and nail the row, using the vertical chalk lines to ensure that every seventh row lines up with the first.

Installing hip and ridge shingles

TOOLKIT
• Utility knife
• Chalk line
• Tape measure
• Hammer

Cutting and applying shingles

Use ready-made ridge and hip shingles or cut 12" squares from standard shingles. Bend each; if cold, warm them first. Snap a chalk line the length of the ridge and each hip, 6" from the center. For a hipped roof, begin with a double layer at the bottom of the hip; work toward ridge, applying shingles with a 5" exposure (right). Each edge should line up with chalk mark. Nail on each side, 5½" from the butt and 1" from outside edge. Shingle the ridge the same way (inset), starting at the end opposite the prevailing wind. Use nails about 2" long. Dab exposed nailheads of the last shingle with plastic cement.

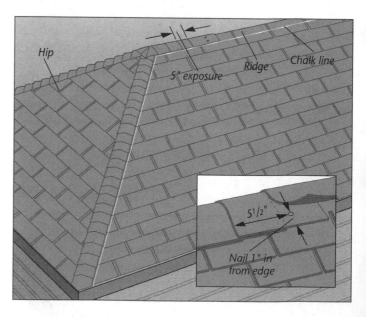

Labels on illustration: Hip, 5" exposure, Ridge, Chalk line, 5½", Nail 1" in from edge

APPLYING WOOD SHINGLES AND SHAKES

Shingles, sawn from chunks (called "bolts") of western red cedar, come in lengths of 16, 18, and 24 inches. Shakes are thicker, and are split by machine or by hand into 18- and 24-inch lengths. Though shingles and shakes come in several grades (suitable for siding as well as roofing), use the Number 1 ("Blue Label") grade on a roof.

When applying either shingles or shakes, always position the tapered end uproof and the thicker end downroof. If the wood has a sawn side and a rough side, install with the rough side exposed to the weather. When applying straight-split shakes (those equally thick throughout), lay them with the smooth end uproof.

Correct exposure for wood shingles and shakes depends on their length and the slope of your roof; see the chart below.

To make straight cuts in shingles, slice through them with a roofer's hatchet. Heavier wood shakes can either be sawn or split along the grain with the hatchet. When making an angled cut for a valley, lay the shingle in place and use a straightedge to mark the angle of cut. Then score the shingle with a utility knife and break it. Saw wood shakes.

Nailing: Use rustproof nails, two per shingle or shake. For shingles, use $14\frac{1}{2}$-gauge with $\frac{7}{32}$-inch heads. Use $1\frac{1}{4}$-inch-long nails for a new roof of 16- or 18-inch shingles; $1\frac{1}{2}$-inch for a new roof of 24-inch shingles; over old roof surfaces use longer nails to reach $\frac{3}{4}$ inch into deck. For shakes, use 13-gauge with $\frac{7}{32}$-inch heads and at least 2 inches long if they have to penetrate $\frac{3}{4}$ inch. When fastening shingles, locate the nails $\frac{3}{4}$ inch in from sides and 1 inch above butt line for the next course. Nails for shakes are positioned 1 inch in from sides.

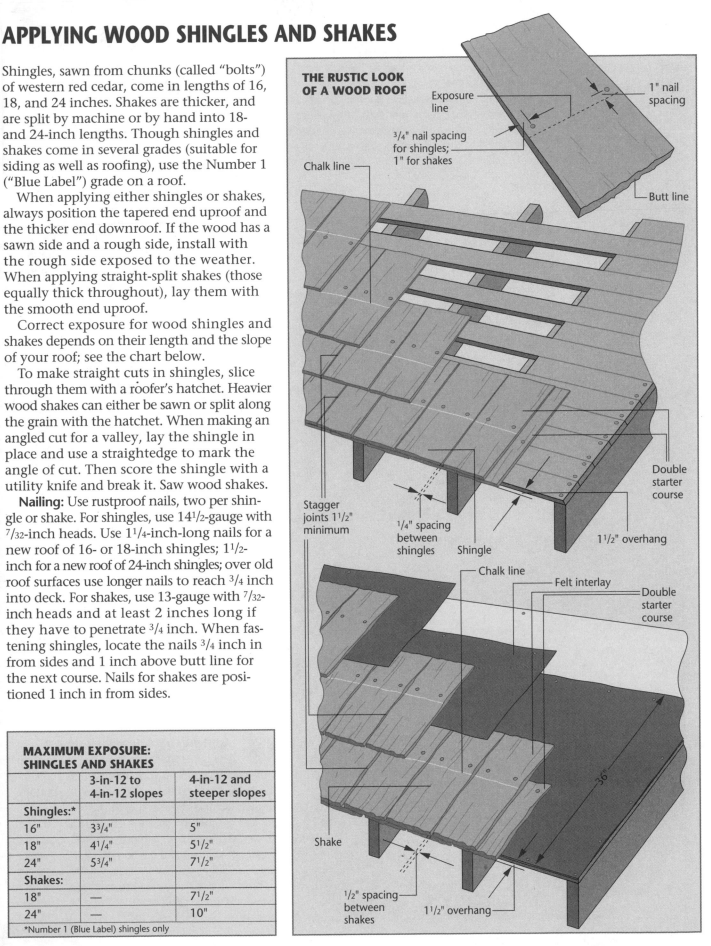

THE RUSTIC LOOK OF A WOOD ROOF

Exposure line

1" nail spacing

$\frac{3}{4}$" nail spacing for shingles; 1" for shakes

Butt line

Chalk line

Double starter course

Stagger joints $1\frac{1}{2}$" minimum

$\frac{1}{4}$" spacing between shingles

Shingle

$1\frac{1}{2}$" overhang

Chalk line

Felt interlay

Double starter course

Shake

36"

$\frac{1}{2}$" spacing between shakes

$1\frac{1}{2}$" overhang

MAXIMUM EXPOSURE: SHINGLES AND SHAKES		
	3-in-12 to 4-in-12 slopes	4-in-12 and steeper slopes
Shingles:*		
16"	$3\frac{3}{4}$"	5"
18"	$4\frac{1}{4}$"	$5\frac{1}{2}$"
24"	$5\frac{3}{4}$"	$7\frac{1}{2}$"
Shakes:		
18"	—	$7\frac{1}{2}$"
24"	—	10"
*Number 1 (Blue Label) shingles only		

Laying wood shingles and shakes

TOOLKIT
• Hammer
• Tape measure
• Chalk line (optional)
• Saw
• Roofer's hatchet

1 Installing starter and first course
Combine these courses by laying the shingles or shakes one on top of the other *(page 85)*. Though roofing felt is seldom required under wood shingles, it is recommended with shakes; their irregular shape allows water to work through the cracks. For wood shakes, therefore, first nail a 36" wide strip of 30-pound felt along the eave (with ³/₈" overhang). When laying the double course, offset the joints between layers by 1¹/₂", and leave a 1¹/₂" overhang at the eaves and rakes. Leave ¹/₄" between shingles and ¹/₂" between shakes for the wood to expand and contract.

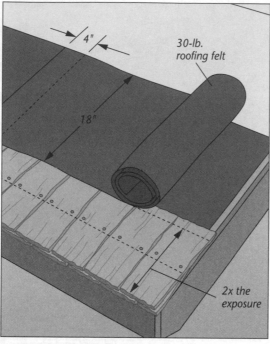

4"

18"

30-lb. roofing felt

2x the exposure

2 Installing successive courses
Align shingles or shakes both vertically and horizontally for proper exposure and coverage. You don't need to snap chalk lines to line up shingles or shakes vertically; simply lay them according to this principle: Offset joints by at least 1¹/₂" so that no joints in any 3 successive courses are in alignment.

To line up wood shingles horizontally, snap a chalk line at the proper exposure over the doubled starter/first course, or use your roofer's hatchet as an exposure guide. Then lay the butts of the next course at the chalk line. Nail the course down and repeat the procedure until you reach the ridge. For wood shakes, install roofing felt interlays over each course *(left)*: From the butt of the starter/first course, measure a distance twice the planned exposure. Place the bottom edge of an 18" wide strip of 30-pound felt at that line, and nail every 12" along the top edge of the felt. Overlap vertical joints 4". Then snap a chalk line on the starter/first course for the proper exposure (or use your roofer's hatchet). Nail the second course, place the next felt, and continue until you reach the ridge. Use short, 15" shakes (ready-made or cut from standard shakes) as the last course.

At the ridge, let the last courses of shingles or shakes hang over; snap a chalk line above the center of the ridgeboard and trim off all the ends at once. Cover the ridge with a strip of 30-pound felt at least 8" wide.

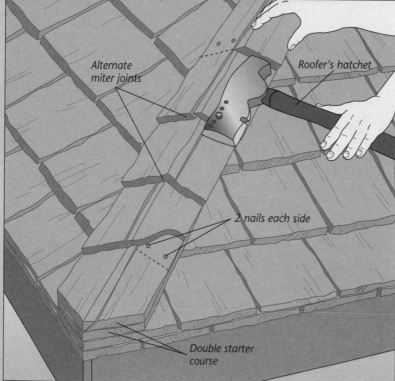

Alternate miter joints

Roofer's hatchet

2 nails each side

Double starter course

3 Applying hip and ridge shingles
Using factory-made ridge and hip shingles (mitering and making your own is a time-consuming task), double the starter courses at the bottom of each hip and at the end of the ridge. Use a roofer's hatchet to check the exposure as you work toward the ridge *(left)*; exposure should equal the weather exposure of the wood shingles or shakes. Start the ridge shingles at the end of the ridge opposite prevailing winds. Use nails long enough to penetrate the layers of material and extend into the ridgeboard (usually 2" or 2¹/₂").

Installing a skylight in an existing pitched roof is a three-part process: you cut and frame openings in the roof and the ceiling, mount the skylight unit, and then connect the two openings with a vertical, angled, or splayed light shaft. An outline of the installation sequence follows. For details, consult the manufacturer's instructions or your dealer.

1. Marking the openings: After planning the layout of your roof opening, light shaft, and ceiling opening, mark the location of the ceiling opening; then drive nails up through the four corners and center so they'll be visible in your attic or crawl space. From the attic, check for obstructions, shifting the location if necessary.

Use a plumb bob to transfer the ceiling marks to the underside of the roof; again, drive nails up through the roofing materials to mark the location.

2. Framing the roof opening: On a day with zero probability of rain, cut and frame the roof opening.

When you work with a skylight that is designed to be mounted on a curb frame, build the curb first; 2x6 lumber is commonly used. Your skylight may have an integral curb or may be self-flashing; if so, you can skip this step.

To determine the actual size of the opening you need to cut, add the dimensions of any framing materials (*see illustration*) to the rough opening size marked by the nails. You may need to remove some extra shingles or roofing materials down to the sheathing to accommodate the flashing of a curb-mounted unit or the flange of a self-flashing unit.

Cut the roof opening in successive layers: roofing materials first, sheathing next, and finally any necessary rafters. Before cutting the rafters, support them with 2x4s nailed to the ceiling joists below. If you're going to need to cut a joist as well, you'll need additional support for the rafter.

To frame the opening, you'll need to install double headers and possibly trimmers. Install the headers with double joist hangers.

If you're installing a curb-mounted unit, position and flash the curb. Install saddle flashing above the curb, apron flashing below, and step flashing along the sides. As each section of flashing is positioned, replace the shingle over it to form an overlap. Toenail the curb to the rafters or trimmers and to the headers. Pay special attention to the manufacturer's instructions concerning flashing.

3. Mounting the skylight: For a curb-mounted unit, secure the skylight to the top of the curb with nails and a sealant. Set a self-flashing unit in roofing cement and then nail through the flange directly to the roof sheathing. Coat the joints and nail holes with more roofing cement.

4. Opening the ceiling: Double-check your original ceiling

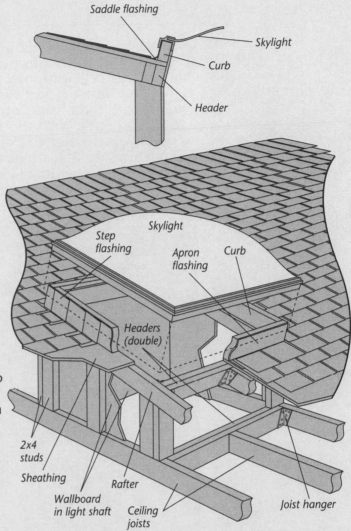

marks against the roof opening and the intended angle of the light shaft. Brace the joists to be cut against adjacent joists with a header. Cut through the ceiling materials and then sever the joists. Then frame the ceiling opening in the same manner as described in step 2.

5. Building a light shaft: Measure the distance between the ceiling headers and the roof headers at each corner and at 16-inch intervals between the corners. Cut the studs to fit the measurements, and install them as illustrated above. This will provide a good nailing surface for wall coverings.

6. Final touches: Insulate all the spaces between the studs in the light shaft before fastening the wallboard to the studs. To maximize reflected light, paint the wallboard white or add mirrors. Trim the ceiling opening with molding strips. Adding a plastic ceiling panel—it can be either manufactured or cut to size—helps to diffuse light evenly.

FINISH CARPENTRY

O nce the shell of your house is built, the rains may rage and the winds may howl. But, after a well-earned celebration, a whole new phase of carpentry, the "finish work," begins. These are the interior details that give a home much of its individuality.

In this chapter we'll show you how to hang a door or window, whether you're building from scratch or remodeling. You'll learn how to build a basic stairway and to put up a ceiling. Finally, you'll choose from a variety of wall coverings and trim that will give your home a clean, finished look.

This panel door is hinged to a frame formed by a head jamb and two side jambs. Door casing seals the frame and ties the structure together. In this chapter we'll show you how to hang a door or to install one that's already prehung.

CLOSING UP THE INTERIOR

Now the work moves indoors—and there is plenty left to be done. Depending on the weather, you may want to consider installing the doors and windows at this point. However, you still have to rough in the interior and do all the fine finish work.

Roughing-in: This is the time when the plumber, electrician, and heating specialist must rough in pipes, electrical wiring and boxes, and the heating system.

Insulation comes next. Our model shows mineral fiber blankets installed between exterior wall studs. If the attic area will remain unfinished, also place insulation between ceiling joists; insulate finished attics between rafters and gable studs. A vapor barrier, provided as a backing on some insulation materials, is positioned between the main living areas and the insulation. A separate sheet can be used instead, or as well.

Finish work: Stairways require proper calculation of headroom, width, and railings. Ceiling materials are fastened directly to the ceiling joists or to a metal or wooden grid suspended from the joists. Gypsum wallboard or plywood sheet paneling is applied directly to wall studs; solid board paneling may first require a wallboard backing, or furring strips as a nailing base. Plaster walls need a gypsum, fiberboard, or metal lath backing. If you choose wallboard as a final covering for either ceilings or walls, you'll need to tape, fill, and then sand the joints between the panels *(page 105)*.

If the finish floor covering requires a separate underlayment—plywood, particleboard, or hardboard—over the subfloor, that's the next step. After the finish floor is down, install interior doors in their openings. Interior trim—baseboards, moldings, and window or door casings as needed—completes the basic job.

Of course, there's still work to be done. Paint and wallpaper head the list; cabinets and countertops need to be installed. Plumbing fixtures must be hooked up to supply and waste pipes; appliances require gas, water, and electrical connections. Finally, it's time to install light fixtures and electrical cover plates. And there, at last, you have it—the modern platform-framed house.

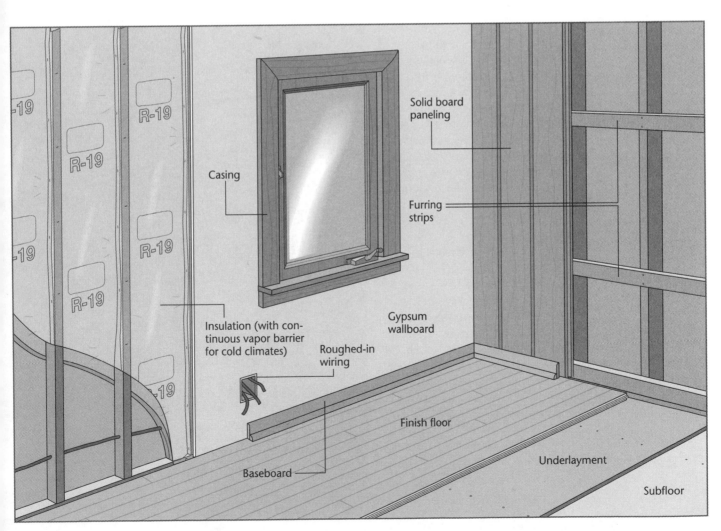

DOORS

Installing a door in the traditional way means constructing a door frame, positioning it in the rough door opening, hinging the door to the frame, and installing a latch or lockset. If you buy a prehung door, much of the work has been done for you: the door comes hinged to the jamb, and frequently casing, lock, latch, and strike plate are included, too. Both procedures are described below.

First, frame the rough opening. In a new structure, you'll do this along with the walls—see Wall Framing on pages 64-66. Remodeling calls for another approach. After removing the wall materials and studs around the opening, frame the opening with the wall in place *(see page 92)*. Before you cut into any wall, be sure that it's nonbearing *(see page 64)*. If it is bearing, then the weight must be supported with a temporary wall. Any electrical wires, pipes, or ductwork must be rerouted. Remove the baseboard to check for wires and pipes.

Modern manufactured doors come in two basic types: panel and flush. Panel doors, as shown below, consist of solid vertical stiles and horizontal rails, with filler panels between. Superior strength and good looks make this style a wise choice for exterior doors, especially at a main entrance. Flush doors are usually built from thin face and back veneers—typically 1/8-inch plywood attached to a solid or gridlike hollow core. This hollow-core type should only be used for interiors. Your dealer may also have the newer composite or steel doors.

Standard interior door height is 6 feet 8 inches; exterior is 6 feet 10 inches. Width and thickness vary: for exterior doors, choose a width from 32 to 36 inches, and a thickness of 1¾ inches. Interior doors are 18 to 36 inches wide and 1⅜ inches thick. Both types are installed in a similar way, with a few extra steps required for weatherproofing an exterior door.

A few rules about doors: they should open into rooms, not stairwells or hallways; they should open at least 90 degrees; they should open into the corner of a room, not the middle; also, make sure closely situated doors won't hit each other.

Hanging a door

TOOLKIT
- Tape measure
- Saw
- Hammer
- Carpenter's level
- Chisel or router with straight bit and hinge template
- Electric drill with spade bit and hole saw, or hand brace with expansion and auger bits
- Combination square

1 ▶ Determining the size of door jambs

A door frame consists of two side jambs and a head jamb. The tops of the side jambs are normally rabbeted to hold the head jamb. You can buy standard jambs at lumberyards. Choose a jamb width slightly larger than the thickness of the finished wall. For example, if the wall is framed with 2x4 lumber and surfaced on both sides with 1/2" wallboard, your jambs should be 4¹/2" wide. Jambs for exterior doors may include integral stop moldings, as shown at right. To calculate the length of the head jamb, add up the following: the width of the door to be installed; ³/16" clearance between the door and each side jamb (³/8" total); and the depth of the side jambs' routed rabbets. Cut the head jamb to this length and then assemble the frame with glue and 2¹/2" nails, or screws.

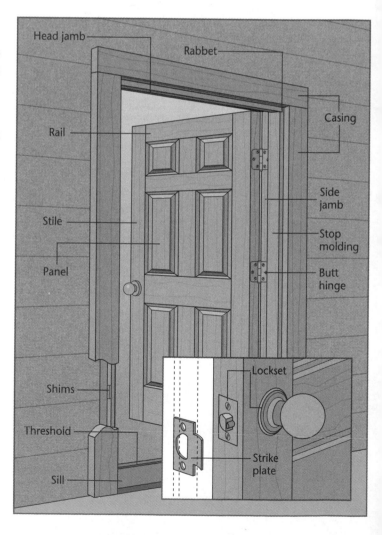

Head jamb · Rabbet · Rail · Stile · Panel · Shims · Threshold · Sill · Casing · Side jamb · Stop molding · Butt hinge · Lockset · Strike plate

2 Centering the door frame

Exterior doors need a sill sloping to the outside and a threshold at the jambs' base. The sill is installed on the finish floor. Remove the sole plate between trimmer studs (*page 65*). Prop up the jamb assembly in the opening; if the floor is not installed, insert a scrap of flooring below jambs. Shim until head jamb is correct height and level. Some carpenters center the frame from front to back and side to side by wedging shingle shims between head jamb and header.

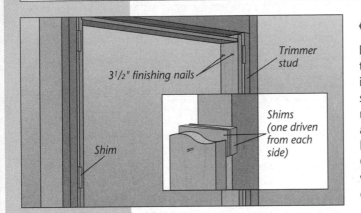

3¹/₂" finishing nails

Trimmer stud

Shims (one driven from each side)

Shim

3 Leveling and plumbing a door frame

Beginning next to lower hinge location, drive 2 shims snugly between side jamb and trimmer stud—one from each side. Nail through the jamb and shims partway into the stud with a 3¹/₂" finishing nail; position nail where the stop molding will cover it. Insert shims next to upper hinge location, check the jamb for plumb, and nail partway. Again, shim, plumb, and nail halfway between top and bottom hinge positions. Now shim the opposite jamb at similar locations, but don't nail where you'll need to cut for the latch. Check frame once more for plumb. Drive nails home and set heads with a nailset. If you're working on an exterior door, nail the threshold between the jambs (unless threshold and sill are a single unit).

4 Installing the hinges

Hinges for interior doors should be about 7" from the top and 11" from the bottom. Exterior and heavy interior doors require a third hinge, between the first two. Use butt hinges: 3¹/₂" long for interior doors (3" for lighter ones); 4¹/₂" for exterior doors. To lay out hinge locations, prop door up in the frame, raising it on blocks to the correct height above the floor. (A quarter laid flat will give you the correct top spacing.) Mark hinge locations on door and jamb simultaneously. (Or, you can install half the hinge on the jamb before putting it up.) Remove the door and cut mortises for the hinges with a sharp chisel (*page 19*) or router and template (*page 20*). Leave ¹/₄" between hinge edge and door's leading edge. Attach the matching hinge leaves to the door jamb and hang the door. Place pin in top hinge first, then in bottom one.

5 Installing the lockset

A template and instructions should be included with your lockset. Place the knob 36" to 38" above the floor. Bore the holes using an electric drill with a spade bit and hole saw; always drill the lock hole first. To prevent blowing out the side of the door, clamp a piece of wood on either side while drilling the latch hole (wood removed for clarity in illustration). Next, close the door and mark the top and bottom of the latch where it contacts the jamb. Position the strike plate there; drill or chisel out a mortise for the latch.

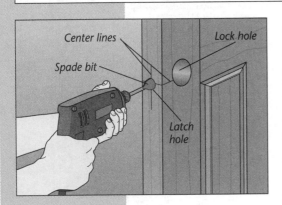

Center lines

Lock hole

Spade bit

Latch hole

6 Nailing stop molding to jambs

This prevents door from closing too far. Unless the frame includes it, begin at hinge side; tack a length of molding from the floor to the head jamb with a 1¹/₂" finishing nail every 12", spacing it ¹/₁₆" from the door face. Tack opposite stop flush with door and place the top stop molding bridging the other two across head jamb. Check everything, then drive in the nails.

ASK A PRO

HOW CAN I FIX A STICKY DOOR?

If the door sticks at the top of the lock side, insert cardboard shims behind lower hinge; if at the bottom, shim top hinge. To correct tight clearance at top and bottom, insert a shim opposite the pin side of each hinge (near right). If it's too loose, insert cardboard on the pin side (far right). If door is very tight on any side, scribe the correct clearance, remove door, and shave to the line with a jack plane.

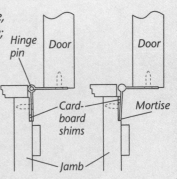

Hinge pin

Door

Door

Cardboard shims

Mortise

Jamb

Attaching the door to rough framing

To complete the installation first remove any bracing, blocking, or stop molding tacked to the unit. Position the unit in the rough opening. If the finish floor is not yet installed, raise the side jambs to the correct level with blocks.

Shim the jambs level and plumb as detailed on page 91. If casing is included on the face side, insert 2 shims from the open back (*page 91,* *step 3*). Fasten the unit to the rough door framing by driving nails through the jambs and shims at least 1" into the framing. Fasten the attached casing to the rough door framing near the outside edge with nails spaced every 16". Make the final adjustments as described on the previous page. Finally, check the clearance, install the lockset, and then add the stop molding.

Remodeling: Framing a doorway

TOOLKIT
- Tape measure
- Carpenter's level
- Prybar
- Reciprocating or compass saw for gypsum wallboard or cold chisel to remove plaster and lath
- Handsaw
- Combination square
- Hammer
- Circular saw (optional)

1 Positioning the opening

Plan an opening large enough for both the rough opening and rough door framing—an extra 1½" on top and sides. (For a bearing wall, see page 95.) Often it's simplest to remove the wall covering from floor to ceiling between two bordering studs (the new king studs) that will remain in place. On taller walls—10', for example—cutting your opening slightly larger than the intended doorway may save extra drywall work later. Try to use at least one existing stud as part of the rough framing. Locate the studs in the area; then, using a carpenter's level as a straightedge, draw plumb lines to mark the outline of the opening on the wall.

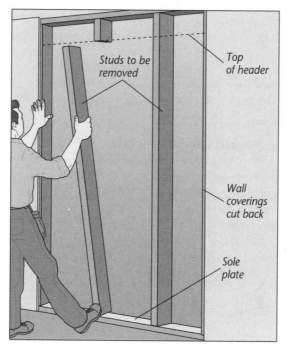

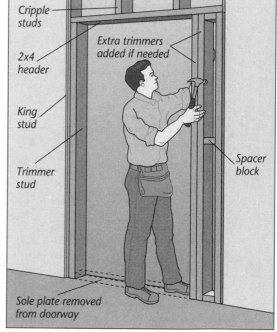

2 Removing wall covering and studs

Remove base molding, check for wires and pipes, and cut gypsum wallboard along outline with a reciprocating or compass saw. Cut only wallboard, not studs. Pry wallboard away from framing. To remove plaster and lath, chisel through plaster, then cut lath and pry it loose. Cut the studs inside the opening to the height required for the header (for a partition wall, use one 2x4 laid flat; for other header sizes, see page 66). Use a square to mark these on the face and one edge, then cut with a handsaw. Pry the studs from the sole plate (*above*).

3 Framing the opening

With wall covering and studs removed, you're ready to frame the opening. Measure and cut the header, and toenail it to the king studs with 2½" nails. Nail the header to the bottoms of the cripple studs with 3½" nails. Cut the sole plate flush with the bordering king studs and pry it loose from the subfloor. Now cut trimmer studs; nail them to the king studs with 3" nails in a staggered pattern. You'll probably need to adjust the doorway's width by adding spacer blocks and an extra pair of trimmers on one side, as shown above.

WINDOWS

The most popular styles of windows are double-hung, sliding, casement, and fixed. The most widely used, double-hung windows, have an upper, outside sash that moves down, and a lower, inside sash that moves up in grooves in the frame. Sliding windows have movable sashes that slide in horizontal tracks. Casement windows, hung singly or in pairs, have sashes that swing outward; the modern ones are operated with a crank. Fixed windows, often called "picture" windows, are stationary units mounted within a frame.

Most movable windows are available as prehung units, complete with sash, frame, sill, hardware, and all the trim except the interior casing, which greatly simplifies their installation. It's best to install one of these windows from the inside. Fixed windows can be purchased prehung, or they can be mounted within an existing frame or a frame you make yourself. We give general installation instructions; follow the directions supplied with your windows, especially for aluminum ones.

This section also shows how to cut and frame a window opening in an existing wall *(page 95)*. You may be dealing with a bearing wall *(see page 64)* or balloon framing *(see page 53)*; both call for additional steps. For details on framing a new wall, see pages 64-66.

Installing a prehung window in a new or existing wall

TOOLKIT
- Carpenter's level
- Square
- Hammer
- For installation in an existing wall, circular saw and appropriate blade for type of siding
- Caulking gun

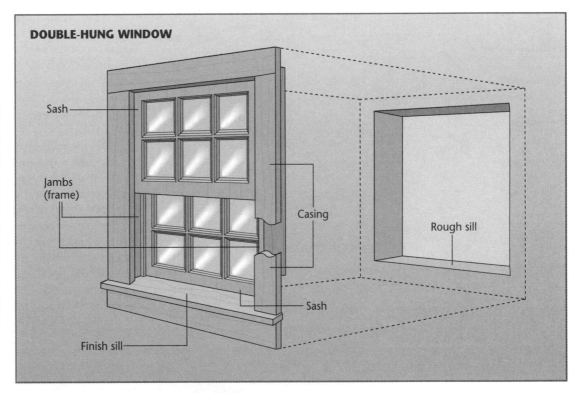

DOUBLE-HUNG WINDOW

Sash · Jambs (frame) · Casing · Rough sill · Sash · Finish sill

1 **Mounting a prehung window in a new wall**
If you're working on a pre-existing wall, go to step 2. Otherwise, depending on the design, secure prehung windows in the rough opening by either nailing through brackets or a flange that surrounds the window; or fastening (with nails or screws) the jambs through the shims into the trimmer studs and header surrounding the rough opening. Windows are normally installed after the sheathing is on, but before the siding is attached.

Center the window in the rough opening *(above)* and have a helper hold it securely against the wall. From inside, raise the window to the correct height above the rough sill with shims or wood blocks. Check the top of the unit with a carpenter's level. Adjust the shims. Start by securing the window at the top of the sides, working down to the bottom. (Starting at the top will prevent the window from falling out while you're working.) Now plumb and level the head and side jambs with more shims. Check the corners with a square. It's important for the window to be plumb and level.

2 Mounting a prehung window in an existing wall

If you're mounting the window in an existing wall, first center the window in the opening; then, using wood shims or blocks, raise it to the desired height above the rough sill. Check the level of the head jamb, then have your helper trace the outline of the flanges or trim. Remove the window. Using a circular saw with the blade set to cut through the siding but not through the sheathing or wall framing, cut along the marked lines; remove the siding. Now cut away the sheathing, followed by the studs. Set the window back in the opening, level, plumb, and fasten it as described in step 1.

3 Finishing the job

Whether in a new or existing wall, unless your roof has a pronounced overhang, your building code may require a drip cap or metal flashing over the top of the window. Thoroughly caulk the joints between the siding and the new window.

Once the interior wall coverings are in place, trim the inside of the window; for techniques, see page 110.

Building a simple fixed window

TOOLKIT
- Router and rabbeting bit
- Handsaw or circular saw
- Hammer
- Screwdriver (optional)

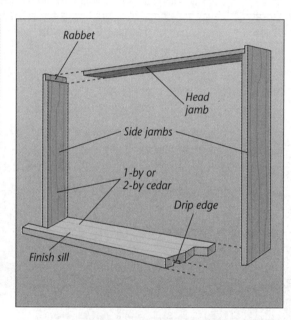

Rabbet

Head jamb

Side jambs

1-by or 2-by cedar

Drip edge

Finish sill

1 Recycling an existing frame or building a new one

To build a simple, solid frame, choose clear, knot-free lumber (cedar is good for an unpainted finish). 1-by lumber (3/4" thick) is the minimum; use 2-by lumber for a large window. The width should match the wall thickness, including outside sheathing or sheet siding and inside wall coverings. You can buy premade wood or metal sills, or make your own, cutting a thin groove below the outside lip to serve as a "drip edge."

Lay out the rabbets at the tops of the side jambs, and cut them with a router, handsaw, or circular saw. Then assemble the frame with finishing nails and waterproof glue. The finish sill should be sloped (14° is standard) to allow water runoff; nail or screw it to the jamb on an angle.

To re-use a casement window frame, remove the existing sash, molding, and hardware. With a double-hung window, pry off the inside stop and remove the lower sash and mechanisms. Pull out the parting strips to remove the upper sash and balance. Do any prep work for repainting now.

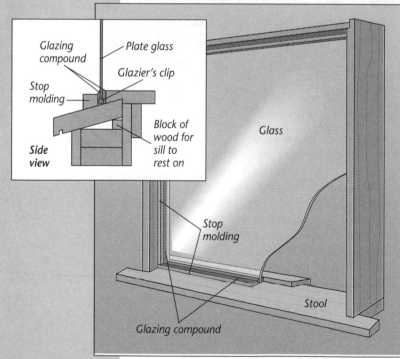

Glazing compound

Plate glass

Glazier's clip

Stop molding

Block of wood for sill to rest on

Side view

Glass

Stop molding

Glazing compound

Stool

2 Installing plate glass

Ask the glass dealer for recommendations on glass type and thickness, then have it cut to fit your frame. You may need small glazier's clips, rubber seals or gaskets, or metal or plastic moldings to space the glass away from the stops and frame. The glass should not touch either frame or stops, but should "float" in a layer of glazing compound (inset). If the installation seems difficult, have the dealer mount the glass in the frame for you.

The installation of a fixed window is similar to a prehung unit secured through the jambs. Position your unit inside the rough opening; then shim, level, and plumb as described on page 93.

TOOLKIT
- Tape measure
- Reciprocating or circular saw with appropriate blade to cut through siding and sheathing
- Combination square
- Saw to cut framing
- Hammer
- Wrench (for balloon-frame house)
- Drill
- Carpenter's level
- Prybar to lever big window into place

1 Marking the location

Check the manufacturer's specifications for the precise width of the rough opening or add ³/₈" to each side of the actual window unit. Mark this width on the wall where the window will go. Examine both the inside and outside of the building to see if you can use at least one existing stud as a king stud, to save work. You'll need to reroute any pipes or wires that cross the opening, then cut through the wall coverings and pry them loose.

Measure the height of existing doors and windows, then add on the ³/₈" shimming space and the height of the header. To determine the cor-

rect header size for your opening, see the chart on page 66 and check local codes. Unless your code demands something heavier, the header for a nonbearing wall can be a single 2x4 or 2x6 laid flat. Using a combination square, mark the total height on the king studs flanking the opening. Transfer the height to the studs within the opening. Mark each stud on the edge and one side. Then, from the marks you've just drawn, measure down the height of the rough opening (or the height of the window unit plus ³/₈"), and add 1¹/₂" for the thickness of the rough sill. Mark the studs again.

2 Supporting the ceiling

If the wall is a bearing wall or is constructed with balloon framing, you must support the ceiling and structure above the opening. Build a temporary wall slightly longer than the width of the opening and about 4' away from the existing wall. Protect flooring with ¹/₂" plywood. Measure height from floor to ceiling and cut 2x4 studs to this dimension, minus 4" for shimming and top and bottom plates. You can assemble the wall on the floor, spacing studs on 16" centers *(page 64)*, or build the wall by installing

the top and bottom plates, cutting the studs to fit, and wedging them in place. While a helper holds the wall plumb, drive shims between sole plate and plywood until the plate is tight against ceiling. Put shims under each stud. This technique also works well with doors.

In a balloon-framed house, also support studs above the opening by placing a 2x8 waler (a horizontal board) against the ceiling and attaching it to studs with lag screws. Wedge 4x4 posts (or posts of two 2x4s) between waler and floor.

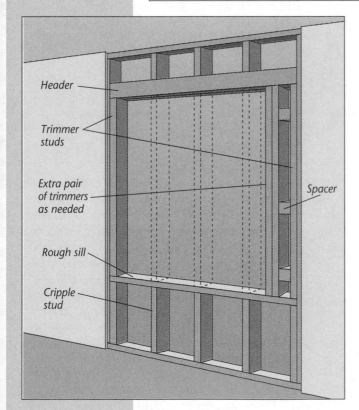

Header

Trimmer studs

Extra pair of trimmers as needed

Rough sill

Cripple stud

Spacer

3 Framing the new opening

Cut studs to be removed at the lines marking the bottom of the rough sill and at the header's top edge; these cut studs are the cripple studs. Measure the distance from the sole plate to the line marking the sill on each king stud; cut two additional cripple studs to this length. Fasten these to king studs with 3" nails. Measure the distance between king studs; cut the rough sill to this length and nail it to each cripple with two 3¹/₂" nails.

For a bearing wall, assemble a header *(page 66)*. Have a helper position the top of the header, crown-side up, against upper cripple studs. Toenail (2¹/₂" nails) the ends of the header to king studs and nail cripples to header. Finally, measure the distance between the bottom of the header and the top of the sill. Cut two trimmer studs to this length and nail them to the king studs with 3" nails. To adjust the width of the opening, block out a doubled trimmer on one side, allowing enough shimming space; add spacer blocks. You can also install a header by preparing it; cutting trimmers to measure; mounting one trimmer; loading one end of the header, and wedging it into place with the second trimmer.

Finish up on a dry day. Drill holes through the wall from inside at each corner of the rough opening; stick nails through to the outside. From outside, mark the rough opening's outline using a level. With a reciprocating or circular saw, cut through the siding and sheathing. For a brick wall, consult a professional mason.

INSULATING THE SHELL

The best time to insulate against the cold is during new construction or remodeling, when the spaces between joists, studs, and rafters are exposed. The instructions on these pages explain how to install mineral-fiber blankets or batts *(page 50)*, the simplest type of insulation to apply in exposed areas. If you need to add insulation to an existing structure in which the spaces are concealed, consult an insulation contractor. Insulating an unfinished attic yields the greatest energy savings relative to its cost. Of course, walls are also very important. If your heating costs are high, don't neglect the area under floors. Insulating foundation walls may also be advantageous in an enclosed crawl space or heated basement that projects well above grade level. The illustration below shows the common areas to insulate.

You'll need a sharp utility knife for cutting blankets or batts and a lightweight hand stapler for fastening them to studs or joists. To insulate dark areas, you'll need at least one portable light. Insulation materials are either dusty or irritating to skin, eyes, nose, and lungs; wear gloves, respiratory protection, plastic goggles, and long sleeves, taped around wrists.

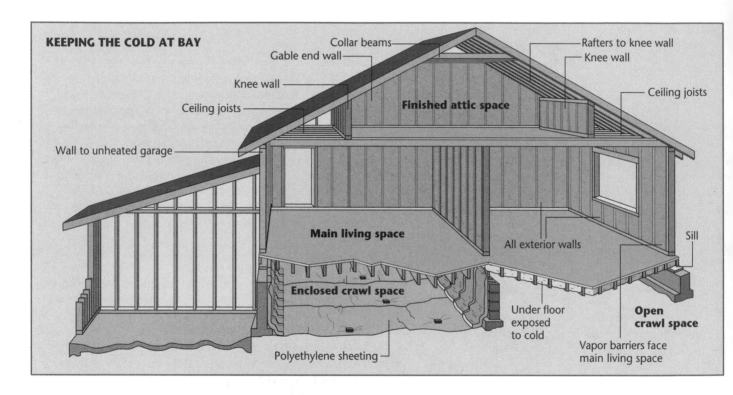

KEEPING THE COLD AT BAY

- Collar beams
- Gable end wall
- Knee wall
- Ceiling joists
- Wall to unheated garage
- Rafters to knee wall
- Knee wall
- Ceiling joists
- Finished attic space
- Main living space
- All exterior walls
- Sill
- Enclosed crawl space
- Under floor exposed to cold
- Open crawl space
- Polyethylene sheeting
- Vapor barriers face main living space

Insulating the attic

TOOLKIT
- Tape measure
- Utility knife
- Stapler

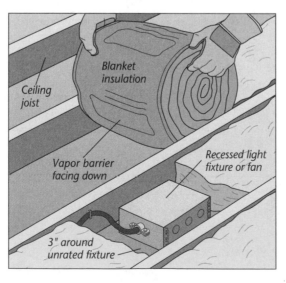

- Ceiling joist
- Blanket insulation
- Vapor barrier facing down
- Recessed light fixture or fan
- 3" around unrated fixture

Installing insulation

Insulate unfinished attics between ceiling joists only. Lay some boards over joists as makeshift flooring. Lay blankets or batts with attached vapor barrier down. With a separate vapor barrier, fasten it first to the sides of the joists. Extend insulation over top plates but don't block eave vents. Leave 3" around unrated heat producing fixtures *(left)*, and around chimneys, stovepipes, and flues. Insulation can be laid over fixtures rated I.C. (insulated ceiling rating). Slit batts to fit around wiring. For a finished attic, insulate between rafters, collar beams, short "knee wall" studs, and gable studs instead of ceiling joists. The vapor barrier faces in, toward the attic. Staple faced batts or blankets directly to the edges of rafters and studs. For unfaced batts and blankets, use wires *(page 97)*.

Insulating the walls

TOOLKIT
- Tape measure
- Utility knife
- Stapler

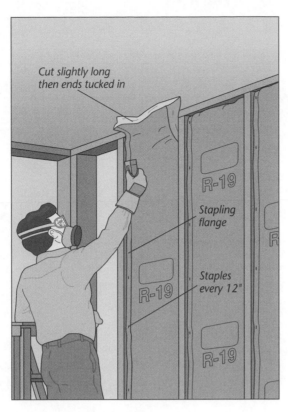

Cut slightly long then ends tucked in

R-19

Stapling flange

Staples every 12"

R-19

R-19

Installing insulation and vapor barriers

Precut 4' batts are simplest to handle when insulating a standard 8' wall with fire blocks at 4' heights, but blankets can be easily cut to length. Split insulation where necessary to fit around wiring *(page 89)*. Size the pieces slightly long to give a tight fit. Choose insulation with attached vapor barriers except in very cold climates, where a continuous barrier should be applied over studs. The barrier should always face the side that's warm in winter, so it's simplest to place insulation from the inside. If you must work from outside, fasten batts in place using one of the methods for floors described below. Peel back flammable barriers 3" from flues, chimneys, electric fans, and other heat-producing equipment. Stuff insulation scraps into cracks and small spaces between rough framing and windows and door jambs, and behind electrical conduit, outlet and switch boxes, and other obstructions. Staple barrier flanges to studs and tuck in loose ends *(left)*. Never force too much insulation into a space, as there must be sufficient loft, or thickness, for it to be effective.

Insulating floors and basement walls

TOOLKIT
- Tape measure
- Utility knife
- Stapler (or wire hangers)
- Hammer

1 ▸ Insulating floors

Work from below to insulate existing floors. Precut 4' batts are easiest to handle in tight spots. Otherwise, cut them to the exact length of each space. If you can find them, "reverse-flange" batts are excellent; you can staple them from below. The most common way to hold standard blankets and batts in place is to lace 18-gauge baling wire back and forth between nails hammered into joists or staple chicken wire to the joists. Or, cut wire braces 1" longer than the space between joists from 13-gauge wire, or even from wire hangers. Hold the blanket or batt in place between joists and bow a wire brace gently up against the fibers at one end. Place a wire every 1$^1/_2$'. Fold up each batt or blanket at the ends of every joist space *(right)*, and abut any adjoining ends snugly.

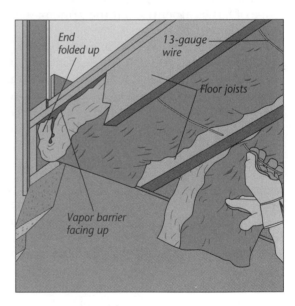

End folded up

13-gauge wire

Floor joists

Vapor barrier facing up

---

2 Weatherproofing the crawl space

To form a vapor barrier in a dirt crawl space, lay 4- to 6-mil opaque polyethylene sheeting over the ground, extending it several inches up the walls and fastening it there with duct tape as shown on page 96. Overlap adjoining pieces and anchor them with rocks or bricks. If the crawl space can be sealed during winter, the cheapest and best protection is insulation draped across the inner surfaces of the exterior walls and along the ground.

3 Insulating a heated basement

To insulate walls, either build a standard stud wall *(page 64)* just shy of each concrete wall, or fur out concrete walls with smaller wooden framing members. Barrier facings on regular blankets and batts are flammable; they cannot be left exposed. Cover them with gypsum wallboard or some other fire-retardant covering permitted by local codes. If you live in a very cold climate, it's important to check with your building department for recommendations before applying any type of insulation to basement walls and foundations.

BASIC STAIRWAYS

Converting an attic or loft, finishing a basement, or adding a deck is likely to mean that you must consider stairs. The type of stairway described here is "rough" (that is, suitable for outdoor, basement, and attic applications). They're easier to build than they look, provided you follow certain basic rules, measure carefully, and plan each detail before you begin construction. Should you need to frame a new opening, or well, in the floor or ceiling for your stairway, see page 62 for details.

Major stairways serving interior living spaces can be a great deal more complicated: these often involve some decorative woodwork or changes in direction and elevation that require considerable skill in planning and execution. Such stairs go beyond the scope of basic carpentry, but the principles are the same as those discussed below.

Three calculations are critical to your stairway plan: stairway angle, tread depth, and riser height. You also have to consider stair width, height of railings, and headroom. See the illustration above for help with these terms.

Angle, treads, and risers: The angle of a stairway is a function of its riser/tread relationship. If the angle is too steep, the stairs will be a strain to climb. The ideal angle lies between 30° and 35°.

Normally the sum of the riser height and tread depth should be 17 to 18 inches. Ideal riser height is 7 inches (many building codes specify a maximum of 7½ inches).

Headroom, width, railings: To avoid hitting your head or having to duck every time you go up or down interior stairs you must provide adequate headroom. Most codes require a minimum headroom (measured from the front edge of the tread to any overhead obstruction) of 6½ feet. About 7½ feet is ideal, both for extra-tall people and to avoid giving the stairway a closed-in feeling.

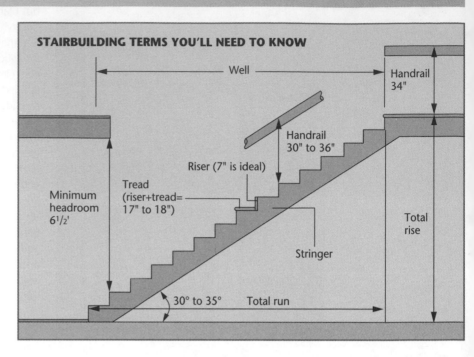

STAIRBUILDING TERMS YOU'LL NEED TO KNOW

Well · Handrail 34" · Handrail 30" to 36" · Riser (7" is ideal) · Tread (riser+tread= 17" to 18") · Minimum headroom 6½' · Total rise · Stringer · 30° to 35° · Total run

The width of the stair is less important and will be dictated largely by available space, but it should allow two people to pass. Building codes usually specify a 30-inch minimum; a width of 36 to 42 inches is preferable.

Handrailings 30 to 36 inches high (measured from the top of the front of the tread to the top of the railing) are comfortable for a person of average height; 34 inches is a good height above floors and landings. Check your local building code.

Materials: Because it provides the greatest strength, the best stringer design is the single-piece stringer with "sawtooth" cutouts for the steps. You'll need knot-free 2x12 dimension lumber long enough to reach from the top landing to the bottom flooring at the correct angle, with 1 foot extra at each end.

For risers, select a knot-free grade of lumber not less than 1 inch thick (nominal dimension). It's common to use 2-inch nominal thickness boards for treads. You may want to purchase bullnosed treads and cut them to length.

Figuring your layout

TOOLKIT
- Tape measure
- Calculator

1 Calculating risers and treads

To determine the number of steps you'll need, measure the vertical distance—in inches—from finish floor to finish floor and divide that measurement by 7", the ideal riser height. If the answer ends in a decimal (as it probably will), drop the decimal and divide that number into the vertical distance; the resulting figure will give you the exact measurement for each of your risers. For example, a total rise of 89"÷7"=12.7 steps. By dividing 89" by 12, you'll arrive at a riser height of 7.4".

Now take the exact riser height and subtract it from the ideal sum for both risers and treads—17½"—to find the exact depth of each tread. For safety, they must not measure less than 10".

2 Making the plan fit

Determine the total run (horizontal distance between top and bottom risers) to see if your plan will fit the space. Multiply your exact tread depth by the number of risers—minus one—to get the total run. If this run won't fit the space, adjust the riser/tread relationship, increasing the rise and decreasing the run—or vice versa—until you achieve a total run that will work. If you increase or decrease the height of each riser, you'll have to add or drop a step and recalculate. If a straight run proves too long, you may have to go to a return (180° change in direction) or L (90°) design.

Building the stairway

TOOLKIT
- Carpenter's square
- Square gauges (optional)
- Handsaw
- Circular saw
- Tape measure
- Hammer

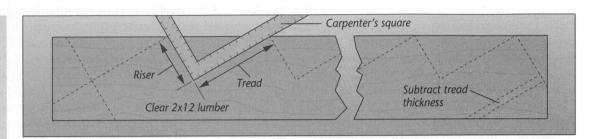

Carpenter's square
Riser
Tread
Clear 2x12 lumber
Subtract tread thickness

1 Laying out a sawtooth stringer

This is similar to stepping off a rafter *(page 70)*. First, mark the height of the risers on the tongue of a carpenter's square; then mark the depth of the treads on the body (or use square gauges). Line up the marks with the top edge of the 2x12 stringer and trace the outline of the risers and treads onto it *(above)*. Cut out the notches, finishing with a handsaw. Because the tread thickness will add to the first step height, measure the exact thickness of a tread and cut this amount off the bottom of the stringer. Check the alignment, then use this stringer as a pattern to mark the second one. If your stairway is 36" or wider, space a third stringer between the end stringers.

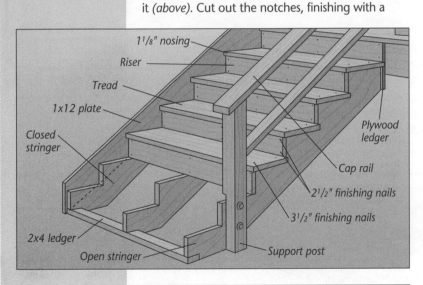

1¹⁄₈" nosing
Riser
Tread
1x12 plate
Closed stringer
2x4 ledger
Open stringer
Plywood ledger
Cap rail
2¹⁄₂" finishing nails
3¹⁄₂" finishing nails
Support post

2 Nailing the stringer

Generally, nailing the top of the stringer to the rough opening's trimmers or headers *(page 62)* is sufficient, but you can increase strength by adding an extra header board, metal joist hangers, or a plywood ledger. At the bottom, either toenail the stringers to the floor or notch them for a 2x4 ledger *(left)*.

If one or both end stringers will be "closed"—that is, attached to an adjacent wall—first nail an additional 1x12 plate to the wall studs: this acts both as trim and as a nailing surface for the main stair stringer.

3 Cutting and nailing the risers and treads

When measuring and cutting risers and treads, remember that the bottom edge of the riser overlaps the back of the tread, and the forward edge of the tread overlaps the riser below it. Giving each tread a 1¹⁄₈" nosing (a projection beyond the front of a riser) lends a more finished appearance.

Nail risers to the stringers, using 2¹⁄₂" nails. Then nail treads to the stringers with 3¹⁄₂" nails. Fasten the bottom edges of risers to the backs of treads with 2¹⁄₂" nails. Gluing treads and risers to the stringer as you nail them will help minimize squeaks.

4 Adding railings

Whether you use a simple length of 2x4 or purchase finished decorative railing, fasten it securely to an inside wall by screwing commercial brackets to wall studs (every third stud). For the open sides of stairways, begin with sturdy posts not less than 2" square; bolt them directly to the stringer. Cap rails for outdoor and rough stairs are usually 2x4s or 2x6s nailed to each supporting post.

CEILINGS

In most homes, the ceilings are not the outstanding feature. Even so, a new ceiling can brighten up a room with light and color.

Mineral and wood-fiber tiles and suspended panel ceilings are easily installed. Gypsum wallboard, today's standard, is not technically complicated to hang, but the large, heavy panels are awkward to handle. The following pages give directions on installing these three ceiling materials. A host of other wall coverings—solid board and plywood panelings and even siding—are suitable for ceilings; simply adapt the directions found in Siding *(page 75)* and Interior Wall Coverings *(page 104)*. In certain cases, another option is to simply omit the ceiling covering and finish the joists and beams.

Tiles: Square ceiling tiles are available in a variety of decorative and acoustic styles. These tiles, most commonly 1 foot square, can be applied either directly to existing, flat ceilings in good shape or to 1x3 furring strips fastened across joists or ceiling with special adhesive or staples.

Suspended ceilings: Easy-to-install suspended ceilings consist of a metal grid supported from above by wire or spring-type hangers. The grid holds acoustic or decorative fiberboard panels. The most common dimension is 2 feet by 4 feet. Transparent and translucent plastic panels and egg-crate grilles are made to fit the gridwork and admit light from above. Recessed lighting panels that exactly replace one panel are available from some manufacturers. All components are replaceable, and panels can be raised for access to wiring, ducts, and pipes.

Gypsum wallboard: Though gypsum wallboard panels can be tricky to install on ceilings, they are the most popular choice because they're inexpensive, they take paint and surface textures well, and one panel covers a large area. A few special techniques will help the work go smoothly—and will lead to a smooth result, as well.

ASK A PRO

HOW DO I FIGURE OUT HOW MANY PANELS OR TILES I NEED?

Tiles are usually sold in packages of a certain number of square feet. Measure the length and width of the room, eliminating areas not to be covered (a skylight, for example). Multiply these figures for the square footage, and buy enough material to cover this area. Add 10% for waste. For a professional-looking job, plan equal borders on opposite sides of the room.

To determine the nonstandard width of tiles or panels needed for perimeter rows, measure the extra space from the last full row of pieces to one wall, and divide by two. This final figure will be the dimension of border pieces against that wall and the opposite wall. To complete your plan, repeat this procedure for the other room dimensions.

Putting up ceiling tiles

TOOLKIT
- Hammer
- Lever
- Tape measure
- Stapler
- Chalk line

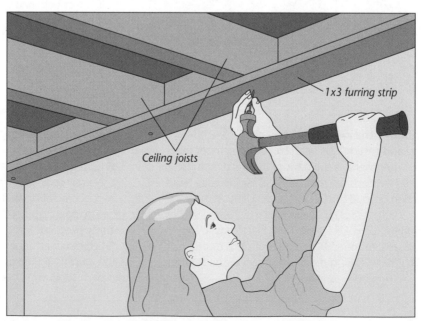

Ceiling joists

1x3 furring strip

1 Building a nailing base

Fasten furring strips to ceiling joists with 2" nails. Position the first strip along the edge of one wall, perpendicular to the joists. Place the second strip so that the edges of the border tiles will be centered on the strip. Then space each succeeding strip 12" on center.

2 ▶ Leveling the furring strips

In the high spots, shim the strips by driving shingles between them and the joists (right). Also level the strips with each other, checking with a straightedge.

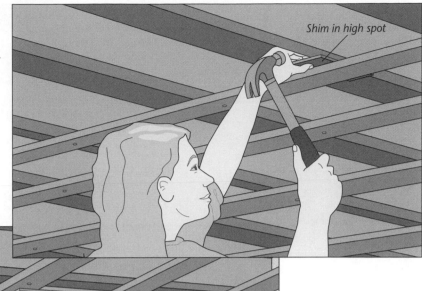

Shim in high spot

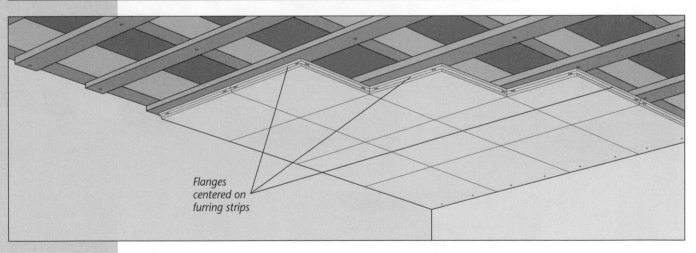

Staples through flanges

Nails to be covered by molding

◀ 3 Installing border tiles

Cut border tiles to size. Place the cut edges against the wall and face-nail where the molding will cover the nailheads. Staple the other sides to the furring strips through the flanges.

Flanges centered on furring strips

4 Installing the remaining tiles

Work outward from the border tiles across the room. Center each tile on the furring strips, as shown above, and staple it in place.

ASK A PRO

TILING OVER A CEILING

If you're applying tiles over an existing ceiling, first mark your layout across the ceiling by snapping a chalk line for each row. Install the tiles by daubing special adhesive on each corner and the center of the back of each tile.

Hanging a suspended ceiling

TOOLKIT
- Tape measure
- Chalk line
- Hammer
- Tin snips or hacksaw
- Utility knife

1 ▶ Installing molding
First, figure the ceiling height —at least 3" below plumbing, 5" below lights; minimum ceiling height is 7'6". Snap a chalk line around the room at your chosen level and install right-angle molding just covering the chalk line.

Chalk line

Right-angle molding

2 Hanging the main runners
Cut the main tees to length with tin snips or a hacksaw. Setting them on the right-angle molding at each end, support them every 4' with #12 wire attached to small eye screws fastened into joists above.

Ceiling joists

#12 wire

Main tee

3 ▶ Adding the cross tees
Lock 4' cross tees to the main tees by inserting the tabs into the slots in the main tees and snapping them in place.

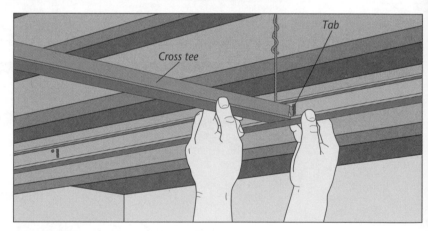

Cross tee

Tab

4 Installing panels:
Slide the panels up diagonally through the grid openings and lower them into place. Install any recessed lighting panels. Cut border panels as necessary with a sharp utility knife. Be sure your hands are clean when handling panels—smudges and fingerprints are hard to remove.

Installing gypsum wallboard on a ceiling

TOOLKIT
- Straightedge or chalk line
- Electric screw gun
- Bell-faced hammer
- Tape measure
- Utility knife
- Wallboard or compass saw
- Perforated rasp

1 Supporting the panels

Because it's necessary to support the heavy panels while fastening them, installing a wallboard ceiling is accomplished much more easily if done by two people. First, position a pair of stepladders, or set up a couple of sturdy sawhorses, laying a few planks across them to serve as a short scaffold to stand on. Then, both carpenters hold their respective ends of a panel in place with their heads. Begin putting in fasteners at the center of each panel; then place the next few fasteners where they will take the weight off your head *(below)*.

2 Installing the ceiling

If walls are being finished with wallboard, apply the ceiling first: the edges of ceiling panels may be supported by wall panels. Methods for installing a wallboard ceiling are basically the same as those for walls *(page 104)*. Choose 1/2"- or 5/8"-thick panels, and fasten them perpendicular to joists with annular ring nails, drywall screws or a combination of nails and construction adhesive. Screws installed with a screw gun is the easiest and fastest method—screw guns may be rented—screw spacings are governed by local codes, but typical spacing is every 7" along panel ends and at intermediate joists (called "in the field"). If you decide to double-nail *(page 105)* space the first set of nails every 7" along the ends and every 12" in the field. Then place a second nail about 2" away from each nail in the first set. Nails should be spaced at least 3/8" in from the edges around the perimeter.

ASK A PRO

WHAT IF I DON'T HAVE A HELPER?

You can construct one or two T-braces as shown at right. The length of the braces should equal the height from the floor to the ceiling joists; when the panel is positioned, the extra thickness will help wedge the brace in place.

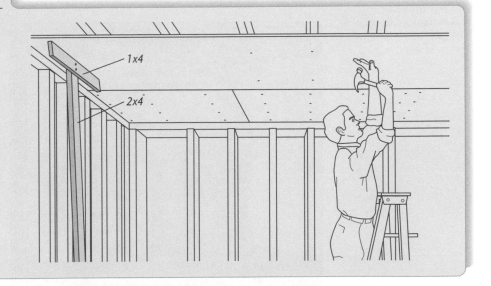

1x4

2x4

INTERIOR WALL COVERINGS

A variety of attractive wall coverings is available, including gypsum wallboard, wood sheet paneling, and solid boards. You can attach wall coverings to new studs, directly over existing wall coverings, or to furring strips fastened to an old bumpy wall.

Arrange to have all wood paneling (and also the trim) stored for at least two days in the room where it will be installed—ideally a week to 10 days. This allows the material to adapt to the room's temperature and humidity, preventing later warping or buckling.

Gypsum wallboard: Cutting and installing wallboard is straightforward, but the weight of full panels can be awkward to work with. Wallboard is easily damaged; take care not to bend or break the corners or tear the paper covering. If your wallboard will serve as a backing for paneling, ceramic tile, or cabinets, you may not need to hide joints and corners. But if you expect to paint or wallpaper, you'll need to finish the wallboard.

Concealing the joints between panels and in the corners demands patience and care. Buy precreased wallboard tape and pre-mixed joint compound. Textured compounds applied later will hide a less-than-perfect taping job,

and any cracks between panels due to shifting will be less apparent. Ask your dealer for recommendations.

Sheet paneling: Sheet paneling is typically decorative plywood, hardboard, or plastic laminate. If you're paneling over bare studs, ask your dealer whether you'll need to back the sheets with gypsum wallboard or other material for rigidity and fire protection.

For a good appearance, cut the first and last panels on a wall the same width unless you're using panels with random-width grooves. Prop up all the panels along the wall to see how they'll fit. Whenever possible, center between-panel joints over door and window openings. At inside corners, plan to butt panels together. Outside corners, unless perfectly mitered, will require two pieces of trim or a corner guard.

Adhesive is preferable to nails—it's fast and clean, and subjects panels to less risk of dents or visible nail holes.

Solid boards: Though solid boards are usually installed vertically or horizontally, consider using a diagonal pattern, or even a pattern designed for exterior siding boards, to give your walls some added visual punch. See the chart on page 77 for some ideas.

Installing gypsum wallboard

TOOLKIT
- Straightedge or chalk line
- Utility knife
- Tape measure
- Wallboard or compass saw
- Perforated rasp
- Bell-faced hammer or screw gun

1 Cutting wallboard

To make a straight cut, first mark the cutting line on the front paper layer with a pencil and straightedge, or snap a chalk line. Cut through the front paper with a utility knife. Turn the wallboard over and break the gypsum core by bending it toward the back. Finally, cut the back paper along the crease. When fitting wallboard around obstructions such as doorways, windows, or out-

lets, carefully measure from the edge of an adjacent wallboard panel or reference point and up from the floor to the obstruction. For small cuts such as outlets, cut the opening about 1/8" to 3/16" bigger than needed. Transfer the measurements to a new panel and make the necessary cuts with a wallboard or compass saw. If the fit is too tight, trim with a perforated rasp.

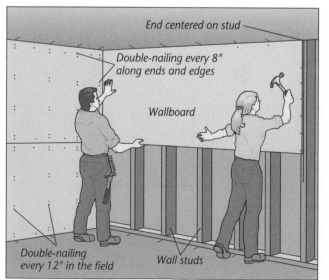

End centered on stud

Double-nailing every 8" along ends and edges

Wallboard

Double-nailing every 12" in the field

Wall studs

2 Installing the panels:

Wallboard panels may be positioned either vertically or horizontally—that is, with the long edges either parallel or perpendicular to wall studs. Most professionals prefer the latter method *(left)*, because it helps bridge irregularities between studs, results in a stronger wall, and is easier to finish. Before installing panels, mark the stud locations on the floor and ceiling. Starting from one corner, lay the first panel tight against the ceiling. (If you choose the horizontal method, panel ends may be either centered over studs or "floated" and tied together with backing blocks.) Stagger the end joints in the bottom row so they don't line up with the joints in the top row.

3 Fastening the panels

Wallboard may be fastened with drywall nails or screws, or construction adhesive and nails, but screws with a screw gun is the most common method.

Fastener spacings are subject to local codes, but typical screw or nail spacing is every 8" along panel ends and edges and along intermediate supports ("in the field"). Fasteners must be at least ³/₈" in from edges. Panels can also be "double-nailed": Space a second nail 2" from each nail in the first set; space these pairs 12" apart in the field. Use a bell-faced hammer, since your goal is to dimple the wallboard surface without puncturing the paper. If you do puncture the paper or miss a stud, pull out the nail and install another one. The hole can be patched and sanded later. It's usually simplest to first tack a row of panels in place with a few nails through each; later you can snap chalk lines to mark the studs, and then finish the nailing pattern.

Taping wallboard joints

TOOLKIT
- 6" and 10" taping knives
- Corner tool
- Putty knife
- Hammer
- Dust mask and hat

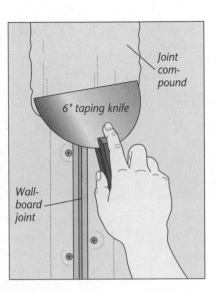

Joint compound

6" taping knife

Wallboard joint

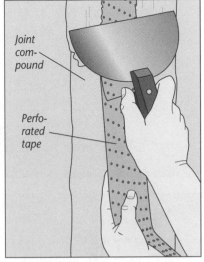

Joint compound

Perforated tape

1 Taping joints between panels

Apply a smooth layer of joint compound over the joint with a 6" taping knife (far left). Before the compound dries, embed wallboard tape into it with the knife (left) and then apply another thin coat of compound over the tape, smoothing it gently with the knife. Use only enough compound to fill the joint and cover the tape evenly.

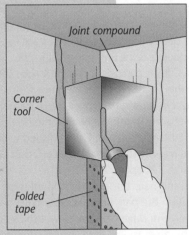

Joint compound

Corner tool

Folded tape

2 Taping the inside corners

Apply a smooth layer of compound to the wallboard on each side of the corner. Tear a piece of tape to length, fold it in half vertically, then press it into the corner with a corner tool or putty knife. Apply a thin layer of compound over the tape and smooth it out.

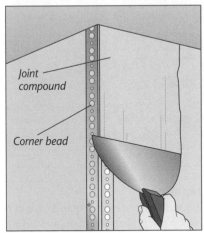

Joint compound

Corner bead

3 Finishing outside corners

Cover exterior corners with a protective metal corner bead cut to length and nailed through its perforations every 12". There's no need to tape (although it will reduce the chances of cracking); simply run your knife down the sharp metal edge to fill the spaces with compound (left).

10" taping knife

4 Applying successive coats

When all the joints and corners are taped, use smooth, even strokes with the 6" knife to cover the nail dimples in the field with compound. When compound has dried (it will look white, not gray), use a 10" knife to apply a second coat, feathering out edges past each side of the joint (left). Let dry. Then sand and apply a final coat, using the 10" or an even wider finishing trowel to smooth out and feather the edges. After the final coat dries, sand with fine sandpaper to remove minor imperfections.

Installing sheet paneling

TOOLKIT
- Hammer
- Carpenter's level
- Rubber mallet or padded block
- Tape measure
- Compass
- Coping saw, saber saw, or block plane to cut irregular panel edge

1 Furring and shimming

Attach furring strips (1x3s or 1x4s) to the wall with nails long enough to penetrate studs at least 1". For masonry walls, use concrete nails or metal shields. Furring strips should be plumb and flat; you can make small adjustments with shingle shims. If the existing wall is severely out of plumb, you may need to shim out furring strips at one end.

The correct spacing of furring strips depends on the type of paneling that will cover them. A typical arrangement is shown below. Check the manufacturer's instructions for recommended nail spacings. Be sure to leave a 1/4" space at both the top and bottom of the wall when applying the strips in case of any unevenness in the floor or ceiling.

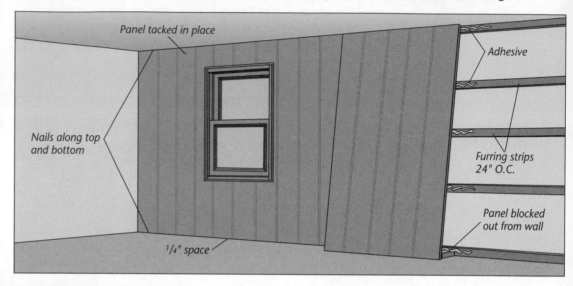

Panel tacked in place

Nails along top and bottom

Adhesive

Furring strips 24" O.C.

Panel blocked out from wall

1/4" space

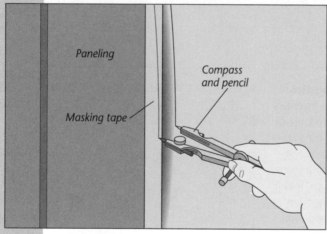

Paneling

Compass and pencil

Masking tape

2 Cutting and attaching the sheets

Work clockwise or counterclockwise starting in the corner adjacent to the most irregular wall. To mark these irregularities on the panel's edge, prop the panel into place about 1" from the uneven surface; use shims, if necessary, to adjust level and plumb. Draw the points of a compass (open to the greatest gap) along the irregular surface so the pencil leg duplicates the unevenness onto the paneling *(left)*. Cut the paneling along the scribed line.

Cut each panel 1/4" short of the distance from floor to ceiling. On furring or exposed wall framing, apply adhesive to the framing in wavy lines, as shown in the illustration above. On a finished wall, apply adhesive directly to the wall, spacing dots the size of 50¢ pieces 12" apart.

Drive 4 finishing nails through the top edge of the panel. Position the panel on the wall, leaving a 1/4" space at bottom; drive nails partway into the wall to act as hinge pins. Pull the bottom edge of the panel out about 6" from the wall and push a block behind it; wait for the adhesive to get tacky. Remove the block and press the panel firmly into place; knock on the panel with a rubber mallet or hammer against a padded block. Drive the top-edge nails all the way in; then nail the panels at the bottom (you'll eventually cover the nailheads and the 1/4" gap with molding). Thin paneling materials require either glue or nails within 1/4" of the panel edges to prevent curling.

3 Cutting an opening

Fitting a panel around any opening requires careful measuring, marking, and cutting. Keep track of all the measurements by sketching them on a piece of paper.

Starting from the corner of the wall or the edge of the nearest panel, measure to the edge of the opening or electrical box; then, from the same point, measure to the opening's opposite edge. Next, measure the distance from the floor to the opening's bottom edge and from the floor to the opening's top edge. (Remember that you'll install the paneling 1/4" above the floor.) Transfer these measurements to the panel; mark the side of the panel that will face you as you cut (face-up for a handsaw, face-down for a power saw—mirror image of the opening in this case). Finally, cut the panel.

Installing board paneling vertically

TOOLKIT
- Tape measure
- Hammer
- Saw
- Carpenter's level
- Nailset
- Putty stick

1 Furring and laying out the boards
Before paneling vertically with solid boards, attach horizontal furring strips every 24" on center, or install nailing blocks at these spacings between studs. Measure the width of the boards and then the width of the wall. Calculate the width of the final board. To avoid a sliver-size board, split the difference so the first and last boards are the same. Cut boards 1/4" shorter than the height from floor to ceiling. When you place the first board into the corner, check the outer edge with a carpenter's level. If the board isn't plumb or doesn't fit exactly, scribe and trim the edge facing the corner *(facing page).*

2 Attaching the boards
Attach the first board, leaving a 1/4" space above the floor (use a prybar as a lever); then butt the second board against its edge and check for plumb before you nail it. Repeat this procedure with all subsequent boards. To make the last board fit easily into place, cut its edge at a slight angle (about 5°) toward the board's back edge. At the inside corners, simply butt adjacent board edges together, scribing if necessary. At the outside corners, you can either bevel the joints for a neat fit (cut the bevels at an angle slightly greater than 45° so they'll fit snugly) or you can butt boards and then conceal the joints with trim.

Installing solid boards horizontally

TOOLKIT
- Tape measure
- Hammer
- Carpenter's level
- Nailset
- Putty stick

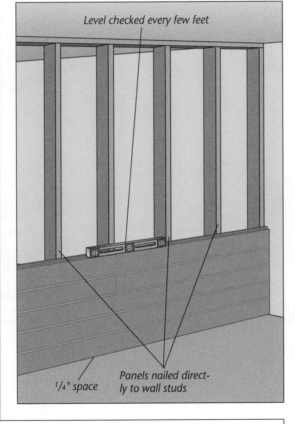

Level checked every few feet

1/4" space

Panels nailed directly to wall studs

 1 Laying out the boards
Generally, you won't need to apply furring unless the wall is badly damaged or out of plumb. You can nail the boards to the studs directly *(left)* or through existing wall coverings. To avoid ending up with a very narrow board at the ceiling, calculate its width and split the difference so it and the first board will be the same width.

ASK A PRO

HOW SHOULD I FASTEN SOLID BOARDS?
Either nail solid boards to your wall surface or use adhesive, but nailing is preferred. Panel type and size determine exact nail placement, as shown. For standard 1-by boards, use 2" finishing nails and recess the heads 1/32" below the surface with a nailset. Cover nailheads, using a putty stick in a matching color.

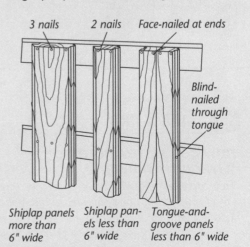

3 nails   2 nails   Face-nailed at ends

Blind-nailed through tongue

Shiplap panels more than 6" wide   Shiplap panels less than 6" wide   Tongue-and-groove panels less than 6" wide

2 Attaching the boards
Start at bottom of wall and work toward the ceiling. Nail the first board temporarily at one end, 1/4" above the floor. Then level the board and complete the nailing. If you need to scribe and trim the board at its ends, follow the instructions opposite (minor inconsistencies can be covered with trim). Working toward the ceiling, attach each board in the same way. Rip the last board to width as required, making sure it will reach the ceiling. If you have trouble fitting the last board, bevel its back edge slightly and pivot into place.

TRIM

Contoured moldings or standard lumber trim along the bottom edge of wallboard or wood paneling not only cover the gaps between wall covering and floor, they also introduce new architectural interest to a room. You may wish to trim the ceiling line and corners, as well. In addition, the edges of both door and window openings need casing. For examples of the types of available molding, see page 40.

A miter box and backsaw are most commonly used for neatly cutting trim. With a miter box, you can cut the precise 45° and 90° angles necessary for most joints. If you're going to do a lot of cutting, or are working with unusual angles, it may be worthwhile to rent or borrow a power miter saw. Contoured moldings may require coped joints at inside corners *(below)*.

Door trim may be either contoured molding or standard lumber. If you choose lumber, plan to butt joints at the top; for molding, you'll have to miter the joints.

Most window units require interior trim around the opening. The standard treatment consists of top and side casings, a stool on top of the finish sill, and a bottom casing—or apron—below the stool.

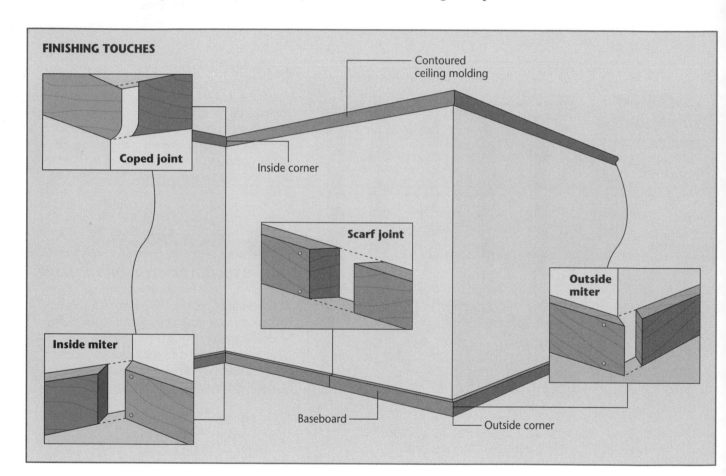

FINISHING TOUCHES

Coped joint

Contoured ceiling molding

Inside corner

Scarf joint

Outside miter

Inside miter

Baseboard

Outside corner

 ASK A PRO

HOW DO I FASTEN MOLDING WITHOUT IT SHOWING?
To attach molding, you have three choices: nail it in place with finishing nails and then recess the heads with a nailset; fasten it with color-matched nails; or blind-nail it. To blind-nail, use a small knife or gouge to raise a sliver of wood that's large enough to hide the head of a finishing nail;

don't break off the sliver. Pull the sliver to the side, nail into the cavity, and then glue the sliver into place. You can tape the sliver down with masking tape until the glue dries. Rub the spot lightly with fine sandpaper to remove all signs of gluing so it will not affect the stain.

Cutting molding and coping a joint

TOOLKIT
- Thin cardboard
- Hammer
- Nailset
- Backsaw
- Miter box
- Coping saw
- Combination square

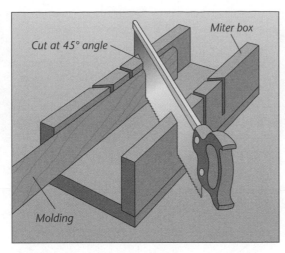

Cut at 45° angle

Miter box

Molding

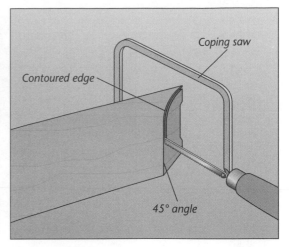

Coping saw

Contoured edge

45° angle

Cutting and attaching straight moldings

Once the finish floor is installed, you can attach baseboards and, if desired, a base shoe *(page 40)*. These moldings should be installed with a slight gap between the flooring and the bottom of the molding; use thin cardboard as a spacer. Nail moldings to the wall studs, not to the floor. Where two lengths of molding join along a wall, miter the ends *(above)* to create a scarf joint *(opposite)*. Nail through the joint to secure the pieces. At outside corners cut matching miters in each piece.

Coping a joint

Contoured moldings will require a coped joint at inside corners for a smooth fit. To form a coped joint, cut the first piece of molding square and butt it into the corner. Then cut the end of the second piece back at a 45° angle. Next, using a coping saw, follow the curvature of the molding's front edge while reinstating the 90° angle *(above)*. With a little practice, you can make the contoured end smoothly match the contours of the first piece.

Installing door casing

TOOLKIT
- Tape measure
- Pencil
- Backsaw
- Miter box
- Hammer
- Nailset
- Carpenter's level

1 ▷ **Installing side casing**
Before installing the casing, pencil a "reveal" or setback line 1/4" in from the inside of each jamb. Align each of the side casings with this line and mark them where they intersect the top reveal line. Ideally, the finish floor should be in place first. If not, remember to leave room for it at the bottom of the casing. Miter the ends from these points. (With flat lumber, you could choose to cut the corners square.) Use 1 1/2" or 2" finishing nails to attach casing to the jamb, and 2 1/2" nails along the rough framing. Space nails every 16" *(right)*.

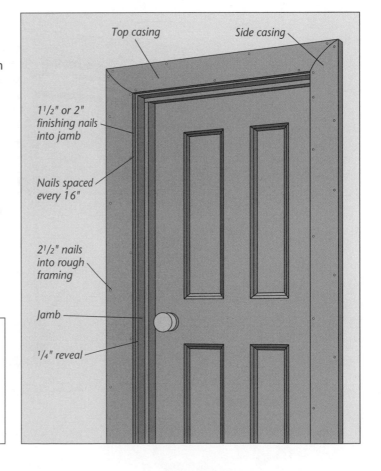

Top casing

Side casing

1 1/2" or 2" finishing nails into jamb

Nails spaced every 16"

2 1/2" nails into rough framing

Jamb

1/4" reveal

2 **Installing top casing**
Now measure for the top casing, from one side to the other. If the door jambs are level and plumb, all should join snugly. If not, you'll have to adjust the angles of the top cuts to fit the side casings exactly. Then nail the top casing into place.

TOOLKIT
- Straightedge
- Pencil
- Tape measure
- Saw
- Combination square
- Hammer
- Nailset
- Backsaw
- Miter box

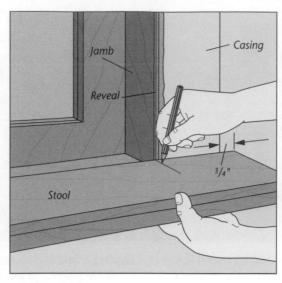

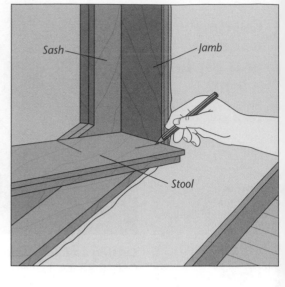

1 Installing the stool

Begin by penciling a 1/8" or 1/4" reveal just inside the side and top jambs; then measure the width of your casing. Add 3/4" to the casing's width, double this figure and add the width of the window; this is the length you should cut the stool. Use either a flat piece of lumber or a preformed rabbeted or flat stool to meet the finish sill.

Center the stool over the opening and mark the center point on the stool and opening. Mark the inside edge of each side jamb on the stool's back edge *(above, left)*. Place one end of the stool against a jamb (the back edge flush with the window's sash) and mark the front edge of the jamb on the stool *(above, right)*. Repeat this process for the other end. Using a combination square, extend each set of marks until they intersect; then notch the stool along the lines. Set the stool in place and fasten it to the finish sill with 2" finishing nails.

2 Installing the side casings

Square off one end of a piece of casing, and set that end on the stool, aligning the inside edge with the reveal. Mark the inside edge of the casing where the head jamb's reveal crosses it. If you're using contoured molding as shown, use a backsaw and miter box to cut the end at a 45° miter. For flat lumber, cut the end square. Nail the casing to the jamb with 1 1/2" or 2" finishing nails, and to the rough framing with 2 1/2" finishing nails. Repeat this process for the casing on the opposite side.

3 Fitting in the top casing and adding the apron

For the top casing, measure the distance between the side casings. Cut the casing to this length, with the ends mitered at 45°, and nail it in place. If you're using flat lumber, cut the top casing straight and long enough to extend a bit past the side casings.

For the apron, cut a piece of molding the same length as the distance between the outside edges of the side casings. Center the apron under the stool, lining up its edges precisely with the casings' outside edges. Nail it to the rough framing with 2" finishing nails.

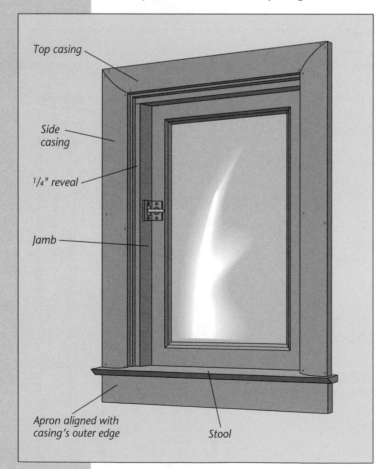

CARPENTRY GLOSSARY

Bearing wall
A wall that supports joists at their ends or midspan, transferring weight to the girder or columns below. All exterior walls are bearing, as well as some interior walls.

Casing
Trim applied around a door or window.

Crosscut
A cut running perpendicular to the direction of the wood grain.

Crown
The higher edge of a warped framing member.

Dado
A channel cut across the grain of a piece of lumber with square sides and bottom.

Decking, roof
Material such as plywood that forms a base for roofing materials.

Eave
The horizontal edge of a roof, overhanging the wall.

Face-nailing
The act of driving a nail through one piece into another with the nail at right angles to the surface.

Fire block
A piece of wood inserted between wall studs to stop the spread of fire.

Flashing
Material that seals a roof at its vulnerable points, such as at valleys and eaves and against chimneys.

Furring strips
Thin strips of wood that are attached to the structure to provide a nailing base for siding, or for ceiling or wall materials.

Girder
A heavy, horizontal framing member set into the foundation walls, supporting floor joists. Also, a beam used to support second floor joists, resting on columns below.

Header
A support piece framing an opening in a floor, wall, ceiling, or roof, at right angles to other framing members.

Jamb
A board that forms the top or side of a window frame or door frame.

Joist
A horizontal framing member placed on edge, as in a floor or ceiling joist.

Joist, band
A horizontal framing member positioned on edge on the mudsill. Runs around the structure's perimeter, supporting the subfloor and sole plate.

Joist, tail
A short joist that meets a header at a floor or ceiling opening.

Lath
A material, usually wood strips or metal, to which plaster is applied.

Level
Exactly horizontal.

Miter
An angled cut that is other than 90°.

Mortise
A shaped cutout in a workpiece, commonly used as a recess for a hinge, lock, or tenon.

Nominal size
The size of a piece of lumber when it is first cut from the log, before being surfaced. Lumber is sold by these sizes.

On center
The distance from the center of a framing member to the center of the one next to it. Normally abbreviated O.C.

Pilot hole
A hole drilled into a piece of stock for a screw or nail to follow, slightly smaller than the shaft of the nail or the threads of the screw. It guides the fastener and prevents splitting. Also, a hole cut in a board to start interior cuts.

Plate
A horizontal framing member lying flat that forms the top or bottom of a wall frame, as in sole plate or top plate.

Plumb
Exactly vertical.

Pressure treatment
A process by which chemicals are forced into wood to make it more resistant to decay.

Rabbet
A 90° notch with two sides; on the edge or end of a piece of stock.

Rafter
An angled framing member that forms part of the sloping sides of a roof and supports the roof deck and roofing materials.

Rake
The angled edge of a roof.

Ridgeboard
A horizontal framing member set on edge that creates the crest of the roof, and to which the tops of the rafters are fastened.

Rip cut
A cut parallel to the direction of the wood grain.

Rise
The vertical distance covered by anything that slopes, such as a roof or a stairway.

Riser
The vertical part of a step.

Run
The horizontal distance covered by anything that slopes, such as a stairway or roof.

Sash
The part of a window holding the glass.

Sheathing
The exterior skin of a house under the siding, typically as plywood or exterior gypsum board. May or may not contribute structural strength, depending on the material, and may or may not provide a nailing base for siding.

Shim
Small piece of wood, usually wedge-shaped, or other material used to adjust alignment, such as wood inserted behind furring strips or cardboard inserted in door hinges.

Shiplap
An edge milling where each edge of a board is rabbeted on the opposite face so that it fits into the adjacent board.

Sill
A framing member lying flat, anchored to the foundation wall, supporting the band joist. Also referred to as mudsill.

Soffit
The area below the eaves, where the roof overhangs the exterior walls. Soffits may be built "open" or "closed."

Square
The achievement of a 90° angle at the point where two pieces of lumber meet.

Steel, galvanized
Steel that has been coated with zinc to prevent rusting.

Stringer
A diagonal piece of lumber supporting a stairway.

Stud
A vertical framing member; also referred to as a wall stud.

Stud, cripple
A shortened stud that meets a header at a wall opening.

Stud, gable
A vertical framing member that fills the gap between end rafters and the top plate.

Stud, king
A full-length vertical framing member installed at a wall opening to which trimmer studs are nailed.

Stud, trimmer
A vertical framing member attached to king studs to form the sides of an opening, supporting the header.

Subfloor
Material such as plywood that forms a base for flooring materials. (An underlayment is generally applied between the subfloor and the flooring.)

Tack
To drive a nail partway, prior to alignment of pieces and final driving of nail.

Toenailing
The act of driving a nail at an angle from one piece into another.

Tongue-and-groove
An edge milling where one edge of the board is machined on both faces to form a groove, and the other edge is grooved, so that the tongue of one board fits into the groove on the next.

Tread
The part of a step that is horizontal.

Trim
Decorative moldings around wall openings or over joints, such as where the wall and floor meet.

INDEX